LAST OF THE GIANTS

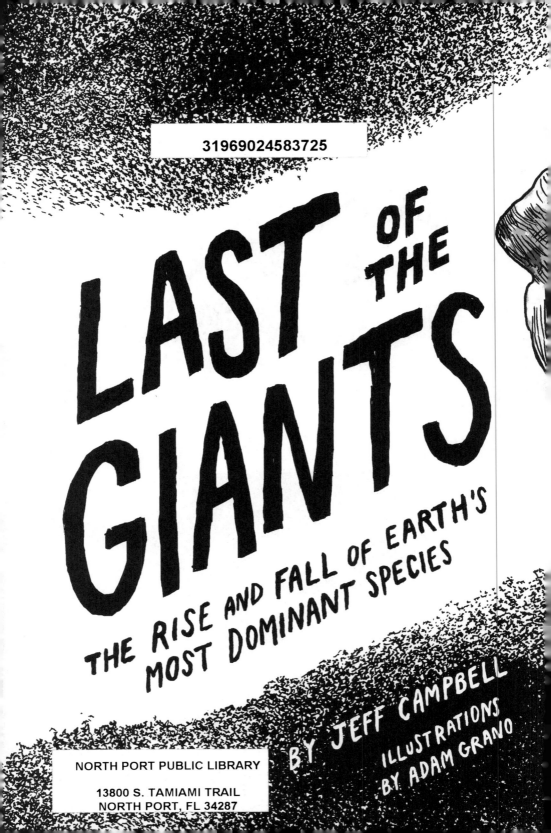

LAST OF THE GIANTS

THE RISE AND FALL OF EARTH'S MOST DOMINANT SPECIES

BY JEFF CAMPBELL

ILLUSTRATIONS BY ADAM GRANO

ZEST BOOKS

Connect with Zest!

- zestbooks.net/blog
- zestbooks.net/contests

- twitter.com/zestbooks
- facebook.com/BooksWithATwist

2443 Fillmore Street, Suite 340, San Francisco, CA 94115 | www.zestbooks.net

/ Animals / Endangered | ISBN: 978-1-942186-04-5 | Publisher: Hallie Warshaw | Editor: Daniel Harmon | Marketing: Emma
Boyer | Design: Adam Grano

Manufactured in the U.S.A. | 4500578032 | DOC 10 9 8 7 6 5 4 3 2 1

CONTENTS

HUMAN
(APPROX. 6 FT.)

MOA

AUROCHS

ELEPHANT
BIRD

STELLER'S
SEA COW

GIANT
TORTOISE

PASSENGER
PIGEON

CALIFORNIA
GRIZZLY

THYLACINE

LION

RED WOLF

TIGER

BAIJI

RHINOCEROS

INTRODUCTION: MEET THE GIANTS

We were lucky, I guess.

For two weeks in late June, my friend Chris and I drove across North America, camping from Long Island, New York, to Seward, Alaska, and we weren't attacked by a single bear.

That's good, right? From Michigan westward, every campground warned us that we were in bear country, and so we obeyed the rules. We hid our food in the trunk of my Plymouth Valiant, we didn't eat in the tent, and we never hiked alone.

Two months after arriving in Seward, I couldn't stand it anymore: we'd been so cautious and careful, *we hadn't seen a single bear.* So I made a solo pilgrimage to the town dump. There, locals told me, I'd find grizzlies. Lots of them.

The locals were correct. When I arrived, a half-dozen massive beasts were pawing the town's refuse, snuffling for prize morsels. I half-hid behind a pine and watched, transfixed, as the bears ambled casually over their lunchtime buffet, their bulk rippling beneath shaggy auburn coats.

Then—I don't know why—I turned around.

Thirty yards away, a brown bear stood tall on its hind legs, arms loose, snout raised, taking in the many pungent odors on the breeze.

My stomach clenched. Between the bear and its lunch stood me. Which was tastier? *Good job*, I thought. *Real smart. Stand alone next to a garbage dump surrounded by hungry bears.*

After one of those movie-cliché moments—in which time suspends and beads of sweat glisten melodramatically—the grizzly nonchalantly humphed to its four feet, as if it could have cared less. Then slowly, *very slowly*, I backed away, inching down the road I'd come. I had to resist the urge to run with all my might. When, finally, the bears were out of sight, I turned and walked with measured steps, ringing a little bell I'd brought for just this purpose and singing in a cracked voice the only song that came into my addled head, "Mary Had a Little Lamb."

That's what you're supposed to do if you ever find yourself alone in bear country: sing, ring a bell, so you don't startle the bears. You may not see them, but you want them to see you.

That was the first time I met a grizzly. I'd seen grizzlies in zoos before, of course, but I felt that didn't really count. I didn't want to just see a bear. I wanted to stand with grizzlies in *their* home, with no fence in between. That's one of the reasons I'd traveled to Alaska to begin with: to encounter true wilderness and wild animals face to face.

I had other encounters: A bald eagle dove and plucked a wriggling trout from Resurrection Bay right in front of me. A towering, antlered moose crashed out of the forest and stopped, eyeballing me with lordly indifference before sauntering on. I woke one morning to a dozen bison munching grass around our tent, witnessed an endless pod of whales swim past our ferry, and heard wolves howl, a spine-tingling chorus that raises your neck hairs no matter how far away they sound.

Why is it so exciting to encounter top predators and enormous beasts in the wild? Why do we travel thousands of miles to do so? And why do we savor these moments, telling the stories over and over?

After all, wild giants are dangerous. They are big for a reason. They evolved either to kill the biggest prey or to fight off the biggest predators. Without a weapon, outside a car, standing in the open, a human is at their mercy.

It's a situation that our fight-or-flight instincts tell us to avoid, and yet it's also one of the most awe-inspiring, moving experiences you can have.

That is, so long as the bear doesn't kill you.

Living with Giants: The Crisis of Coexistence

At one time, you didn't have to travel far to meet a grizzly in the United States. Grizzlies occupied nearly every mountain and valley across the western half of North America, and they ruled as one of the continent's top predators. Not anymore. Over the last 350 years, we have mostly tried to get rid of this animal, which is a dangerous beast to live with. Yet now we realize that nature can suffer when grizzlies and other giant species are gone, and we often miss these magnificent creatures.

As naturalist Aldo Leopold once lamented, "Relegating grizzlies to Alaska is about like relegating happiness to heaven; one may never get there."

This book tells the stories of thirteen giant species who once dominated our world but who suffered loss and extinction after they met us. It explores our complicated relationships with the fierce carnivores and large herbivores who always get our attention—those daunting animals who are too powerful, and sometimes too deadly, for us to ignore.

This book seeks to understand the fates of these species in part by re-creating what it was like when people first met these tremendous animals. What was the world like when lions, tigers, wolves, and grizzlies flourished? When herds of aurochs and rhinos filled the landscape? When giant tortoises packed so close you couldn't see the ground?

Inevitably, trouble. Giant animals are awe-inspiring, but they make difficult neighbors. They are invariably hard to live with. And so at times humans have pushed wild animals aside because we wanted their habitats for ourselves; at times we have hunted them relentlessly for food; and at times we have exterminated large carnivores, like the grizzly, as competing predators and pests.

As a result, our feelings about these animals are often intense and deeply conflicted. We love them and hate them, admire them and fear them, desire them and drive them away—sometimes all at once.

We also notice when they disappear. Today, giant species are vanishing right before our eyes, along with the wilderness that is their home, and this is another important reason to tell these stories: they provide a clear window for understanding the much larger extinction crisis that is currently unfolding across the globe. This crisis started about 500 years ago, and it's been getting worse ever since. In recent decades, this wave of extinctions has become so widespread and pronounced—affecting all types of species, from the very largest to the microscopic—that it's been given a name, "the sixth extinction."

What's happening to cause these extinctions? Why are so many species suddenly failing right now? What role do humans play in this crisis? What is the danger, to us and to nature, when species fail? And what can we do to save species before they go extinct?

By examining these thirteen species, this book explores these vital, complex questions. We don't have all the answers. In fact, we sometimes have very few definitive answers. But our first challenge is to understand what's happening—to name the problem correctly—for only then can we ask the *right* questions, the ones that yield the most effective answers.

In this, giant, dominant species are particularly helpful, since they illustrate dramatically that the extinction crisis is, when you get right down to it, really a crisis of coexistence. The problem we face today is how to live in sustainable ways with all wildlife, and even with landscapes themselves. Where once giant species stood in our way and made life harder for human society, now we have become Earth's single most dominant species, and the urgent problem facing many animals, especially giant animals, is how to adapt to and coexist with us.

These thirteen species aren't the whole story, but taken together, they help chart the impact of people, of us, on our planet over the last five centuries, during which human attitudes toward wildlife and nature have changed tremendously, shifting from primarily self-interest, competition, and exploitation to increasing self-awareness, caring, and conservation.

Which is a good thing. Because the short answer to how we can save giant animals and slow the extinction crisis is for us to change how we think about and live with wildlife.

Who Are Giant Animals?

First of all, what is a "giant" animal, and how did I select these thirteen species?

Of course, *giant* is not a scientific or biological term. It doesn't define a specific type of animal. Instead, I have used this adjective loosely as a guiding concept. Naturally, *giant* means big, so when selecting species, sheer size was important—but not always and not all by itself. Equally important was the species' impact on nature and on us. I chose animals who have dominated their ecosystems—perhaps because they live at the top of the food web—and who have had a profound influence on human experience and culture. Whatever their size, these species are the quintessential "charismatic animals" that inspire awe and wonder in us.

In terms of size, ten of the species qualify as *megafauna*. This *is* a scientific term that refers to any animal 100 pounds or larger. By this definition, *we* are megafauna, and the megafauna in this book range from 200 to up to 8,000 pounds. At least six include representatives that are the largest of their kind, while three are among the largest mammals to exist in the historical era and qualify as *megaherbivores*—massive vegetarians who weigh at least a ton, or 2,000 pounds.

Top or *apex predators* also qualify as giants since, by definition, they represent the largest, fiercest carnivores in their ecosystem, the ones that no other predator dare attack. However, of the six top predators in this book, only four also qualify as megafauna (and weigh over 100 pounds). The other two—the red wolf and the thylacine—don't, or didn't, get much larger than 75 pounds. But these animals still dominated their environments, and humans have treated these species as if they were the most vicious carnivores who ever existed.

Then, I've included one species that was neither a top predator nor a megafauna: the passenger pigeon. Modest in size even for a bird, the passenger pigeon could fit in your coat pocket, and just about every predator dined on it, so what is it doing here?

In part, it's here to illustrate that there's more to being a "giant" than the size of the individual animal. As a collective, passenger pigeons were a hurricane-like force of nature. They flocked by the millions, even the billions, so that their passing blotted out the sun. Passenger pigeons once dominated the eastern half of North America, and they affected human culture as much as bison, grizzlies, or wolves.

Three final criteria also influenced my choices. One was variety. In total, these species span the globe, touching every continent, and they include mammals, reptiles, and birds, carnivores and herbivores, species on land and in water. They include familiar animals, whose histories might be surprising, and unusual species you might never have heard of—like the moa, aurochs, thylacine, and baiji.

Species were also chosen that lived into the modern era, meaning within the last 500 years—not coincidentally, right about the time of the great age of European open-ocean exploration that Christopher Columbus kick-started in 1492 with his voyage to the New World. This is about when scientists believe the sixth extinction began.

Finally, all the species are joined by loss. Each species has experienced extinction on some level. Seven species are entirely extinct, and six species have suffered the extinction of one or more subspecies (while other subspecies survive). Extinction dates guide how the book is arranged: by using the date of extinction of either the full species or a subspecies, the stories are ordered from the earliest extinction to the most recent.

These last two criteria are why no whales, elephants, or great apes appear in this book. Thankfully, despite being endangered, in some cases critically endangered, these species haven't yet experienced any extinctions in the modern age.

If we want to keep it that way, we have work to do.

A Long Relationship: Megafauna Then & Now

We've known all the species in this book a very long time, and each species existed for millions of years, sometimes tens of millions of years, before modern humans evolved. This ancient human and evolutionary history is also part of these stories.

Where did the Steller's sea cow come from? Why did the elephant bird become so huge? What made tigers such successful predators in the first place?

Then, once the first humans came along, what happened when they met these animals? What did people do when faced with herds of 12-foot-tall moa pounding across grasslands? What myths did they tell about the mighty aurochs and the graceful baiji? Did we ever coexist in peace with lions and thylacines?

Originally, giant species defined their landscapes, and early human society, in order to succeed, frequently had to solve the challenges these animals posed. Do these early encounters show that conflict with certain species was inevitable? Or did something change in modern times that caused a species' demise? Most of all, could we have done something differently to avoid extinction?

What's striking is that, quite often, the signature attributes that once allowed a giant species to become dominant—to outcompete others and reach the top—are the very ones that have caused us the most trouble and that are liabilities when we coexist.

This is, perhaps, one of the most important lessons: if we value and want to preserve giant animals in the wild, we will have to put up with what we consider their most difficult traits.

In addition, this book discusses an earlier extinction event that relates to our modern crisis. All the species in this book lived during the great age of megafauna that defined the Pleistocene—the geological epoch right before ours, which began about 2.6 million years ago. During this age, the earth was chock-full of legendary, colossal creatures: woolly mammoths and mastodons, short-faced bears and sabertooth cats, carnivorous kangaroos, giant ground sloths, and 1-ton lizards.

These behemoths ruled the world in which humans evolved, and yet these creatures don't rule any longer. Most of these enormous animals eventually disappeared. Starting about 50,000 years ago and lasting until about 10,000 years ago, about half of all the largest species on Earth died out. This is an extremely curious, even mysterious event. What could have possibly happened during that time that would have caused this wave of extinctions?

Scientists have focused on two things. One is that, within this 40,000-year period, our planet experienced the last ice age, which was marked by periods of severe climate change as the earth rapidly cooled and later warmed. The other is that the first modern humans, Cro-Magnons, began their steady migration across the globe, settling on every continent. Dubbed the mammoth hunters, Cro-Magnons were the first human species to develop the skills, weapons, and intelligence to hunt the biggest prey and fight off the most dangerous predators. They were wildly successful, and we are their children.

This moment marks our "first encounter" with many of this book's species, and our evolution within this world of giants has left a lasting legacy on us: in certain essential ways, it made us who we are. In boxed spreads in between the animal stories, I explore what we know about the Late Pleistocene extinctions and the rise and fall of these earlier giants. Scientists still heatedly debate the causes of the Late Pleistocene extinctions, but the parallels to today are eerie: a similarly deadly combination of human impacts and climate change are imperiling Earth's animals.

Wrestling with Extinction: Causes & Conservation

All these stories about giants provide lessons about coexistence that can help us and guide us in our conservation efforts today. One main reason to tell extinction stories is to understand what has happened in the past so we can avoid extinctions in the future. The continued survival of many species depends on us.

My hope is to show that extinction stories and conservation stories are actually the same story about our evolving relationship with animals. One story becomes the other at the moment our awareness and attitudes change and we act to help species who are being harmed. Several of the animal profiles highlight our conservation efforts to save endangered species today, and it's possible that some of the extinct species in this book might still be with us if we had become more aware and acted more effectively sooner.

This isn't to say or imply that extinction is all our fault or that humans alone can always stop extinction from happening. That's not fair or accurate. As these stories show, sometimes we don't realize we're causing harm, and we don't mean to, yet we still do. Many factors can be at work, and humans can't control everything. Sometimes, despite our Herculean efforts to save an animal, the species still fails.

Plus, extinction, like death, is a fact of life. No species lasts forever. Ultimately, extinction occurs when a species can't overcome or adapt to some critical problem, such as the arrival of an unfamiliar predator or a major change in its habitat. This goes on all the time. Every species must "evolve or die," as it were. The only constant is change.

The reason extinction is considered a crisis today is that so many more species are going extinct so much more quickly than normal. This indicates that we are experiencing an unusual, global problem. In the epilogue, "Written in the Earth: The Sixth Extinction & the Anthropocene," I discuss the overall numbers in more detail: I provide current species counts and extinction rates, and I also explain why counting species is so difficult and can be so controversial.

Yet for all the debates over numbers, scientists generally agree that most extinctions today are the result of some combination of four main causes: habitat change, pollution, introduced invasive species, and human hunting or killing. All play major roles in this book, and all relate to us.

Habitat change is by far the most serious and affects the most species, and the majority of habitat impacts in modern times are due to humans. We've steadily converted the world's wilderness into fields and fodder, suburbs and cities. We've now filled the globe with over 7 billion of ourselves—and all the meals, houses, cars, and industry that means—and in the process we have crowded out many species.

In addition, climate change is transforming habitats and driving species toward extinction. Human activity contributes to global warming as well, even if it isn't the sole cause, and unfortunately, climate change will continue to cause extinctions even if we never cut down another tree.

What can we do? The stories highlight all the ways we are currently trying to help, protect, live with, and restore endangered species—along with our attempts to resurrect extinct ones. De-extinction, as it's called, can border on science fiction, and it includes cloning, gene splicing, and crossbreeding hybrids. Entire "frozen arks" of preserved DNA await the perfection of these techniques, so that one day we might welcome back the woolly mammoth and re-create any species the earth might lose.

That day is not here yet. Traditional conservation is still the main approach, though it's not so traditional anymore, either. Captive-breeding programs throw a lifeline to species on the brink, while "rewilding" projects attempt to reintroduce top predators and large herbivores into landscapes where these species have been driven out. That said, the simplest strategy remains the most effective: giving wild animals enough space and enough freedom from human interference to live the lives they evolved to lead.

Most of all, the unbelievable devotion of a great many people to protecting wildlife and wilderness gives us many reasons to hope that humanity can meet this crisis. Turn to "Call to Action" for a list of resources for more information and ways to get involved.

Conservation and coexistence aren't, and may never be, easy. They mean, at various times, making more room for animals, paying the costs, giving up traditions, revising our beliefs, and occasionally, particularly with giants, learning to live with trouble.

Why Giants Matter

In the end, does it matter that the species in this book went extinct? What's the difference? Do we really need them or any endangered species?

These are not rhetorical questions. They are some of the most important questions we can ask. If we don't identify reasons to care, both personally for ourselves and as a society, then we won't be inspired to act on behalf of wildlife. Conservation and coexistence are expensive. They cost time, money, and effort. We need to know that species are important and necessary and worth those costs. In one form or another, we must always ask these questions and come up with satisfying answers.

Here are several good reasons why giants matter.

The first is that large, charismatic species often *already* matter to us. Whether because of our long history with a species, or out of pure affection for an animal, or out of reverence for life itself, we frequently care without having to be convinced. Animals such as rhinos, elephants, tigers, giant pandas, and baiji have inspired worldwide conservation efforts simply because people treasure them. They are like family. Sentiment can be dismissed as impractical, but for many, love is reason enough.

However, the most practical reason is that giant species frequently play an outsize role in their ecosystems, one that's equivalent to their weight. Of course, all species in an ecosystem matter because all species coevolve together and live in interdependent communities. Yet top predators and large herbivores often have more influence over an ecosystem's dynamics. Animals who play these roles are often dubbed keystone species.

When these animals disappear, many species may suffer, and ecosystems are more likely to fall out of balance. In other words, the species at the top of the food web—who are always the largest animals—affect many other species, both flora and fauna.

Conserving giant animals and top predators is often key to preserving wilderness and biodiversity in general, and these species can be a handy measuring stick for evaluating an ecosystem's health. When giants are healthy, ecosystems tend to thrive; when they are not, ecosystems often suffer. This isn't universally true, but it's one reason that saving giants is so important. Doing so can sometimes go a long way to saving many species, even the smallest ones we can't see.

Since quantifying the *exact* impact of losing a particular species in an ecosystem can be very difficult, many people also cite the "precautionary principle" as another reason to save wildlife. As Aldo Leopold said, "To keep every cog and wheel is the first precaution of intelligent tinkering." It's always wisest to conserve all the parts of an ecosystem on the assumption that all are needed. As several stories and that old saw about Humpty Dumpty demonstrate, it's much harder to recover and restore what was than to preserve what is.

Further, we don't always know how far ecosystems can bend before they break, and some breakdowns are more severe than others. With so many species failing today, the wider concern is that certain ecosystems might become so dysfunctional that they won't properly support human needs, such as for agriculture, raising livestock, and providing fresh water. Preserving the full diversity of wildlife supports the biosphere that supports us.

Giant animals are also important because they represent the crown jewels of evolution. Relatively speaking, giant species are rare. They take millions of years to evolve, and just the right circumstances, and the world only contains so many. Giants are complex, beautiful, and often smart. As I've mentioned, *we* are giant animals, and we know that certain others— like whales, dolphins, elephants, great apes, wolves, horses, big cats, bears, and so on—are among the most intelligent, emotionally aware, and social animals that exist.

When we look a lion or a grizzly in the eye, we don't wonder whether they can think. Their eyes twinkle with consciousness; their actions betray curiosity, memory, and awareness. Instead, we only wonder *what* they think as we interact with them and communicate intuitively, nonverbally. Giants matter because intelligence matters.

Which leads back to our crazy desire to risk wild encounters. Giant animals are wondrous and fascinating because we see something of ourselves in them, and that's not anthropomorphism. Giant species see us, communicate with us, teach us about existence and awareness. Our lives would feel incomplete if we never connected with them, directly, heart to heart. We don't trek across continents to meet squirrels. We don't scuba dive to visit plankton. We don't take African safaris for the mosquitos. We want our pulse to race with the fear, excitement, and awe of meeting our fellow giants, especially those creatures bigger, stronger, and more daunting than ourselves.

The stories of giant animals in this book are just one small piece of the larger story about the impact of people, of us, on our planet. Whenever magnificent animals disappear, our lives are impoverished. And yet these stories also exemplify the reassuring truth that caring and action can make a positive difference, every time. ⤳

AUSTRALIA

TASMANIA   NEW ZEALAND

MOA: THE WORLD'S BIGGEST "CHICKEN"

EXTINCTION: up to thirteen species of moa were mostly extinct by 1500; the last moa went extinct possibly one to three centuries later

The Maori of New Zealand are some of the most famous cannibals in human history. In their fierce warrior culture, eating one another became an everyday reality of war. But it wasn't always that way.

Their story starts with an unlikely journey. Polynesian peoples sailed across the then-unknown waters of the South Pacific, probably from the Society Islands in the mid-1200s, until they reached New Zealand, a pair of islands that until that moment had never known a human footfall. By doing so, the Maori didn't just discover a semitropical paradise—a worthy reward for their breathtakingly dangerous voyage—they stumbled upon one of evolution's most fascinating experiments.

Land of Walking Birds

Approaching New Zealand for the first time, the Maori would have been hit by a symphony of noise. According to early accounts, the islands were deafening, particularly at dawn and dusk, for that is when Earth's avians always open up their throats and sing. Untouched New Zealand was an unprecedented, unique home for birds, and their majestic cacophony, over 60 million years in the making, must have cascaded down the shore in an overwhelming, heart-pounding avalanche.

Naturalist Joseph Banks described awakening to birdsong on the morning of February 6, 1770, while anchored a quarter mile offshore: "Their voices were certainly the [most] melodious wild musick I have ever heard, almost imitating small bells but with the most tuneable silver sound imaginable."

As they beached their boats and leapt out, the Maori would have discovered a big surprise: here, many birds walked. On New Zealand, nearly every bird family developed one or more flightless or poorly flighted species, including pelicans, parrots, pigeons, penguins, wrens, ducks, geese, owls, crows, and swans. These grounded flocks, having long given up the air because there was never any need to take to it, would have barely bothered to amble out of the way of these newly arrived strangers.

Even among this cornucopia of birds, the Maori would have noticed the moa, which dominated New Zealand. Moa were a type of ratite—the name for any flightless bird without a keel (an extension of the breastbone where wing muscles attach)—which today includes emus and ostriches. On New Zealand, moa had been flightless for so long that they had completely lost their wings, and they had divided into a vast and varied congregation of species.

The giant moa—*Dinornis giganteus*—was the tallest bird that ever lived. Stretching 12 to 13 feet from talon tip to feathered crown and weighing 550 to 600 pounds, it was as tall as an elephant and as heavy as a tiger. A slow-running "herd" of giant moa would have shuddered the ground. If moa were like Africa's ostriches, they probably didn't voice a "tuneable silver sound," either; they more likely hissed, grunted, and roared like an angry lion when upset. This wasn't a bird to trifle with.

An estimated nine to thirteen species of moa once existed, divided among two or three moa families. There may have been more species, but scientists can't quite make up their minds about moa taxonomy (or the classification of species and subspecies). Moa ranged across nearly every landscape on both North and South Island. They lived in humid forests and dry grasslands, along the coast and in the mountains. They came in small, medium, and large sizes. The smallest moa was only 3 feet tall and

45 pounds, about the same as the dodo on Mauritius.

Spectacularly successful, moa were preyed on by only one predator: the Haast's eagle, the largest eagle that ever lived. With a nearly 10-foot wingspan, the Haast's eagle could break a moa's thick neck in a single strike. Maybe—who knows?—seeing this giant raptor cruising the sky, and contemplating walking birds twice as tall as a human, the first Maori had second thoughts about this particular beachfront property. Nervous or not, they settled in and made themselves at home.

Maybe they sensed an opportunity. New Zealand was unique not only for what it possessed but for what it lacked. Having separated from other landmasses about 80 million years ago, New Zealand had no land mammals—until people came along. Thus, the Maori found oodles of seals and fish, veritable cities of frogs, a good number of lizards and reptiles, two species of bats (the only mammals), and birds of all types literally everywhere, but no mammals like themselves. No deer, monkeys, pigs, buffalo, bears, tigers, wolves, apes, or rats. No tortoises or crocodiles.

As paleontologist Tim Flannery wrote, New Zealand embodied "what the world might have looked like if mammals as well as dinosaurs had become extinct 65 million years ago, leaving the birds to inherit the globe."

Further, because of its long isolation, most animal life on New Zealand was endemic, meaning it existed nowhere else. These islands were such a rare crucible of evolution that, as anthropologist Jared Diamond wrote, they were "as close as we will get to the opportunity to study life on another planet."

Giant, Flightless & Fearless

This raises the question, where did moa come from? They had no wings and couldn't swim, so how did they get to New Zealand, which is 1,300 miles southeast of Australia, or the back end of nowhere? Why did moa get so big in the first place, and how did they become New Zealand's dominant species?

The origins of the moa, and its relation to other living ratites, have long befuddled scientists. In 2014, DNA research may have finally cracked the case. It turns out that the moa evolved from a relatively small, winged bird that flew to New Zealand about 60 million years ago, and then it steadily grew until it was too big to fly.

Scientists had long assumed that moa must be closely related to kiwis, a small flightless species that's also native to New Zealand, or perhaps moa were close kin to other large ratites like the ostrich, the emu, the rhea, or the cassowary. Nope—none of the above. DNA shows that the moa is most closely related to the tinamous, a small South American bird that can still fly, though it mostly lives on the ground. Meanwhile, New Zealand's kiwi is most closely related to Madagascar's even-more-massive elephant bird.

How exactly did *that* happen?

First of all, over the long history of avian life, bird species have evolved to become flightless numerous times—when this happens, flightless birds sometimes come to resemble one another due to what's called convergent evolution. Sometimes, different species that occupy equivalent ecological niches, or play equivalent roles, will develop similar physical attributes and behavior, since they are solving similar lifestyle problems. As we'll see, this is why Australia's thylacine resembled Eurasia's wolf, and why Mascarene giant tortoises looked like Galápagos giant tortoises. Today, even though ostriches and emus look like siblings, their genes tell us otherwise, and neither is a near relative of the extinct moa. All are distinct species that evolved separately to look alike.

The reason the moa got so big, while the tinamous remained small, was due to ancient New Zealand's relative lack of other species, particularly large animals or predators. That first ancestral moa flew in and found few competitors for resources. Nothing stopped it from having the run of the place. So over millions of years, the original moa split into a variety of new species, each adapting to fill "empty" ecological niches. Some moa reached high, some stayed low; some preferred shrubs, some trees, and some grasses. This process—in which one moa species became a dozen species of vastly different sizes and habits—is called adaptive radiation. This process is very common among bird species on remote islands.

"THE GIANT MOA—*DINORNIS GIGANTEUS*— WAS THE TALLEST BIRD THAT EVER LIVED. STRETCHING 12 TO 13 FEET FROM TALON TIP TO FEATHERED CROWN AND WEIGHING 550 TO 600 POUNDS, IT WAS TALL AS AN ELEPHANT AND AS HEAVY AS A TIGER."

However, all moa became flightless to the point that their wings atrophied, and even these vestigial wings disappeared. This is a testament to their species' great age. While almost every bird that found New Zealand also developed a flightless species, only the moa lost its wings. You might think that flying is too cool to quit (I, for one, can't imagine not using wings if I had them), but that's not how nature operates. Flying takes a lot of energy, and when birds don't have to fly, they often stop. On New Zealand, with no terrestrial predators to worry about, many birds claimed the ground, which was a smart adaptive strategy. The energy saved by not flying could be put to other uses, like eating and reproducing.

Thus, moa diversified to become New Zealand's equivalent of rhinos, giraffes, kangaroos, sheep, and goats, with a different moa species occupying each ecological niche. All were herbivores, and they ate everything: grasses, leaves, twigs, seeds, fruits, shrubs, and so on. Their long deadly talons were effective defensive weapons, but they were mostly used, scientists speculate, to dig for roots, insects, and grubs.

Only their beaks and feet weren't covered in feathers. This was probably protection from New Zealand's cold winters. We can only speculate about their plumage and color: moas were probably a ruddy or reddish brown, but pure white, purple, and yellow moa feathers have also been found, some 9 inches long.

Moa habits are also obscure. Fossil evidence and oral history suggest that moa bred once a year, laying one or two eggs, and the male may have incubated the eggs along with the female. They ran well but were probably slower than today's ostriches, which can reach 40 miles per hour.

Also unknown is how many moa populated New Zealand before the Maori arrived. Judging by the piles of bones, a lot. Conservative estimates are from 70,000 to 150,000 moa overall, with about twice as many moa on South Island as on North.

No Wings, But It Tastes Like Chicken

What did the Maori think upon seeing the moa, and how important was this bird to them? Well, *moa* in Polynesia is a common word for the domestic chicken. After their long voyage, what the Maori probably thought was, *dinner*.

It's possible that the Maori brought domestic chickens with them to New Zealand; Polynesian wayfarers often carried them. If they did, the Maori quickly ate these scrawny fowl and forgot about them; we've found no fossil evidence of domestic chickens on New Zealand. In naming this bird, it's almost as if the Maori said, now *this* is a chicken!

The Maori then proceeded to turn the coasts of New Zealand into essentially one huge, ongoing barbecue for the next 200 years. Moa were hunted on a comparable scale to the slaughter of bison in North America. During this period, moa were estimated to constitute from a quarter to a half of the Maori diet.

Not that they ate moa every night. The Maori diet was initially diverse. They also hunted marine mammals like fur seals, sea lions, and elephant seals. Using moa bones for fish hooks, they caught tons of snapper off the coast, and they ate dozens and dozens of other bird species. For a time, New Zealand's spectacular abundance must have seemed endless, and the Maori population grew exponentially.

One tremendous cooking site on North Island shows evidence of three moa species and fifty-five other bird species, many now extinct. On South Island, one well-used butchering site contains the remains of 30,000 to 90,000 moa. Overall, we've found evidence of over 73 significant moa-hunting sites (and 300 in all), most dating from 500 to 800 years ago. Great mounds of moa bones still remain scattered across the countryside, as if the cook fires were lit only yesterday.

In hindsight, it's easy to see that the Maori grew too quickly and over-exploited New Zealand's resources. Today, we are well aware of the fragile limitations of island ecosystems, but the Maori probably were not, and the consequences were tragic.

For instance, the Maori targeted mature, adult moa and ate their eggs in equal measure. This undermined the moa's ability to breed twice over, which accelerated their population decline. The Maori also left a lot of meat on the bone: abundant evidence exists of wasteful practices at butchering sites. After a hunt, Maori would drag legs to the roasting pits and leave the rest of the body to rot. This indicates that moa were once so plentiful the Maori could be choosy about what to eat.

This wastage also implies that the moa must have been easy to hunt. You don't waste food that's hard to get. A gigantic 12-foot moa—faced with an unfamiliar ape waving a stick—might have naively let itself be clubbed to death. Isolated island species who have never seen humans, or even mammals, often don't recognize them as a predator. The innocence of undiscovered island species is well chronicled. Moa certainly learned to fear humans, but how long did it take before self-protection became a habit? Maori lacked bows and arrows, and we have yet to find any specialized

Island Dwarfism: The Incredible Shrinking Giants

Not all animals aspire to be big.

Millions of years ago during the Pleistocene, when giant mammals migrated to tiny islands, they sometimes got small, evolving to become mini versions of their enormous continental cousins. Big species adapted to the suddenly constrained living space and more limited food supply of their new homes by shrinking.

Nowhere was "insular dwarfism" more notable and bizarre than on ancient Mediterranean islands. Corsica, Sardinia, Sicily, Crete, Cyprus, the Balearics, and others were all colonized by large mammals, who probably walked or waded to these islands during ice ages when sea levels were low. When sea levels rose again, the animals became marooned, and for generations afterward, they became ever more modest until their size matched their reduced circumstances.

Every Mediterranean island seemed to have its own species of pygmy hippo (similar to Madagascar's) and pygmy elephant. Related to African elephants, these dwarf pachyderms stood only 3 to 5 feet tall and weighed about 450 pounds, give or take. So, technically, they were megafauna, but it's hard to take an elephant seriously when it's the same height as the average ten-year-old child.

Sicily had several species of pygmy elephants, and these Lilliputians may have contributed to myths about the Roc—the legendary giant bird, perhaps modeled after Madagascar's elephant bird, that could lift and smash elephants. Madagascar's elephant bird, after all, was twice the weight of *these* tiny specimens.

Sardinia, meanwhile, held a dwarf mammoth, and Crete had seven or eight species of pygmy deer. Possibly related to the Pleistocene's half-ton Irish elk—one of the largest deer that ever lived, with some of the biggest antlers—Crete's stubby-legged cousins ranged from a reasonable 5.5 feet tall to a truly minuscule species that reached only 16 inches at the shoulders. Still, the little guy stood proud: its impressive antlers were 31 inches long.

moa-hunting weapons. Apparently, all the Maori needed to hunt giant moa were clubs, wooden spears, snares, and the aid of companion dogs.

Over the first three centuries of Maori settlement, New Zealand experienced a large wave of extinctions, which eventually included a quarter of its bird species. Starting about 800 years ago, one of the first to go was the Haast's eagle. Scientists speculate this raptor died out because its main prey—the moa—was disappearing, but humans may also have targeted this predator directly. In addition, New Zealand's marine mammals became completely hunted out, leaving beaches empty, and even ocean fish stocks declined near shore.

By 1500, the good times were over. The archaeological evidence shows that most moa species were by then extinct, and the age of moa hunting was finished, just like that. However, some moa probably remained scattered among inaccessible valleys and mountains; dating when the very last moa died is difficult and controversial. Tantalizing evidence exists that handfuls of birds may have outrun the grim reaper for centuries.

Yet as the defining species of New Zealand's landscape, and as a food source for an entire people, the moa was gone as the sixteenth century dawned. Too late, the Maori realized their mistake, which they immortalized in their famous lament:

Ka ngaro, i te ngaro, a te moa: "Lost as the moa is lost."

Famine, War & Meat

During their first few hundred years on New Zealand, the Maori were a happy, peaceful bunch. They proliferated, feasted on plentiful roasted meats, and lived in large, apparently harmonious villages. At least, we find no archaeological evidence of organized conflict until the 1400s, when the first forts were built. This timing coincides with the swiftly declining populations of New Zealand's birds, seals, and fish.

The cost of this peaceful interlude was high. Most of the extinctions of New Zealand's unique fauna were clearly caused by people, and certainly overhunting was the primary cause of the moa's extinction. Moa couldn't breed fast enough to keep up with the killing. Plus, stuck on an island, unable to fly, moa had nowhere to run. The very attribute that had allowed moa to rule New Zealand—their prodigious size, along with the tradeoffs of being huge (see page 80)—had worked against them.

However, deforestation and habitat loss also played roles. Over their first two centuries, the Maori put a torch to 40 percent of the island's forests to clear land for themselves and to cultivate native plants. Also, two invasive species—rats and dogs, the first an inadvertent stowaway with the original Maori, the second their trusted companion—probably preyed on bird eggs and played a small part in the moa's decline.

By the 1500s, the crowded Maori villages dispersed; too many humans and too few resources were causing conflicts that drove people apart. The Maori had little agriculture. Besides some tropical fruits, they grew a meager, finger-size type of sweet potato, and they cultivated and collected the roots of a native bracken fern. Previously the neglected side starches of the Maori banquet, these plants became prized foods to be defended with your life. Indeed, Maori forts were originally built to protect their painstakingly collected stores of potatoes. But the Maori also needed meat. So they ate dogs and roasted rats, until eventually...

If only they had kept a few chickens.

By the mid-1600s, the Maori had transformed into a culture of violent, tattooed warriors. Not only was war as regular as rain, but it provided necessary sustenance. For Maori, cannibalism became an entrenched custom of battle, in which an accepted spoil of victory was eating the enemy's dead. Mostly, this appears to have been a way to feed the troops, but eating one another was occasionally necessary to stave off famine.

The biography of a famous Maori chief, Te Rauparaha—written in 1869 by his son, Tamihana—includes numerous matter-of-fact references to cannibalism. After one battle around 1820, Tamihana wrote, "The bodies of the slaughtered were covered in a heap until later, when the party would return and dismember them… Te Rauparaha told how he had won the battle, saying that Tukataro, Karewha and ten other men were killed and that they should go back to eat the bodies."

Of course, Maori went to war for all the usual reasons—power, land, revenge, and honor—and Maori society was complex and beautiful. It knew times of peace and planting. Yet cannibalism wasn't occasional or accidental. It became an accepted part of Maori culture, and it's hard not to connect this with the demise of the moa and the impoverishment of New Zealand's landscape. As a general rule, people don't eat people unless they have no other choice.

The first European to find New Zealand was Dutch explorer Abel Tasmin in 1642. He did not actually land in New Zealand, which is understandable: a dinghy sent to greet the island's native peoples was attacked, unprovoked, and the dead sailors were dragged into the forest, presumably as food. Tasmin dubbed the place "Murderer's Bay" and left.

The next European visitor, British explorer Captain James Cook, didn't arrive until 1769. He was greeted with a different Maori expression: *Haere mai ki uta kia patua.* "Come ashore and be clubbed." In 1835, after exploring the Galápagos, Charles Darwin visited during his famous voyage aboard the *Beagle,* but he was soon happy to leave New Zealand. Darwin wrote, "I should think a more warlike race of inhabitants could not be found in any part of the world."

Then, over the next century, the Maori suffered a tragic fate that sadly resembled what happened to the moa, and which was repeated on many Pacific islands (including Tasmania, last home of the thylacine): the native peoples were overwhelmed and overrun by invading European colonists who wanted the islands for themselves. The British waged war on the Maori and eventually defeated them. This, along with the scourge of introduced diseases, drove Maori society to the brink of extinction, but that is another story.

The Last Moa

When Captain Cook anchored off New Zealand in 1769, he supposedly saw a strange giant bird running along the beach and disappear into the woods. Most today discount this story as apocryphal, a fanciful imagining, since they assume all moa were extinct by then.

And yet...

Western scientists didn't realize that New Zealand had once harbored enormous walking birds until the 1840s, when they first discovered moa bones. Before then, the Maori had neglected to mention the moa to Europeans. Apparently, Maori oral history had preserved few details about moa or their own moa-hunting traditions—as if as a culture they'd forgotten about the species that once defined their lives. Rather, Maori more often told stories of a mythic creature, also called a moa, with the body of a chicken and a human face.

However, when pressed by nineteenth-century scientists, individual Maori told intriguing if conflicting tales. Some Maori assured listeners the moa were long gone, while others claimed to have hunted moa themselves into the late eighteenth century. One Maori, Kawani Paipai, described various hunting methods. One approach was to chase a moa until it was entrapped and encircled. Then, when the giant bird lifted a powerful, deadly claw to defend itself, men from behind would strike its standing leg. Once grounded, the moa was easily killed with spears. Another method was to spear and injure a moa and simply keep chasing it until it collapsed of exhaustion.

In addition, dozens of written accounts of moa sightings by Europeans came to light, dating from 1770 and continuing through the 1800s. Whalers and sealers in New Zealand claimed to have dined on moa and seen the monstrous beasts running along beaches. In the 1820s, a certain George Pauley said he stumbled into a 20-foot-tall moa; each was so startled by the other that they ran in opposite directions.

In 1861, a survey party reported seeing fresh, three-toed footprints 14 inches long. In 1868, someone claimed to know of a small moa killed out of a flock of half a dozen. In 1878, a farmer said his dog flushed a moa out of the scrub, which then stared at them for ten full minutes. Even as recently as 1950, an expedition reported seeing two birds who looked like emus on New Zealand.

In some uninhabited valley, might a clutch of moas *still* peck the grass?

It's exciting to imagine, but the truth is, we've yet to find any physical evidence of living moa after Europeans arrived in New Zealand, such as moa bones butchered with iron tools or moa bones mixed with pig bones (since Captain Cook brought the first pigs). Further, the nineteenth-century Europeans who interviewed the Maoris aren't reliable sources themselves; their records are tainted with confusions, corruptions, misinterpretations, and obvious errors. In their accounts, facts get mixed up with fiction, and the Maori stories they recorded can't be fully trusted. None of the European sightings can be verified. All might be tall tales and wishful thinking.

In the end, whether the last moa perished in 1500, 1650, or the 1880s, the 60-million-year-old evolutionary experiment that was New Zealand is long gone. Even when Joseph Banks heard New Zealand's "melodious wild musick" in 1770, the islands were a pale echo of their original selves, and today that concert is over. ⌁

AUROCHS: THE ORIGINAL WILD BULL

EXTINCTION: the last aurochs died in 1627

The aurochs has the ironic distinction of being the first extinction that humans ever documented. The aurochs went the way of the dodo in 1627, while the dodo—history's second documented extinction—didn't go the way of itself until the 1660s.

Why ironic? Because the wild aurochs (which despite the *s* is both singular and plural) is the parent species for all domestic cattle, and domestic cattle are the most successful and important species on earth. In all, nearly 1.5 billion cattle representing perhaps a thousand types encircle the globe today, one for every five human beings, and without domestic cattle, civilization as we know it would not exist.

Yet the success of its well-behaved children is primarily what did the aurochs in. That's gratitude, huh?

Giants of Cave Painting

Aurochs have always held a special place in the human imagination. The species caught our attention early and never let go.

The same can be said of many giants. Big wild animals are almost invariably the focus of prehistoric figurative rock art. We can only guess at the art's purpose—it may be ritualized hunting magic, or hunting instructions, or spiritual communication, or storytelling, or artistic expression—but our obsession with giant animals rings loud and clear. They rumbled across crowded prehistoric landscapes and defined our early existence.

The aurochs (*Bos primigenius*) is one of fourteen species depicted in France's Chauvet Cave, whose art dates to at least 32,000 to 30,000 years ago, and some say it may be 36,000 years old. This makes it the oldest cave painting in Europe and among the oldest anywhere. Aurochs are also featured in the famous cave paintings at Altamira, Spain (dating from 22,000 to 14,000 years ago), and at Lascaux, France (dating from 17,000 years ago). In Lascaux, the Great Hall of the Bulls showcases four aurochs, one stretching 17 feet long and among the largest animals ever depicted in cave art.

Was this aurochs to scale? Twice the size of any known aurochs, it would have been equivalent to an Asian elephant. However, Caesar, the famous Roman emperor, wrote that aurochs were "little smaller than elephants in size," and a twelfth-century account also called them "as big as an elephant."

Could certain individuals have been that massive? Humans are notorious exaggerators, so probably not, but we don't really know because no one took a tape measure to a living aurochs when they had a chance.

Indeed, though beautiful and even lifelike, ancient art only hints at the living animal. Later paintings and illustrations of aurochs aren't very accurate either. That's all we possess besides bones. So today, researchers must measure fossils, chew their pencils, and guesstimate how big the earth's original bovine really was, rump to horn tip and hoof to withers (or the tops of the shoulder blades).

What's clear is that aurochs were significantly larger than domestic cattle and "squarely built." Weighing up to 3,000 pounds, an adult bull likely stood 5.5 to 6.3 feet tall at the shoulders. Its body length roughly matched its height, to which was added a huge head and stupendous horns: a pair of ivory-colored, spiraled, forward-curving daggers ending in sharp black tips that could reach 3.5 feet long.

In modern terms, it's like taking the original, classic Volkswagen bus, chopping a few feet off the back end, replacing the rearview mirrors with swords, and there's your aurochs bull, a ton-plus of rock-solid, grass-chewing meanness.

No wonder they caught our attention.

Female aurochs were noticeably smaller, by a foot or more all around. This gender size difference is known as sexual dimorphism, and it's a common trait among herd-living herbivores.

Since even the ancients painted in color, one thing we're more certain of is their hide. Bulls were black or a rich blackish brown and females were more reddish brown. Both genders also had a light-colored stripe running down their back, and they had a tousled mop of shaggy, curly hair between their horns.

For some reason, among the animal's many daunting attributes, this incongruous frizzy forehead inspired the most fear in us. One sixteenth-century hunter wrote that it "makes the animal horrible to behold," a sentiment echoed by others.

Another incongruity: aurochs were legendary for their unyielding nature. They weren't just big; they stared you down. They never gave in, meeting every challenge and every challenger head-on. And yet of all the megaherbivores depicted in those ancient caves—including elk, bison, red deer, elephants, rhinos, hippos, and so on—only aurochs and horses were domesticated.

After the woolly mammoth and the woolly rhino went extinct, the aurochs was left as Europe's largest land mammal, and yet somehow we persuaded this powerful, unrelenting behemoth to relax and come live with us.

Wild Mother of a Thousand Children

That ancient humans learned how to domesticate wild animals is self-evident: anyone with a dog or cat, or who rides a horse, lives with the proof. How did people do it? That we can only guess.

Chauvet Cave: "They Have Been Here!"

On a chilly December afternoon in 1994, in southern France's Ardèche valley, three friends and amateur spelunkers—Jean-Marie Chauvet, Éliette Brunel, and Christian Hillaire—chipped away at a jumble of limestone rocks. Chauvet had noticed that the crevices exhaled air, a good sign that hidden caverns lay beyond.

They widened the opening enough for Brunel, the smallest, to squeeze through, and she confirmed that some vast sunken grotto awaited their discovery. The others followed, and the trio descended carefully onto the stalagmite-covered cave floor.

As they crept gingerly deeper into the earth, Brunel caught a glimpse of a wall marked with purposeful red lines and shouted, "They have been here!"

They were ancient humans, Cro-Magnons, who well over 30,000 years ago used the vaulted chambers within this quarter-mile-long cavern to create the Sistine Chapel of cave art.

The sophistication, complexity, and age of the Chauvet Cave art stunned archeologists. These figures are among the world's oldest known human-

The wolf was the first wild animal to morph into an entirely new, domestic species, the dog. This doesn't mean we tamed a few individuals now and then; even lions can occasionally be tamed. Rather, generations of tamed wolves steadily evolved to become genetically different, until each new generation was born preferring to live with people. With the wolf, this process happened very slowly, over thousands, and perhaps tens of thousands, of years, sometime between 30,000 and 14,000 years ago. At some point when prehistoric humans were painting in caves, the dog joined us, perhaps sitting alertly by the artist's side.

Then, 13,000 to 11,000 years ago, what's known as the Neolithic revolution began. We domesticated the first wild grains (rye and wheat), and we domesticated goats, sheep, and pigs. With these, humans shifted for painted images, yet they are not the crude doodles of first-time artists. Cro-Magnons had by then developed a powerful, symbolic visual language that they wielded with almost unmatched skill and grace.

As the original discoverers wrote in their recent memoir, "We crouched on our heels, gazing at the cave wall, mute with stupefaction."

In all, Chauvet Cave contains over 400 images, and over half are of cave bears, mammoths, woolly rhinos, and lions. Yet the plethora of mega-fauna includes aurochs, bison, hyenas, panthers, leopards, horses, red deer, ibex, and musk ox. Chauvet is unique for its wealth of predators, some of whom also visited the cavern. The bones and skulls of cave bears and ancient wolves litter the ground.

Even though Chauvet Cave is closed to the public, there are two vivid ways to experience it. One is to watch the 2010 movie *Cave of Forgotten Dreams* by Werner Herzog, who spent six days filming inside. The other is, if you happen to be in southern France, to visit the Caverne du Pont d'Arc, a $62.5-million re-creation of Chauvet Cave that was unveiled in 2015.

the first time from hunters to herders, from foragers to farmers. Instead of living on the move, chasing our meals, and migrating with the seasons, we settled into permanent villages, stored food for the winter, and got busy with our epic work: civilization.

What we needed, though, was more muscle. Goats, sheep, pigs, and dogs were great, but they wouldn't pull a plow or a cart. Who might do that? Hmmm…

The aurochs was domesticated between 10,500 and 8,000 years ago, and humans performed this magic trick of turning aggression into agree-ableness not once, but possibly three separate times. The first was about 10,500 years ago in the Fertile Crescent of the Middle East, along the Tigris and Euphrates Rivers. Then we did it again in northern India about 9,500 years ago. Then we possibly did it a third time in North Africa some 9,500 to 8,000 years ago.

Afterward, cattle became living tools and the engines of the agricultural revolution. They were our tractors and trucks, plowing fields and hauling the harvest. They mowed pastures, eating hard-to-digest grasses, and their manure fertilized crops. Their milk, meat, and hides fed and clothed each expanding generation of people. Cattle came to define wealth and prosperity, and they carried us on their broad shoulders into the modern age.

Over the next 7,000 years, cattle were herded into every corner of the globe. As humans bred cattle for specific jobs in new habitats, their forms multiplied, becoming perhaps a thousand breeds in all (some of which have since disappeared).

By contrast, aurochs evolved into three subspecies, and their habitat only dwindled. Cattle directly competed with aurochs for the same types of grasslands, and as people cleared forests and created new pastures, aurochs were driven away so cattle could thrive.

Aurochs originally ranged across almost the entire temperate middle of Eurasia, from the Atlantic to the Pacific Ocean, from Great Britain south to India and along the North African coast. Then like water draining from a tub, with the drain itself in central Europe, the aurochs disappeared: first from East Asia, then from India, and then the Middle East. From 1300 BC to AD 400, aurochs vanished from Great Britain, Greece, Italy, France, Spain, Sweden, and the Netherlands. By 1300, it was gone from Germany, Hungary, and eastern Russia.

As the fourteenth century unfolded, Poland was the only place with aurochs.

Most people didn't mind. Cattle were essential to us, not aurochs. And the truth was, wild aurochs could be a real pain.

But even by this late date, the extinction of the aurochs wasn't inevitable. Rather, its demise epitomized how human attitudes toward wilderness and wildness had evolved.

Once there was only wilderness, and we were simply part of it; that's what we painted on cave walls. However, when we learned how to domesticate plants and animals, we learned how to create something other than wilderness, a world shaped by us, a world built *for* us. In the process, we became domesticated ourselves, and getting rid of wilderness, taming wildness inside and out, came to seem like our most important job.

The aurochs' wild, unpredictable nature embodied precisely what humans wanted to stamp out.

Don't Poke the Bull

So what was it about the aurochs? Was it really the crazed, snorting monster of legend?

Yes and no.

Actually, aurochs didn't seem to be a problem if you left them alone. Several firsthand accounts from the early 1600s testify to this. In 1634, one person wrote, "When not provoked, they will allow a human being or even a wild animal easy passage." In 1602, someone who'd clearly encountered an aurochs wrote:

> An aurochs is not afraid of humans and will not flee when a human being comes near, it will hardly avoid him when he approaches it slowly. And if someone tries to scare it by screaming or throwing something, this will not scare it in the least, but while it stays in its place it will actually open its mouth, widen it and close it again quickly, as if it is making fun at the human for this attempt. When it is standing in the road or somewhere else, one must go around it, even if one is driving a carriage, since it will not move off the road by itself. When challenged they become very hot-tempered, but if the person who has provoked it stretches out on the ground, nothing bad will happen to him, since they spare those who are stretched out, just like lions, with remarkable kindness.

Whether or not the writer personally tested this theory, he paints an interesting portrait: impassive, placid, unbothered, the aurochs feared nothing, not even us, who perhaps amused it. Having evolved to be more than a match for the nastiest predators of the Pleistocene, maybe the aurochs looked at us, thinking, *Grow some claws and teeth, then we'll talk...*

Perhaps this is a clue to how we domesticated the aurochs. So long as we were friendly, the animal tolerated us, even displaying "remarkable kindness." Many wild animals don't, no matter how nice we are. Tolerance of humans is an extremely rare trait among wild creatures.

But we didn't leave the aurochs alone. We poked it, hunted it, and provoked it to fight. When angry, the aurochs was an unrelenting beast, and overcoming such fury became a badge of honor and a way to prove one's courage. Perhaps people felt this proved their superiority over wildness itself.

This urge remains. To imagine facing an aurochs, imagine being a Spanish bullfighter or one of those daredevils in the streets of Pamplona when the bulls are let loose to run every year. Today, Spanish bulls are considered the most direct descendant of the aurochs. It's the domestic breed that has retained more of the aurochs' wild genes and behavior, just as certain dogs are more wolf-like. These encounters are the modern versions of what people have been doing for millennia.

Perhaps the earliest reference to a bullfight is in the epic poem *Gilgamesh*, which dates to at least 2000 BC. Gilgamesh defeats the Bull of Heaven in a mythic battle that may indicate a tradition of bullfighting already existed. Bullfights later emerged in ancient Turkey, Egypt, Crete, Italy, and Spain. Almost without question, the aurochs' signature move—the blindingly fast charge, horns down, in order to gore the enemy and toss the opponent into the air—is the one used by Spanish bulls today.

The distinctive art of bull jumping arose in Knossos on Crete; this acrobatic act of heart-stopping bravery was immortalized in Minoan art. The Romans also used aurochs in their arena battles and considered hunting aurochs a male rite of passage. As Julius Caesar wrote in 53 BC: "They kill [aurochs] after they have caught them in pitfalls. The young men season themselves to do this work and... those that have killed the most are greatly praised, after the horns have been displayed in public as evidence."

Hunting aurochs almost didn't seem worth it if you didn't get one of these talismans or trophies. The three treasured items were the horn, the "heart bone," and the hairy forelock. Aurochs horns were intricately carved, gilded with silver and gold, and used as drinking vessels or sounding horns. The heart bone is cross-shaped cartilage that exists in the heart of all bovines.

The forelock was the most coveted prize of all, at least among Polish hunters in the fifteenth and sixteenth centuries. Woven into belts, they were considered valuable gifts that supposedly aided childbirth. Most gruesome of all, the forelock was taken while the aurochs was injured but still alive. As a hunter wrote in 1557, it was "torn off dying aurochs after the skin has been cut loose in a circle."

The only trouble? By 1557, only about forty aurochs were left alive to hunt.

Last Stand in Poland's "Great Wilderness"

Prehistoric Europe was mostly a dense, dark, impenetrable forest, broken up by marshy patches and stubbly grasslands like a badly shaven beard. In the Middle Ages, people experienced it as a terrible "Great Wilderness" that pretty much defined everything they hated about the wild: it was ugly, unruly, dangerous, a barrier to travel, and antithetical to human society. Century after century, people hacked away at this forest, replacing it with fields, roads, and cities. By 1300, only a few scraps had escaped the razor outside Warsaw in central Poland.

This is where the aurochs made its last stand, in the forests of Wiskitki and Jaktorów. By the fourteenth century, so few aurochs were left that the monarchy of Poland decreed that henceforth hunting aurochs was reserved for royalty. Further, in the early 1400s, a well-organized game-keeping service and the entire village of Jaktorów were founded expressly to care for the aurochs. The gamekeepers were sixteen "hunters" whose job was to protect the aurochs from poachers, feed the aurochs hay in winter, count them,

"IN MODERN TERMS, IT'S LIKE TAKING THE ORIGINAL, CLASSIC VOLKSWAGEN BUS, CHOPPING A FEW FEET OFF THE BACK END, REPLACING THE REARVIEW MIRRORS WITH SWORDS, AND THERE'S YOUR AUROCHS BULL, A TON-PLUS OF ROCK-SOLID, GRASS-CHEWING MEANNESS."

and keep the animals from straying outside the forest. In exchange, game wardens were exempt from taxes, equipped with horses and weapons, and given farmland.

It was a cushy, privileged job, and it meant the aurochs was the first wild animal to be protected in the wild. Yet these good intentions weren't shared by everyone.

Evidence of the aurochs' last days is chronicled in a series of royal "inspection reports" from the late 1500s and early 1600s. In bureaucratic language, they document the abuse of power, petty corruption, and everyday self-interest that allowed the aurochs to perish at the hands of the very people who'd been asked to preserve the species.

Apparently, villagers engaged in numerous forbidden or outlawed activities: they cut trees for timber, grazed their cattle, and allowed pigs to forage for acorns in the protected forest. This upset the aurochs' habitat and took the aurochs' food. In 1564, the first inspection report said, "Much of these forests has already been destroyed by the people… They ride violently and do not let themselves be caught… In addition to this, the herds of cattle of the nobility and the farmers are found in these forests, which graze there, as a result of which, according to the hunters, the aurochs do not breed well; … the calves die and few survive the winter."

In 1564, thirty-eight aurochs were counted; by 1599, twenty-four. However, the gamekeepers multiplied, dividing their spoils and territory, to the point that they likely outnumbered the aurochs. Most of all, they were obviously turning a blind eye to illegal shenanigans, perhaps because they were profiting themselves. The 1599 report stated bluntly that the gamekeepers "do not honour their obligations."

One report pleaded: "We demand that the inhabitants… do not herd cattle and do not mow grass for their own use… This village was not established and given liberties so much for their cattle, as for the aurochs and their welfare. The starost [local leader] has to ensure that our forests, where the aurochs live, are not destroyed by said subjects, so that the aurochs may retain their former habitat."

If the Polish monarchy was listening, its response was not recorded. In 1602, only four aurochs remained. At the time, gamekeepers claimed a disease caught from domestic cattle killed the rest. That can happen, but this might have been an excuse to hide illicit poaching and their own negligence.

In 1620, the last bull died, leaving only a single aurochs cow, who died in 1627. A few captive aurochs in zoos may have outlived their wild brethren, but none survived much longer.

What the Heck: Rebreeding Aurochs, Rewilding Europe

A world with cattle but no aurochs is like a world with dogs but no wolves. Almost since the aurochs went extinct, people have wanted the species back. Few things exemplify the transformation of human attitudes toward wilderness in modern times than efforts to restore this great icon.

Today, the dream of re-creating the aurochs is the cornerstone of a movement to "rewild Europe." Of course, rewilding involves more than one species, and it's impossible to remake an entire continent. Instead, conservationists imagine restoring in about a dozen places something closer to the original diversity of plants and animals that once defined Europe's long-lost Great Wilderness. To achieve this, wild cattle are considered a keystone species, since the aurochs' presence and impact helped shape the very character of Europe's ancient wilderness (see page 80).

In the 1800s, people first proposed carefully crossbreeding domestic cattle species in order to re-create the aurochs. Called back breeding, this method amounts to rewinding domestication. Instead of selectively breeding aurochs to create a smaller, gentler, human-loving cow, you selectively breed domestic cows to tease out their enduring wild genes and, trait by trait, reconstruct in a single animal the bigger, wilder original.

This was first attempted in the 1920s and 1930s by two German brothers, Heinz and Lutz Heck. Their father ran the Berlin Zoo, so they had access to lots of cattle breeds. They mixed and matched types until, in short order, they each came up with an animal they thought successfully resembled the extinct aurochs.

Not quite. The Hecks congratulated themselves too quickly. No one today regards "Heck cattle" as reborn aurochs, and the Hecks' work is considered sloppy, incomplete, and inaccurate. However, they showed that back breeding *could* work, and Heck cattle have proven to be survivors. Over 600 still live in Dutch, German, and French nature reserves.

In 2008, the Taurus Foundation decided to try again, as one among several efforts within the Rewilding Europe program. Today, the Tauros Programme is currently in the process of back breeding cattle to create a brand-new species of wild animal. As the foundation's director, Ronald Goderie, wrote, "The end result will look like an aurochs, live like an aurochs, behave, eat, mate, defecate and eventually die like an aurochs."

In other words, by doing all these things, this animal will perform the same ecological function in the wild as the aurochs once did, even though this animal won't actually be an aurochs. Unlike a clone, it won't be an exact copy. So this animal will be given a new name, *tauros*, which is the Greek word for "bull." Further, once the tauros is released into the wild—hopefully by the year 2030—scientists will stop meddling with its genes and allow natural selection and evolution to shape the animal.

As this new-old version of wild cattle ranges across Europe, the tauros will be left free to adapt as it must to survive in our twenty-first-century version of wilderness, just as the original aurochs once adapted to life in the Pleistocene.

If that happens, the final irony for the aurochs will be this: its children will have rebirthed the parent. For the first time in history, domestic animals will be used to re-create a wild one, and this lost species can come down from those prehistoric cave walls and stand tall in the landscape once again. ⤳

THE PLEISTOCENE EXTINCTIONS: RISE OF THE MAMMOTH HUNTERS

For centuries, fossils were a confusing mystery. These mineralized bones clearly didn't belong to any animals people recognized, so where did they come from? At various times, mammoth bones were believed to be pieces of unicorns, giant rats, sea monsters, and Alexander the Great's elephants. Mammoth teeth were suggested to be the molars of Catholic saints.

In 1796, famed paleontologist Georges Cuvier cracked this riddle and figured out that these broken femurs and loose teeth actually belonged to unknown, bizarre creatures who no longer existed. Then, over the nineteenth century, people came to understand a shocking truth: many of these enormous animals had thundered across continents only yesterday, geologically speaking, and humans had lived with them.

In 1876, naturalist Alfred Russel Wallace captured our ambivalent reaction to this sobering news. He wrote, "We live in a zoologically impoverished world, from which all the hugest, and fiercest, and strangest forms have recently disappeared. And it is, no doubt, a much better world for us now they have gone. Yet it is surely a marvellous fact, and one that has hardly been sufficiently dwelt upon, this sudden dying out of so many large mammalia, not in one place only but over half the land surface of the globe."

Indeed, we have been wrestling with this "marvellous fact" ever since. We still ask ourselves: What happened? How crazy was the world when these species lived? What caused the extinction of so many tremendous animals?

And is it possible that humans did it?

The Mystery of the Megafauna

The Late Pleistocene extinctions unfolded in a sequence of waves from about 46,000 to 10,000 years ago. Different continents experienced extinctions at different times, and the severity or number of extinctions varied in each place. Yet on each continent, only the biggest animals went extinct, and each time, almost all the extinctions seem to coincide with the first arrival of Cro-Magnons, our ancestors.

If this were *CSI: The Pleistocene*, the lead actors would be snapping off their gloves and wrapping the investigation. Cro-Magnons had the motive (survival) and the weapons (stone-tipped spears and bows and arrows), and they were present at the scene of the crime. Case closed? Not so fast.

The third-act surprise is that scientists still don't agree on what happened. They debate the evidence, dispute each other's dates, and argue for different culprits, such as climate change, habitat change, epidemic diseases, and competition among species.

Meanwhile, some just cross their arms and declare that it's flat impossible that small bands of human hunters with simple weapons could undermine everything from sabertooth cats to glyptodonts to goannas to woolly mammoths—all of them daunting beasts who'd successfully overcome myriad upheavals over millions of years.

On the surface, it just doesn't make sense. How is it that we and all the species in this book survived this period, but the hugest, fiercest, strangest animals did not?

In the Beginning: Africa

Once upon a time, our ancestors were prey to the top predators of Africa. Early humans evolved as one among several species of apes, branching off about 2 million years ago, and these distant relatives were probably eaten by sabertooth cats, Nile crocodiles, and perhaps great white sharks. Word is still out on when humans learned to swim.

Africa's plains and forests were chock-full of dangerous, gigantic creatures: in addition to multiple big cats—including cheetahs, leopards, and several lions—the continent held the biggest elephants, hippos, warthogs, hyenas, and rhinos that ever lived. Early humans no doubt avoided these animals at all costs, what with their claws, horns, hooves, brawn, and bad attitudes.

Instead, early humans scavenged like their nearest relatives, chimpanzees, eating plants and roots and small animals. Eventually, our cousins, the Neanderthals, migrated to Europe, and another human line, the Denisovans, traveled to Asia, but neither became top predators. Even up to about 100,000 years ago, *Homo sapiens* were not much more than "skilled chimps," as Jared Diamond has written.

Then something changed. Our brains got bigger, for one. Diamond proposes that our throats also transformed, allowing humans to speak and develop language. Whatever the switch was, a light went on. We can't say if this shift was truly sudden or gradual, but by 50,000 years ago, early humans became inventors. In ways they'd never done before, they started expressing themselves and regularly killing animals many times their own size.

We call these peoples Cro-Magnons, and physically, they closely resembled us. In pants and a cap, males would look like unshaven baseball fans. Cro-Magnons changed the rules that the human species had always lived by. Then they went out and conquered the world.

Cave Painters & Mammoth Hunters

One goal of this book is to imagine our first encounters with giant species, but in Africa, that first encounter isn't even what we could call a first encounter. It was a recognition of our place within the circle of life: human-ish apes lived within the familiar web of relationships that defined nature. They were moderate-size omnivores who were in turn meat for larger predators.

No one eats us anymore, not as a standing menu item. For that, we can thank Cro-Magnons, who became so good at killing that they transcended the dynamics of the food web. In a sense, our true first encounter with giant animals occurred when Cro-Magnons looked lions, cave bears, and mammoths in the eyes as equals. Despite our lack of size and natural weapons, we learned that we could be a top predator and that no animal was too big for *us* to eat.

How did that happen?

In short, to condense a complex process into a single moment: Cro-Magnons created ranged weapons and a variety of specialized tools. They lashed stone spear points to wood shafts, wove ropes into nets, and eventually developed the bow and arrow. They made fish hooks and needles out of bone, sewed fur clothes, and built houses, sometimes with mammoth bone walls. They started regularly hunting dangerous animals like Cape buffalo, elephants, and mammoths. Presumably, this only happened once humans could successfully defend these carcass buffets from other, competing scavengers.

Cro-Magnons created art, such as pendants, statues, and necklaces. Even spear points were beautiful. But most of all, cave paintings are a tantalizing window into the suddenly innovative, creative Cro-Magnon mind. In France's Chauvet Cave, a few skillful lines of black pigment from over 30,000 years ago re-create lion prides stalking bison, woolly rhinos clashing head-on, and the regal profiles of mammoths, aurochs, cave bears, and more. No squirrels, no insects. Only giants.

We don't know what purpose these paintings served, but Cro-Magnons obviously felt deeply about giant animals. These paintings seem to express, not fear or hunger, but fascination, even loving admiration and awe. Has the human species always felt this way, but until then had no means to express it? Or was this a new feeling, perhaps of connection, one borne out of a new awareness and a new place among animals?

The Eurasian Extinctions

Missing on these cave walls are Neanderthals. This is probably because Neanderthals no longer existed. Cro-Magnons arrived in Europe by at least 40,000 years ago to find their cousins already there. These two hominid species then shared this landscape for a long time until, about 35,000 to perhaps 28,000 years ago, Neanderthals vanished.

Dating the extinction of Neanderthals is disputed and controversial, but we do know this meeting resulted in more than a few hybrid Cro-Magnon–Neanderthal children: modern genetic tests show that most people today carry 1 to 4 percent Neanderthal genes. Further, some Southeast Asian peoples carry up to 6 percent Denisovan genes, another closely related hominid species.

Yet Cro-Magnons didn't only mate with their distant relatives; they competed with them and possibly killed them. Despite the fact that Neanderthals were stronger—they were a race of chinless, jockey-size Arnold Schwarzeneggers—Cro-Magnons were the human species who survived. However it happened, Neanderthals and Denisovans now count as megafauna extinctions.

As for other animals, from about 30,000 years ago up to about 12,000 years ago, about a third of the giant species in Europe and Asia went extinct. This mostly matches the timing of the last ice age, a bitter long winter that endured from 30,000 years ago to about 14,000 years ago. This also matches the steady march of Cro-Magnons across this vast, contiguous landmass.

Among the species who disappeared are three species of elephants, two species of rhinos, the cave lion, a spiral-horned antelope, a camel, a giant deer, and the Irish elk. The woolly mammoth was driven farther and farther north. The mammoth died out in Europe 12,000 years ago, and in Siberia 10,000 years ago. The last woolly mammoths survived on Wrangel Island, off of mainland Siberia, until about 4,000 years ago.

Not every giant disappeared. In Africa, where Cro-Magnons started, almost no megafauna went extinct during this time period. Most of the great beasts who lived 50,000 years ago live there now. This is why Africa is famous as the last continent to possess nearly its full roster of megafauna. Meanwhile, Eurasia still possesses an impressive collection: tigers, elephants, rhinos, brown bears, polar bears, horses, reindeer, moose, bighorn sheep, yaks, and more.

In the end, the Eurasian extinctions seem to be a mix of impacts. The ice age certainly transformed habitats on an enormous scale, and this probably led to declines in many species. At the same time, our direct ancestors were arriving as a brand-new type of predator and targeting the largest animals. For some giants, this one-two punch may have been too much. ↘

AFRICA

MADAGASCAR

ELEPHANT BIRD: A LEGEND COME TO LIFE

EXTINCTION: the elephant bird's extinction date is unknown, but is speculated to be in the mid-1600s

When it was first discovered, Madagascar was like Arthur Conan Doyle's fantasy novel *The Lost World* brought to life. Like Australia and New Zealand, this enormous island—the earth's fourth largest—was a land that time forgot filled with giant prehistoric creatures that existed nowhere else.

Today, that surreal world of majestic ancients has vanished. In the 2,000 years since humans arrived, Madagascar has lost fully 80 percent of all its giant species. Metaphorically speaking, it's as if the most important and exciting pages of the book have been ripped out. We struggle to understand where those animals came from, where the Malagasy people came from, what those people did, and why so many large species vanished.

Nevertheless, despite its losses, Madagascar remains one of the earth's rare jewels of biodiversity. At the same time that we look back in wonder at what Madagascar once was, we are working hard to hang on to the glorious creatures who remain.

The Mystery of Origins: A Peculiar Ark

Imagine this: you set sail from Indonesia, or India, or East Africa—all three are possible origins for Madagascar's first human residents—and arrive expecting… what?

Since Africa is a mere arm's length away, 250 miles across the Mozambique Channel, maybe you expect a mini-Africa, with herds of antelope, wildebeest, and African buffalo stalked by lions and cheetahs, along with zebras, hyenas, gorillas, and chimpanzees.

Maybe you anticipate a Southeast Asian forested island, with elephants, rhinos, tigers, leopards, and monkeys.

Maybe, knowing something about continental drift, you suspect the presence of Australia's ancient species, the monotremes (egg-laying mammals like the platypus) and marsupials (mammals who nurture fetuses in pouches like kangaroos; see page 139).

Not even close. None of those animals ever lived on Madagascar.

Instead, the forests teem with a bewildering array of primates you can't have seen before because they no longer exist anywhere else. These lemurs—as science will call them—stare back with wild, colored eyes and expressive features. Some are as big as gorillas, have human-like faces, and lope along the ground; some hang onto tree limbs like giant sloths; and others are so small they could hop into your open palm.

Lemurs arrived on Madagascar some 50 to 60 million years ago, presumably when one or more were washed away from an African beach on a mat of vegetation. Afterward, lemurs went extinct in Africa when, much later, a separate branch of primates evolved—monkeys—who outcompeted them. However, Madagascar remained free of monkeys—and of apes, and us, and all but a few predators—and so lemurs thrived.

But lemurs aren't the only odd creatures you find. The rivers are crowded with giant crocodiles and pygmy hippos. These species you recognize, but one is too big, the other too small. Then the seemingly boulder-strewn grasslands reveal themselves covered with herds of grazing giant tortoises and patrolled by the most intimidating presence of all: a 10-foot-tall, striding feathered monster weighing half a ton, with a long, serpentine neck and a deadly hatchet of a beak.

This last, the elephant bird (*Aepyornis maximus*), was the largest bird that ever lived, and it weighed over 1,000 pounds. New Zealand's moa was taller, but it was a willowy swan by comparison: in a face-off, Madagascar's behemoth would have had the moa's lunch.

Where did all these strange creatures come from, and why were so many familiar creatures missing?

We still only understand bits and pieces of this long story. Originally, Africa, South America, India, Australia, and Antarctica formed a single supercontinent in the Southern Hemisphere called Gondwanaland. This steadily went to pieces, due to continental drift, over the course of 500 million years. Madagascar separated from Africa about 150 million years ago and from India about 88 million years ago. At this point, dinosaurs still strode the earth, and the first primates wouldn't open their eyes for another 20 million years.

Thus, most of the land animals we know and love evolved long after Madagascar was an island; few ever reached it. Scientists presume that Madagascar's pygmy hippo, giant tortoise, and Nile crocodile somehow swam over. Actually, Madagascar's giant tortoise kept swimming and populated the Indian Ocean's other, smaller islands.

In all likelihood, the hippo arrived normal size and shrank. Madagascar's pygmy hippo stood 2.5 feet tall at the shoulder, short enough to squeeze under a dining room table. Sometimes, big species adapted to the restrictions of island life by becoming smaller (see page 28).

However, when small continental species migrated to islands that were free of the usual predators, they sometimes became gigantic: Madagascar's lemurs and elephant birds are prime examples. The biggest lemur reached 450 pounds, and every single one of the island's extinct lemur species was bigger than the cute tiny lemurs we know today from the animated *Madagascar* movies. That film would be a little different if giant lemurs were the stars.

The most unlikely transformation, though, involved the elephant bird. DNA evidence today confirms that this species evolved from a flying bird. Like the moa, it eventually grew too big to fly, though it kept its vestigial wings. Scientists long assumed the elephant bird was most closely related

"NEW ZEALAND'S MOA WAS TALLER, BUT IT WAS A WILLOWY SWAN BY COMPARISON: IN A FACE-OFF, MADAGASCAR'S BEHEMOTH WOULD HAVE HAD THE MOA'S LUNCH."

to Africa's large ratite, the ostrich; surely, they must have shared a parent species who walked across Gondwanaland before Madagascar separated. In fact, the elephant bird's nearest genetic sibling is New Zealand's flightless kiwi, the *smallest* living ratite—and for that to happen, their shared parent species must have been a flying bird. The most likely reason that the kiwi didn't become big like the elephant bird is because the moa probably got to New Zealand first and was already occupying all the "giant walking bird" niches.

On Madagascar, the elephant bird had no such competition, and it occupied almost every habitat and diverged into perhaps a dozen species, but we know so little about this bird that we can't confirm the number of species, how they differed, and their specific ranges.

Madagascar, as big as California or Texas, has been dubbed the "eighth continent." This honors not just its size but Madagascar's overwhelming richness of endemic species: 99 percent of Madagascar's frogs, 91 percent of its reptiles, 80 percent of its vascular plants, 46 percent of its birds, and every single lemur occur nowhere else.

In this unique world, it is as if, as scientist Alison Jolly has written, "time has broken its banks and flowed to the present down a different channel."

The Mystery of Extinction: The Malagasy

Now riddle me this: if the modern human species evolved in East Africa, why did it take us so long to reach Madagascar? It wasn't until the height of the Roman Empire, when we reset our calendars with the birth of Christ, that people finally sailed here.

The prevailing theory, much debated, is that people from Indonesia probably hopscotched west along the coast until they reached East Africa before sailing into Madagascar about 2,000 years ago. It could have happened very differently. The only clues we have are the Malagasy people themselves, whose physical attributes, language, and culture are such an interwoven mix of Indonesian, African, Persian, and Chinese influences that we can't properly tease them apart anymore.

How the first Malagasy lived and what they ate are also mysteries. Madagascar is a hot, humid place that doesn't preserve bones and other archaeological evidence very well. We have found very few fossils of Madagascar's extinct giant species, and none older than 26,000 years. We have found no archaeological sites of human evidence before 900 years ago. Unlike on New Zealand, there are no vast piles of elephant bird bones, no butchering sites, no roasting ovens stuffed with lemurs and pygmy hippos, no hunting or warrior culture, no eyewitness accounts. We also don't know the original Malagasy word for *elephant bird*. We can't say if they called it "chicken" or "giant walking thunder death."

In terms of Madagascar's animals, the main thing we know is that nearly every species over 25 pounds went extinct within about 1,500 years of human arrival. Fifteen species of lemur over that size, every hippo, every giant tortoise, and every elephant bird—gone. The only true giant to survive to the present day is the Nile crocodile.

So what happened?

We happened, obviously, but this isn't the usual island tale of overeating and indigestion. If that alone was the cause, we'd expect more evidence, in terms of hunting tools, discarded bones, and a culture built around the elephant bird meal plan.

Instead, the best we can guess is that a perfect storm of sudden changes drove large species to extinction before they could adapt. Some killing and eating occurred; a few bones of pygmy hippos and elephant birds show butchery marks.

Also, with the elephant bird, we know the Malagasy ate their eggs. These eggs are legendary. They were 1 foot long and 9 inches in diameter. Measure a football and consider the bird that popped that out. It was the largest egg that ever existed, larger even than dinosaur eggs, and roughly equivalent to 150 to 200 chicken eggs. You could feed a village with the omelet made from just one. Plus, elephant birds laid their eggs on open ground, within easy reach; until we arrived, no animal ate them or could crack them. We also know that, after sopping up the yolk, the Malagasy used the broken eggshells as drinking cups.

The importance of this egg-eating is that the Malagasy could have undermined the elephant bird's reproductive rate even if they rarely hunted the birds. Invasive species probably also attacked the eggs. Over the years, the Malagasy brought dogs, cats, sheep, cattle, rats, the palm civet, and probably the bush pig, among others. Madagascar's ancient species had coevolved for millions of years and likely couldn't cope with these modern invaders and scavengers. As Malagasy herded cattle into interior grasslands, this drove native species out of their preferred habitats and further hurt their survival.

The Malagasy also used fire to burn the forests and grasslands for their own ends. They planted rice in newly cleared land and increased pasture for livestock. Scientists vigorously disagree over how much of Madagascar was originally covered in forest, and thus how transformed the island became, with its bald top and eroding gullies. Still, to some degree, habitat loss must have played a role in the extinctions.

One cause that is easily discounted is climate change. For tens of millions of years, Madagascar's creatures had successfully weathered numerous ice ages and thaws. No forecast from 2,000 years ago would have troubled them.

Cryptozoology: Hunting the Snark

If science is the art of separating fact from fiction, cryptozoology is the effort to prove that fantasy is fact.

Cryptozoology is the study and pursuit of mythic, legendary, and folkloric creatures that are alleged to exist but have never been found, such as Bigfoot, the Yeti, and the Loch Ness monster. But it also includes the hunt for surviving members of long-extinct species, like dinosaurs, the woolly mammoth, and the thylacine.

In cryptozoological parlance, all these unfound animals are known as "cryptids," and just because we haven't discovered them yet doesn't prove they don't exist. Dedicated cryptozoologists live by the motto "The absence of evidence is not evidence of absence." This makes them very hard to discourage. The disappointment of not finding things comes with the territory.

Then again, occasionally, wild tales about unlikely beasts turn out to contain a kernel of truth. Legends about Mediterranean islands full of cyclops were spread by people misinterpreting the origins of extinct dwarf elephant skulls. Folklore about "land crocodiles" in Indonesia led to the 1910 discovery of the Komodo dragon, which is the largest living lizard. Two other once-mythical and now well-known creatures are the mountain gorilla and the central African okapi, a stripe-legged relative of the giraffe.

As many true believers will tell you, once a mysterious animal is found, it's no longer cryptozoology. It's just zoology.

That said, most of the time cryptozoology is pursued with tongue firmly in cheek. It's simply good fun to search for mermaids, the Jersey devil, and the chupacabra. It's also nice to imagine that our maps, Google or otherwise, still contain enough fuzzy areas where fantastical giants might roam.

To join the hunt, check out the following:

- Cryptomundo (http://cryptomundo.com/cryptozoology/breaking-news/)
- *Cryptozoology News* (http://cryptozoologynews.com)
- *The Fortean Times* (http://www.forteantimes.com)
- *Journal of Scientific Exploration* (http://www.scientificexploration.org/journal/)
- Unexplained Mysteries (http://www.unexplained-mysteries.com)

The Mystery of the Roc:
The World's Largest Egg

That might be the end of our story, except for some famous legends, and enticing rumors, about Madagascar's extinct megafauna.

Arab merchants, who called Madagascar the Island of the Moon, began trading with the Malagasy around the ninth century. Eventually, they brought back gargantuan eggs, too big to believe, along with frightening tales of the terrible bird who laid them. In the thirteenth century, Marco Polo heard these stories while traveling through Arabia and concocted his own version of the infamous Roc.

"They are just like eagles but of the most colossal size… They are so huge and bulky that one of them can pounce on an elephant and carry it up to a great height in the air. Then it lets go, so that the elephant drops to earth and is smashed to a pulp. Whereupon the gryphon bird perches on the carcass and feeds at its ease. They add that they have a wingspan of thirty paces and their wingfeathers are twelve paces long and of a thickness proportionate to their length."

Marco Polo had never seen Madagascar and didn't have a clue what he was talking about, but as myth, the Roc was terrific.

Then nothing else was heard about the elephant bird until 1658, when Étienne de Flacourt, the former French governor of Madagascar, published a survey of the island's flora and fauna. In it, he described several unheard-of creatures; the *mangarsahoc* was clearly the pygmy hippo; another, which the Malagasy called the *tretretretre*, was a giant lemur. Another Flacourt called the *Vouron patra*: "This is a large bird which haunts the Ampatre, it lays eggs like those of an ostrich, the people of these regions cannot catch it, as it seeks out the most deserted place."

Throughout his account, Flacourt wrote in the present tense and presumably used descriptions from actual eyewitnesses. It's a slim branch for such a heavy conclusion, but researchers consider Flacourt's account credible, and thus it probably confirms that at least a few individuals from each of these species remained alive until the mid-1600s.

After that, it was another 200 years before European scientists discovered that a shard of truth hid beneath the Roc's wild legend. In 1851, eggshells and a few elephant bird bones were unearthed on the Madagascar coast and put before confused French scientists. "Mon dieu, c'est incroyable!" cried French naturalist Isidore Saint-Hilaire (or something to that effect). After regaining his composure, Saint-Hilaire gave the species its scientific name.

Afterword, survey expeditions were mounted to find the bird. They came up empty-handed, and that seemed to be that. Science had arrived too late. Or maybe… scientists just weren't looking in the most deserted place.

The Mystery of Modern Sightings: Lemurs & Coelacanths

After the turn of the twentieth century, no self-respecting scientist was still looking for Madagascar's elephant birds and giant lemurs. Everyone knew they no longer existed, so searching for them would only court mockery and charges of cryptozoology.

Then, in 1938, something amazing happened: a living dinosaur was discovered in the waters around the Comoros Islands, off Madagascar's northwest coast.

Alright, that's an exaggeration. The coelacanth isn't literally a dinosaur, but this prehistoric fish once lived with them before going extinct about 65 million years ago—or so we thought until modern-day fishermen starting catching them. At 6 feet long and up to 240 pounds, and sporting lobed fins that may have been precursors to the arms and legs of land animals, the coelacanth isn't exactly a darting minnow. How could we possibly have overlooked this watery beast as it prowled beneath our fishing boats for, oh, the entirety of human existence?

How, indeed? After the coelacanth's discovery by a young museum curator, Marjorie Courtenay-Latimer, local fisherman shrugged and admitted that, sure, they occasionally caught this ugly fish. So what?

Here's what: Not everyone recognizes the significance of what they see, and scientists sometimes ignore "fish stories" at their peril. In 2000 off the coast of South Africa, scuba divers discovered a "colony" of coelacanths who were, conveniently enough, already living within a protected marine park. That made things easy: we'd already been protecting this prehistoric endangered species and didn't even know it.

So, was anyone else spreading far-fetched rumors about unknown animals in and around Madagascar? In fact, yes. Rural Malagasy have been telling stories about hearing and seeing large, secretive forest creatures since the 1870s, and scientists have pooh-poohed them. What if these stories are true?

In 1876, a German zoologist was sent a tanned animal hide from Madagascar that he couldn't identify. Locals said it was from a *tsy-aomby-aomby*, a "not-cow-cow." According to their stories, this secretive animal sounded suspiciously like a pygmy hippo, except that it apparently ate people. The German scientist eventually went looking for it, gave up, and dismissed the story as folklore.

In 1995, American naturalists digging for fossils in Madagascar's Belo sur Mer kept hearing Malagasy stories about modern-day encounters with *kilopilopitsofy* and *kidoky*. Giving in to curiosity, they interviewed six people, five of whom described hearing and/or seeing one or both of these creatures, some multiple times. A few stories dated to 1946 and 1952, most dated to 1976, and a couple were from recent years.

To a remarkable degree, these separate, firsthand, eyewitness accounts shared similar details. The Malagasy knew their wild animals, and when questioned, they could distinguish known animals from these secretive, legendary ones. The *kilopilopitsofy* could only be a pygmy hippo. And the *kidoky*—with a human face and bounding gait, and about the size of a seven-year-old girl—sounded strikingly like a particular species of extinct giant lemur.

No one described seeing an elephant bird. One man proclaimed the *vorombe*, or "big bird," to be extinct "like the dinosaurs."

But who knows?

Well, we know one thing: Madagascar still has over a hundred species of lemurs. They aren't giants, but they are marvelous, unique ring-tailed creatures. They are also the most endangered mammal group in the world. A quarter of lemur species are categorized as critically endangered and half as endangered, meaning that the threat of imminent extinction hangs over seven out of ten lemur species. Naturally, we'd love to discover a lost world of giant lemurs, pygmy hippos, and elephant birds in some unexplored ravine, but first things first: we have to protect those rare, irreplaceable species we know still exist. ⤵

BERING
ISLAND

PACIFIC
OCEAN

STELLER'S SEA COW: ELEPHANT OF THE OCEAN

EXTINCTION: the last sighting and killing of a sea cow, and its presumed extinction, was in 1768

On November 6, 1741, Captain-Commander Vitus Bering was returning home to Siberia when his storm-damaged ship, the *St. Peter*, ran aground on an unknown, uninhabited island in the North Pacific. The theme song to *Gilligan's Island* didn't play in anyone's head because TV hadn't been invented yet, and this wasn't a pleasure cruise.

Bering was trying to complete the last leg of his epic exploration of the then-uncharted waters and lands of the Arctic. His was the first European voyage to reach Alaska, and his historic journeying mapped, documented, and opened up this icy region for the first time.

Before Bering could celebrate, however, he had to get home, and the chances of that had just taken a turn for the worse. But this unplanned stop would yield yet another historic discovery, since this inhospitable rock turned out to be the last refuge of what was then the world's second-largest mammal, second only to whales.

That discovery turned out to be an unexpected blessing for Bering's crew, even as it became a tragedy for the animal. Thankfully, Bering had with him a heroically dedicated naturalist, Georg Wilhelm Steller, whose meticulous journals recorded almost everything we will ever know about this species, along with preserving the harrowing tale of how Bering's ship-wrecked crew survived.

Shipwreck, Scurvy & the Sea Cow

After storms injured the *St. Peter*, but while it was still at sea, the ship's sailors argued over what to do: upon seeing land, some officers wanted to wreck on purpose, assuming (or, more likely, praying) that this must be Kamchatka, the mainland.

Steller, as the voyage's only scientist, vigorously disagreed, but he was overruled, and Bering deliberately ran aground. Disembarking the next day, Steller confirmed their fateful error.

How could Steller tell? Signs were everywhere. The orientation of the coastline was wrong, as were the treeless mountains and the unnatural tameness of the blue foxes and sea otters. Perhaps most of all, in the bay where they'd crashed was a marine mammal that, he wrote, "I had never seen before."

Crowding the near-shore waters, floating serenely and half-submerged, the manatee-like creatures resembled nothing so much as massive, over-turned, barnacle-encrusted boats, many reaching 25 feet long (equivalent to orcas). Like herds of fat cows, the animals munched kelp incessantly, only stopping to periodically lift their stubby, heavily bristled faces and clear their throats, punctuating the subarctic air with a concert of huffs and snorts.

The truth about the men's circumstances hit hard. Many despaired, while others refused for months to believe that this was not Kamchatka. Steller, however, calmly and methodically went to work.

Steller first built an underground dwelling, which he'd seen Kamchatka's indigenous peoples, the Kamchadals, create to survive the winter. Steller also tended to the sick. Many of the crew were already suffering from scurvy—a common scourge among sailors of that era, whose cause (a lack of vitamin C) was then unknown. Steller fed them fresh sea otter meat, and at other times "scurvy grass," another remedy Steller had learned from the Kamcha-dals. In doing so, he became the first European to identify a cure for scurvy, though his findings went ignored for decades.

The first few weeks were horrific. As the men emptied the injured ship, they piled possessions on the beach next to dead bodies awaiting burial.

Dying men, "still alive and helpless," lay everywhere. Steller wrote in his journal: "want, lack of clothing, cold and dampness, weakness, sickness, impatience, and despair were daily guests."

In particular, the foxes harassed and attacked the sailors relentlessly. The foxes were "so malicious," Steller wrote, "they dragged apart all the baggage, ate the leather sacks, scattered the provisions, stole and dragged away from one his boots, from another his socks and trousers, gloves, coats, all of which yet lay under the open sky and for lack of ablebodied men could not be protected… There was nothing they did not sniff at and steal from." Indeed, the foxes "made us laugh in our greatest misery by their crafty and comical monkey tricks."

On December 8, one month after landing, Captain-Commander Bering died. Later, Bering's name would be bestowed upon this island and upon the strait he discovered between Siberia and Alaska. Ultimately, thirty-two men would perish, leaving forty-six survivors among the *St. Peter*'s original crew of seventy-eight.

From December to May, the men huddled in five underground dwellings and ate a diet of sea otter and fry cakes (using rescued flour from the ship). Yet every month they had to travel farther to hunt. They soon killed most of the sea otters from nearby areas, and those otters who were left learned to scatter at the men's approach. By March, no otters existed within almost 40 miles of their dwellings on the north shore, and the men had to make an arduous, overland trek some 10 to 30 miles to the island's south shore to get food.

By spring, the men started to build a new ship out of the soggy bones of the old one. Without a new vessel, they were doomed. However, hunting had become so difficult and time-consuming that it was undermining their efforts.

The solution floated right in front of them. The herds of giant "sea cows," as the sailors dubbed them, were their constant companions, every day crowding the bay where the *St. Peter* had wrecked. Always eating, they came right up to the beach and rubbed against the rocks. They were so

"A DOCILE, SOCIAL BEHEMOTH, THE STELLER'S SEA COW MIGHT STILL BE CROWDING NORTH PACIFIC SHORELINES TODAY EXCEPT FOR HUMAN APPETITES."

unbothered by humans that you could reach out and pet their rough, bark-like skin. They weighed, Steller estimated, about 8,000 pounds—someone later calculated that a single animal could feed thirty men for a month. To the malnourished sailors, they must have bobbed in the harbor like cartoon roast chickens.

But how to kill them? They were too huge to club like a seal or sea otter. In mid-May, Steller and the crew tried to use an iron hook and a long rope "to cut into this huge, powerful sea animal and to pull it ashore," Steller wrote. Yet the sea cow's tough hide rebuffed their hooks, and when it didn't, the animals simply swam away, taking the hook and rope with them.

A month later, in late June, Steller strategized a new technique "in exactly the manner of Greenland whaling." After they repaired their yawl, or longboat, a harpooner and five men rowed quietly next to a herd. The harpoon was attached to a long rope, with a portion coiled in the boat and the rest running to the shore, where it was held by the remaining forty men. Once the harpooner struck, the men on shore pulled on the rope, and the men in the yawl attacked with "large knives and bayonets," wounding the distressed animal however they could, blood geysering in all directions. Once sufficiently weakened, the animal was pulled in and beached at high tide. Then, at low tide, with the sea cow accessible across dry sand, the men approached and "cut off meat and fat everywhere in large pieces, which with great pleasure we carried to our dwellings."

Here, they discovered what ancient peoples millennia before had no doubt learned: the sea cow was extraordinarily delicious and good for you.

The unrendered fat was like "the best Dutch butter," Steller wrote, and once boiled into oil, it was sweeter and tastier than beef fat, with the character of olive oil, and "we drank it by the cupful." The meat itself resembled beef and could be as tender as veal, with "the remarkable characteristic" of not going rancid even after two weeks or more in the summer heat. Steller speculated that the sea cow's diet must have acted like a preservative.

In particular, Steller wrote, "It was evident that all who ate it felt that they increased notably in vigor and health. This was noticeable especially in some sailors who had relapses and had been unable to recuperate up until now. With this, all doubts were now ended about what kind of provisions we should go to sea with; and by means of sea animals it pleased God to strengthen us human beings who had suffered shipwreck through the sea."

The Swimming Elephant

In retrospect, we might wonder whether God remained pleased—for within twenty-seven years, in 1768, the Steller's sea cow was extinct. It is the only North Pacific sea mammal to have gone extinct in modern times, and the swiftness of its passing following discovery is almost unrivaled. Among marine mammals, it's unheard of. That it went extinct so quickly was due to a very unlucky set of circumstances, the first being its discovery by shipwrecked explorers!

Steller's impression was that the animal was "found at all times of the year everywhere around this island in vast numbers." That certainly was true, but it was misleading. The Bering Island sea cows—along with a second population on neighboring Copper Island—were actually the last tiny remnant of a once-vast and ancient species that had survived into modern times only because Bering Island was what the sailors most feared—uninhabited.

About a million years ago, the sea cow (*Hydrodamalis gigas*) evolved into its modern form, but the species represents an unbranched cascade of evolutionary adaptations that extends back 20 million years. About 50 million years ago, the order of Sirenians—which includes sea cows, manatees, and dugongs—branched off from other hooved, browsing herbivores. At first, Sirenians were semiaquatic, grazing on grasses on land and in water. By 28 million years ago, they gave up land completely and adapted to a life spent swimming, their vestigial hind limbs eventually morphing into flipper-like tails.

This is why, strange as it seems, Sirenians are more closely related to elephants and mammoths—or Proboscideans, their large herbivore cousins who stayed on land—than they are to other marine mammals, like whales and dolphins.

Ultimately, the Sirenian order developed into at least sixty species in four families, and from an origin on the South American continent, they spread to virtually every ocean around the globe. Nevertheless, all the species except one—the Steller's sea cow—were acclimated to tropical waters and warm climates. About 2 million years ago, the climate cooled and glaciers encroached everywhere, and most Sirenian species couldn't adapt and went extinct.

The sea cow, however, adjusted to this unfortunate change in temperature in two ways: by preferring cold-water kelp (over warm-water grasses) and by becoming massive—growing nearly twice as big as their warm-water cousins, the manatees and dugongs.

Fossil records show that ancient sea cows exceeded 32 feet in length, even bigger than those Georg Steller encountered. Further, Steller noted that, by spring, the ribs of the sea cows were visible under their thick hides. Apparently, the subarctic winter was hard on everyone, sea cows and sailors included. Despite the sea cow's adaptions, they weren't thriving in this harsh environment. These are additional clues that the Bering Island population was a remnant, one that survived in a less-than-optimal environment because, presumably, they had been driven from better habitats and had no other choice. At one time, sea cows spread through coastal bays across the entire northern Pacific Ocean, from Baja California in Mexico all the way to Japan.

We are lucky that fate chose Georg Steller to be the Bering voyage's scientist. For one thing, in his circumstances, most scientists might slack off. And who wouldn't? Steller was, after all, hopelessly marooned and half starved. But Steller never stopped examining, recording, and questioning, trying to fill in the yawning gaps in knowledge that then existed in mid-eighteenth-century natural history. Steller knew that everything he saw was valuable, and he kept recording right up until they left Bering Island.

Later, Steller's accounts of his discoveries added to zoology, geology, ethnography, and medicine. He profiled the four marine mammals that defined Bering Island: the sea cow, sea otter, fur seal, and sea lion. Steller was also the first to suggest that a land bridge (which would also take Bering's name) must have once connected the continents, allowing ancient humans to migrate east from Siberia into North America. Steller surmised this now-famous theory simply by reading the region's geography and by comparing the physical features and cultures of indigenous peoples in Siberia and Alaska.

This same migration of early humans also led, we presume, to the demise of the sea cow across most of its ancestral range. Nothing else accounts for their decline. The sea cow had already survived extensive climate changes to dominate Pacific Ocean beaches, and until we came along, the only predators that probably ever bothered it were sharks.

Thick Hide, Big Heart

On July 12, 1742, Steller fully dissected his first sea cow, a female, and recorded the entirety of her skeletal structure, organs, and inner workings. He measured her in every aspect: recording the length and width of the tail, head, lips, tongue, internal organs, and more. The heart was about 2 feet long and 2 feet wide and over 34 pounds, or about the size and twice

Hardtack & Scurvy:
A Sailor's Diet in the Age of Exploration

During the era of European open-ocean exploration, from the 1500s through the 1800s, your ship's reach extended only as far as your food and water carried you. Forget wind filling the sails. What mattered was filling a sailor's belly.

Yet that belly subsisted on a monotonous menu of "salt meat, dried pease, oatmeal, hardtack and a little butter and cheese, with beer, wine or watered spirits to wash it down," writes researcher Janet MacDonald. Canning wasn't invented until the mid-1800s, so meats came two ways: dried or salted. Vegetables were pickled.

Hardtack was a dense, bland cracker baked multiple times to be long lasting. Sailor's dubbed them "sea biscuits," "cabin bread," and "worm castles," since they often became infested with weevils.

Fresh fruits and vegetables were virtually unheard of. Sailors might catch fish, but otherwise fresh meat was rare. The low bar set by a ship's rations might be one reason sailors waxed poetic about the deliciousness of giant tortoises and sea cows.

the weight of a one-year-old child. The intestines, stretched out, measured 5,968 inches—that's right, he checked to the inch. At nearly 500 feet, the intestines were twenty times the animal's length.

In this daunting labor, Steller had to plead with and pay the begrudging sailors for help. If we ever doubt Steller's dedication to science, these measurements alone are proof enough.

The sea cow's outer hide was truly bizarre. Steller compared it to a "cuticle" and called it "black, mangy, wrinkled, rough, hard, and tough." It was "more like unto the bark of an ancient oak than unto the skin of an animal," and this "coat of mail" could turn an ax. This hide protected the sea cow from the batterings of waves, rocks, and ice that it regularly endured

But it wasn't just taste. Fresh meat from tortoises and certain marine mammals, including sea otters, kept scurvy at bay. Sailors actually became healthier when they ate these animals. Stick too long to a normal ship's diet, and you wound up dead.

Scurvy was a common, rampant disease that could decimate a crew. Today, we know that scurvy is caused by a deficiency of vitamin C (which is produced by some animals), but for centuries people didn't understand this link.

Scurvy became gruesome as it advanced. A person's skin grew yellow, teeth fell out, and they developed open wounds and bled from mucus membranes. In 1741, Georg Steller wrote about scurvy-riddled sailors on Bering Island: "The gums were swollen up like a sponge, brown-black and grown high over the teeth and covering them." The pain was so intense that sailors couldn't eat, and so they starved.

Steller's scurvy treatments weren't the only ones people ignored. In 1747, British surgeon James Lind realized citrus prevented the disease, but the Royal Navy didn't prescribe fresh lemons and limes until the 1790s.

After that? Healthy English sailors earned a new nickname: Limeys.

while feeding along these frigid shores.

Beneath the outer hide, the sea cow had a second skin that was similar to ox hide, and beneath this was a layer of fat from 4 to 9 inches thick. From end to end, the sea cow was shaped like a spindle, with a comically small head, a bloated, rounded middle that was over 20 feet in diameter, and a solid, perpendicular tail. Buoyant to a fault, sea cows perpetually floated, even sleeping on their backs. Steller never saw a sea cow fully submerge.

As a result, sea cows were like living islands. Parasites burrowed into the exposed cuticle's whorls and wrinkles, and these organisms were food for gulls, who in classic symbiotic fashion perched on the sea cow's back and snacked.

Another unique feature was the sea cow's mouth, which had two sets of lips. The outer set had bristles "as thick as a dove's quill" and were so tough and hard from constantly tearing kelp off rocks that the sailors found the lips inedible no matter how long they were cooked. Further, the sea cow lacked teeth. Instead, two ridged and furrowed bony plates, or "solid tooth masses," masticated the kelp.

"The strangest feature of all," Steller wrote, "is its arms, or, if you please, its front feet." Steller wasn't sure what to call the sea cow's short front appendages, which lacked bones, fingers, or any trace of a nail or hoof. They were "something like claws," with the underside covered in "short and densely set bristles like a scrub brush." Yet they were marvelously dexterous and expressive. "With these forefeet, it swims ahead, beats the seaweed off the rocks on the bottom, and when, lying on its back, it gets ready for the Venus game, one embraces the other with these as if with arms."

Steller was a clear-eyed, rigorous, and implacably objective scientist, yet his descriptions of sea cow behavior are strikingly evocative, even loving. Rather than anthropomorphic projections, these may reflect something close to the truth, that sea cows were themselves highly emotional and perhaps intelligent mammals, which their relation to elephants, however distant, might suggest.

Here is what Steller wrote about "the Venus game": "The female swims gently to and fro in the water, the male following her. The female eludes him with many twists and turns until she herself, impatient of longer delay, as if tired and under compulsion, throws herself upon her back, when the male, rushing upon her, pays the tribute of his passion, and they rush into each other's embrace."

From his observations, Steller felt sea cows were monogamous and had only one calf at a time once a year. Within herds, they maintained family groups of a father, mother, and several young, which were always flanked by adults for protection. That sea cows displayed "an extraordinary love for one another" was evident in numerous ways, large and small.

Most dramatically, when one sea cow was attacked by the sailors, the others invariably tried to help it escape. "Some of them try to upset the boat with their backs, others bear down upon the rope and try to break it, or endeavor to extract the hook from the back of their wounded companion with a blow from their tails, and several times they proved successful."

Once, when a female was harpooned, her mate at first struggled in vain to free her and then followed as she was pulled to shore, "even though we struck him many blows," Steller wrote. Even after the female died, her mate unexpectedly swam up to her side "as swiftly as an arrow." Then, for the next two days, the male returned several more times, even when little was left but an eviscerated carcass.

The sea cow, Steller wrote, was mute and "utters no sound, but only breathes heavily and seems to sigh when wounded." Though silent, this individual's heartbreak was unmistakable to the scientist.

On August 14, 1742, Steller and the other forty-five surviving members of the Bering voyage set sail in a newly built boat, one stocked with provisions that included five barrels of sea cow meat. Three days later, on August 17, they sighted the Kamchatkan mainland, which was a mere hundred miles away. Ten days later, the ship anchored in Avacha Bay, the harbor of their departure.

Harvesting the Sea Cow

News spread quickly. In particular, descriptions of the Commander Islands, flush with fur-bearing animals, their bays stocked with a prodigious, easily caught food source, sparked an immediate rush by Russian fur-hunting expeditions. Every year from 1743 to 1763, nine-month-long expeditions targeted the islands, trapping fur animals and eating sea cow almost exclusively.

By 1754, the sea cows around Copper Island were gone. In 1755, a Russian mining engineer, Peter Jakovleff, raised an alarm with Kamchatkan authorities, saying that if hunting restrictions weren't put in place, the Bering Island sea cows would soon follow. To make his case, Jakovleff described the extremely wasteful hunting methods, in which parties of only a few men would mortally wound a sea cow, wait for it to die, and then hope it washed in on the tide before it rotted. In this way, five times as many animals were killed as were used.

Of course, Jakovleff's prescient warning was ignored. The concept of sustainability, or even of resource management, was as foreign to the eighteenth century as the iPad. Most believed that nature was simply endless and enduring, too abundant to use up. While shipwrecked on Bering Island, the stranded sailors sometimes hunted sea otters solely to get more pelts as "money" to gamble with at cards.

By 1763, eight years after Jakovleff's warning, the Commander Islands were seriously depleted of both fur-bearing animals and sea cows. Expeditions declined. The last known sighting, and killing, of a sea cow was by an expedition in 1768. Four years later, a 1772 expedition confirmed that no sea cows existed around Bering Island.

How many sea cows had there been? Using known expedition records and Jakovleff's percentages, scientists have calculated that there must have been at least 2,500 to 3,000 sea cows around the two islands when Steller first encountered them.

Some have suggested an additional cause for the sea cow's extinction: namely, that as sea otters declined, sea urchins must have proliferated, and sea urchins could have overrun the kelp beds the sea cows depended upon. In this case, sea otters were a keystone species, and their disappearance may have helped unravel this ecosystem's quilt of relationships.

However, sea cow hunting was so intense, and so far beyond what the population could sustain—perhaps seventeen times greater—that any loss of kelp probably had minimal impact.

Finally, could any sea cows have escaped the slaughter? The North Pacific remains a lightly inhabited, formidable place. In 1854, there was an alleged sighting, and two more arose in the twentieth century: in 1962 and 1977. Most likely these were misidentified wayward elephant seals, since there was nothing elusive nor secretive about the creature who bears Steller's name.

Fat, slow, and shore-bound, the sea cow lived in plain sight, near land, never submerged, and its only defense was its size and thick skin, which is why it was so easy to hunt, even by ancestral peoples. A docile, social behemoth, the Steller's sea cow might still be crowding North Pacific shorelines today except for human appetites.

Giant Cousins: Dugongs & Manatees

Today, the Sirenian order has only four species remaining in two families. The most widespread is the dugong, which lives in equatorial regions from Africa to the Indo-Pacific Islands.

There are three species of manatee: the African manatee, the Amazonian manatee, and the West Indian manatee, the last of which has two subspecies, the Florida manatee and the Antillean or Caribbean manatee.

Manatees and dugongs are large creatures, but they were dwarfed by the Steller's sea cow. Manatee adults can reach up to 13 feet long and 1,300 pounds, while dugongs are smaller, rarely exceeding 10 feet and 1,000 pounds.

All four species of Sirenians are listed as vulnerable. While their populations are diverse, the main threats they face are from human impacts, either from direct hunting or, most commonly, from accidental boat collisions. As a rule, Sirenians are slow-moving herbivores who gather near shore and in the mouths of freshwater rivers.

Thus, if sea cows still existed, one thing is certain: they would get in our way. Today, Bering Island is home to about 800 people, and shorelines crowded with tank-size mammals would be a constant hazard and disruption. That said, Copper Island (today called Medny Island) remains uninhabited.

Sea cows might have had that place all to themselves. ⌇

THE PROS & CONS OF BEING GIANT

Bigger must be better, right?

In fact, not always, and the dynamics of size help explain what seems, if not impossible, then extremely unlikely: that a relative handful of Cro-Magnon hunters could have eliminated dozens and dozens of prodigious, dangerous species across the globe over 10,000 years ago.

These dynamics also help explain the particular role that big species often play within ecosystems and why it's important to conserve giant animals today.

Lord, Monarch, King & Keystone: The Upside

The best and most obvious reason that species evolve to become huge is that—putting humans aside for a moment—no one ever threatens the largest creatures. Top predators are those carnivores who are too big and deadly to become anyone's meal, and who in turn feast on the biggest prey in an ecosystem.

Meanwhile, megaherbivores—those animals who weigh over a ton, but who typically range from 2 to 6 tons—are simply too enormous and dangerous to be eaten, even by top predators. Megaherbivores grow so big they go beyond being prey, except on rare occasions and/or when they are still young. No big cat, sabertooth or otherwise, is a match for a healthy, adult aurochs, rhino, elephant, or mammoth.

Giant animals eat better. Top predators feast on more sizes of prey, and megaherbivores typically enjoy the widest range of vegetation. Giants *have* to eat more, to maintain their weight, which means they usually become generalists who can adapt their diets as necessary. Top predators like lions also get to keep more of what they kill: no competing scavengers can steal their carcass. Even better, top predators can take the carcasses of others. Scavenging is easy when you're the king.

That bulk also helps giants survive the lean times, the droughts and winters, as well as conserve heat in cold weather, which is a real plus when ice ages arrive. Giants are robust and dominant: they push aside competition and often influence the very character of their ecosystem. Animals who perform this role are called keystone species, and though not all keystone species are giants, nor are all giants keystones, many times they are.

For instance, the threat of being eaten influences a wolf's main prey— the diet, skills, and habits of deer and elk evolve, in part, to avoid the wolf's bite. This in turn influences the habits, habitat, and abundance of many other species that the wolf couldn't care less about, like trees and birds. The wolf's presence creates ripples of influence that affect which plants and animals prosper.

Meanwhile, megaherbivores and massive herd animals—like bison and mammoths—shape the land itself by their passage, diet, and habits: by what they eat, where they poop, and how much they stomp and tear down. These great beasts "manage" ecosystems and plant growth, dispersing seeds and determining if grasslands, woodlands, or a mosaic of types will exist. It's not just that everyone gets out of a giant's way; giants can determine who and what lives where and how they interact.

The reverse is that, if a giant species goes extinct and no other animal steps in to perform a similar role within that ecosystem, then the character of that ecosystem may utterly transform: a prey species might overpopulate without a top predator to keep it in check, or a forest might take over grasslands once a megaherbivore is gone. These changes ripple out, creating havoc for, and sometimes endangering, many other species.

In all these ways, giants earn their honorary titles as Lords of the Jungle and Monarchs of the Mountain. If they aren't, who is?

Larger, Fewer & Slower: The Downside

This begs the question: If bigger is so much better, why don't *all* animals evolve to be giants? Animals obviously don't pick their size, not deliberately, so how come some species evolve to be lion and mammoth size and some remain bite-size, like rabbits and squirrels?

The truth is, the dynamics of the food web mean that there's room at the top for only a few giant species. As species coevolve, they find success in different niches, and competition keeps other species out. Invariably, in any ecosystem, we find that species at the bottom, so to speak, are the smallest and most abundant (like plants and insects), and at each higher level, species get larger in size and fewer in number.

The largest animals nearly always number the fewest, since they eat the most and need the biggest range or territory; in other words, fewer can live within a particular habitat. This unfolds somewhat differently for large predators than it does for large herbivores, but one thing is the same: evolving to become big has a downside.

Inevitably, as animals get larger, they breed more slowly. They reach maturity later, don't breed as often, and don't have as many young. A giant tortoise doesn't start breeding until it's twenty years old, and some large species might give birth to a single offspring only once every two to four years.

Thus, it's lonely at the top, but is that really a problem?

It can be. If an ecosystem or habitat changes dramatically and quickly, giant species may not adapt fast enough to survive. In those rare tumultuous moments of environmental upheaval, a smaller population of slow-breeding giants has less chance of avoiding extinction, and they are often the first species to go. A woolly mammoth eats grass, but if the grasslands dry up and blow away, the mammoth's size and strength mean nothing.

Similarly, if a new predator comes along who can suddenly kill a slow-breeding megaherbivore—like, say, Cro-Magnon hunters killing woolly mammoths—that predator doesn't have to kill every single individual to cause the species' extinction. Even if early humans were the sole reason woolly mammoths went extinct, it wasn't because they killed every animal. All they had to do was kill more mammoths each year than the mammoth population replaced through breeding. Over tens of thousand of years, even modest annual declines will eventually lead to extinction.

From the human's perspective, successful mammoth hunts may have been rare. But they may have been successful just often enough to send mammoths into a long, slow decline that only got worse as Cro-Magnons prospered and kept pursuing mammoths wherever they migrated next.

Thus, here's the tradeoff in a nutshell: being big helps individual animals survive in the short run, but it puts the species more at risk in the long run.

Further, giants may influence ecosystems, but they don't make the rules. All species in an ecosystem live as an interdependent whole, and giants need the very species they dominate. If a predator's main prey disappears—because habitat change causes the extinction of that species, or, say, ancestral human hunters kill most of the red deer and Irish elk for themselves—a top predator like a sabertooth cat will struggle. Sabertooth cats might survive on other, smaller prey for a while, but not as well, and if this continues over a long period of time, that population may steadily wither until it dies.

Perhaps Cro-Magnons didn't face off against the Pleistocene's top predators directly, but the increased competition could still have helped cause those species to decline.

Long Live the Insects

On the other hand, squirrels, rabbits, and insects don't live long, and many species eat them, but because they are numerous and breed fast—as smaller species must, to keep ahead of the larger animals who prey on them—they have a better chance that some will make it through ecological turmoil and adapt to new circumstances.

You know the meteor that killed all the dinosaurs 65 million years ago? Most of the earth's insects survived that cataclysm. Today, there are uncounted millions of insect species, and their combined mass equals the weight of all people. It's an old joke, but think about that the next time you squash an ant or a cockroach: which species is going to have the last laugh in another 65 million years?

As daunting as individual giant animals are face-to-face, giant *species* are surprisingly vulnerable. This is one lesson of the Late Pleistocene, when the megafauna that had dominated the world for millions of years suddenly met a scrawny, spear-throwing, rule-breaking ape. ⤳

AFRICA

ALDABRA SEYCHELLES

MASCARENES

MADAGASCAR

INDIAN OCEAN GIANT TORTOISES: ANTEDILUVIAN OLD SOULS

EXTINCTION: five of the six species of Indian Ocean giant tortoises were declared extinct between the 1750s and 1800

"The day was glowing hot, and the scrambling over the rough surface and through the intricate thickets, was very fatiguing; but I was well repaid by the strange Cyclopean scene."

On September 17, 1835, naturalist Charles Darwin was picking his way across Chatham Island in the Galápagos when he ran across a pair of 200-pound giant tortoises.

"One was eating a piece of cactus, and as I approached, it stared at me and slowly walked away; the other gave a deep hiss, and drew in its head. These huge reptiles, surrounded by the black lava, the leafless shrubs, and large cacti, seemed to my fancy like some antediluvian animals."

Giant tortoises are ancient, cold-blooded reptiles, living relics from the age of dinosaurs, and we can't help but wonder, what do they remember? What do they know?

"Their tranquil nature; their imperturbable, zen approach to life; their wizened faces; their ancientness give them an almost supernatural air," anthropologist Craig Stanford has written. "Tortoises seem controlled by a different force of gravity than the rest of us, with an internal clock that runs on some otherworldly schedule."

Indeed, no other animal lives at the pace of a giant tortoise. They are grumpy, bow-legged Methuselahs; crusty, boulder-shaped lawnmowers. After a week sitting among the giant tortoises on Aldabra—due north of Madagascar—Stanford wrote, "Their desire to get into your lap to be scratched endlessly is one of the most endearing traits I can imagine in a reptile. To be looked in the eye by such a creature is to look into an old soul."

The Rise of the Reptilian Cow

Who doesn't like a good scratch? Especially after 220 million years inside the most absurd evolutionary adaption a vertebrate animal ever concocted: a shell. A tortoise is no boneless crustacean. Somehow, nature fused this reptile's ribs on the outside and moved its shoulders and pelvis inside, and voilà—a several-inch-thick, double-hulled Captain America shield. The perfect defense for a plodding vegetarian in a world of swift, toothy predators.

About 65 million years ago, these original tortoises split: those we now call turtles became amphibious, while tortoises remained on land. Afterward, tortoises migrated step by unhurried step across every continent, a leisurely stroll that took a mere 15 million years.

Along the way, giant tortoises evolved into the equivalent of reptilian cows and rhinos; they perform the same ecological function as other large grazing animals, such as dispersing seeds and managing plant growth. They also had a tendency to get swept out to sea. Though not built for water, giant tortoises can still swim, and luckily enough, they inadvertently colonized several remote islands.

Giant tortoises in East Africa went extinct about 2 million years ago (perhaps in part because early humans found them easy to catch and tasty to eat), but long before that happened, some were swept to Madagascar, where they flourished. Then, a few million years ago, some Madagascar giants got swept 500 miles east to Mauritius, one of three Mascarene Islands. Some of those tortoises later swam to the other two Mascarene Islands,

Rodrigues and Réunion, and over time, these tortoises evolved into five different species.

Then, less than 125,000 years ago, more Madagascar giants got swept northward to the Seychelles, Comoros, and Aldabra Islands; together, these are considered a single species (*Aldabrachelys gigantea*)—the only Indian Ocean giant tortoise still in existence.

A world away, in South America, the same thing happened to completely different species of giant tortoises: between 3 and 10 million years ago, some got swept out to the volcanic Galápagos Islands, which they bobbed among and colonized, evolving into perhaps fourteen species.

These ocean-going migrations are remarkable, but not nearly as amazing as the animal itself. It is no stretch to call it an old soul. They are the earth's longest-lived vertebrate species. Giant tortoises commonly live past 100; certain individuals have been known to live for 130, 170, 180, and even allegedly over 200 years. Whales *might* live that long, and beyond those two species, only humans regularly break the century mark, though some fish and reptiles can reach 100. Among other mammals, only elephants and apes regularly live past age 60.

Such huge size and old age result in a singular lifestyle: giant tortoises have a ridiculously slow metabolism and late maturity. They don't start reproducing until they are over twenty years old, and they remain fertile until late in life, laying a few eggs every year. It's like your great-great-grandmother having kids.

Mating is also about the only time giant tortoises make noise. Except for the occasional cranky hiss at nosy scientists, giant tortoises are virtually silent, yet during mating, males can be heard long distances emitting "blissful groans" and a "hoarse roar or bellowing."

Above all, giant tortoises are tough as nails. Washed ashore on a desert island? *Whatever.* In that situation, a cow, us, any mammal would overrun its environment in short order—remember the shipwrecked sailors on Bering Island? Giant tortoises lived on impoverished Indian Ocean islands for millions of years, growing to vast herds of tens of thousands, yet they maintained ecological balance and harmony.

How? First, all cold-blooded reptiles have low metabolisms, since they regulate their temperature externally. They don't need as much food as mammals, and by becoming huge, giant tortoises increased this advantage. Large size helps regulate body temperature, and tortoises learned to deliberately slow their metabolism in times of drought, entering a state of torpor or hibernation. They also store huge amounts of fat and gallons of water inside their shells, allowing giant tortoises to go without eating or drinking for many months, even over a year.

Tortoises have another survival mechanism called diapause. This allows a tortoise embryo to actually stop developing in the egg until conditions are optimal for hatching. Eggs might incubate for a year while waiting out the bad times.

Per Aesop's fable, giant tortoises don't hurry, not for anything, but they are determined to finish the race. As their great champion, naturalist Albert Gunther, observed: "Once started in a certain direction no obstacles can stop them. Not infrequently they ascend very steep, rocky hills. Sometimes their shells are broken, and occasionally they are killed, by rolling down these inclines, but if uninjured after these falls they will make repeated efforts to re-ascend until crowned by success."

These unflappable, curmudgeonly ancients have invariably inspired a playful fondness in us. Weeks after his first encounter, on October 8, 1835, Darwin wrote: "I was always amused when overtaking one of these great monsters.... It would draw in its head and legs, and uttering a deep hiss fall to the ground with a heavy sound, as if struck dead. I frequently got on their backs, and then giving a few raps on the hinder part of their shells, they would rise up and walk away."

Tortoise Soup & the Age of Exploration

Too bad, once humans arrived in the Mascarenes, giant tortoises had nowhere to, uh, run. Like some real-world version of *Survivor*, giant tortoises had outwitted, outlasted, and outplayed all other species until our tribe showed up.

"THESE HUGE REPTILES, SURROUNDED BY THE BLACK LAVA, THE LEAFLESS SHRUBS, AND LARGE CACTI, SEEMED TO MY FANCY LIKE SOME ANTEDILUVIAN ANIMALS."

—CHARLES DARWIN

Long before, giant tortoises had vanished from the earth's continents due to the usual collection of reasons, including hunting by early humans. Fast-forward to historic times, and people had completely forgotten these giants existed.

Then, a dozen years after Christopher Columbus ran headlong into the New World, Portuguese sailors swung around Africa's Cape of Good Hope looking for a sea route to India. What they found first, on several journeys between 1505 and 1510, was Madagascar and the Mascarene Islands.

For the next 200 years, as people plied the busy trade route to the Far East, the three Mascarene Islands were variously visited, claimed, and ignored by European nations. In the mid-1600s, the Dutch tried to establish several colonies on Mauritius and failed. Finally, the French claimed and colonized Mauritius in 1715, and ever since, the Mascarene Islands have maintained a human presence.

Meanwhile, visiting sailors feasted and stocked up on island species. This included, perhaps most famously, the dodo, but explorers and traders weren't detouring to the Mascarenes to dine on tough-fleshed pigeons. They came for giant tortoises, which were exquisite.

"There are vast numbers of them," wrote Henri du Quesne in 1689 of the Réunion giant tortoise. "Their flesh is very delicate and the fat better than butter or the best oil." Another called the Réunion tortoise "one of the most delicate morsels which man can eat."

In 1697, buccaneer William Dampier wrote that tortoises are "so sweet that no Pullet eats more pleasantly," and in 1708, François Leguat wrote, "The flesh is very wholesome, and tastes something like mutton. The fat is extremely white, and never congeals or rises in your stomach, eat as much as you will of it. We all unanimously agreed, 'twas better than the best butter in Europe."

In 1761, Canon Pingré stayed on Rodrigues for over three months, and in that time, "we ate practically nothing else: tortoise soup, fricassee of tortoise, tortoise casserole, tortoise mince balls, tortoise eggs, tortoise liver.... These were almost our only dishes." Didn't that get boring? "The meat seemed to me as good on the last day as on the first."

It was, perhaps, a brave person who first cracked open a giant tortoise, but any reluctance vanished after the first bite. "Hideous and disgusting as is their appearance," US Navy captain David Porter wrote in 1813, "no animal can possibly afford a more wholesome, luscious, and delicate food than they do."

As the world's navies discovered, fresh tortoise meat prevented scurvy, and one fed a lot of sailors. Adult tortoises exceeded 200 pounds, and some could be colossal; the largest on record was a captive giant tortoise that weighed over 900 pounds. In addition to meat, one tortoise could provide up to 12 pounds of rendered fat and 2 gallons of drinkable, sweet water, stored in a sack at the base of the neck.

Plus, left to itself, a giant tortoise never seemed to die. Living tortoises were piled into cargo holds by the hundreds, stacked one on top of another, where they would remain alive without food or water for months on end and yet remain as fresh as the day they were caught. In the age before canning and refrigeration, this was nothing less than miraculous. Whaling vessels claimed to keep living tortoises like this for over a year before putting them in the pot.

In this way, the giant tortoise's own evolved traits became its undoing. The same adaptions that allowed it to thrive on desert islands made it a portable packaged meal that sailors could pry open, heat, and serve when ready.

Shell Game

The history of whaling and open-ocean voyaging would no doubt have unfolded very differently without the giant tortoise. We have no way of knowing how many giant tortoises originally existed on Indian Ocean islands and in the Galápagos, but they defied counting. For centuries, they were the main source of fresh food on any ship.

Even as late as 1708, François Leguat described herds of thousands packed so tightly "that you can go above a hundred paces on their backs without setting foot on the ground. They meet together in the evening in shady places, and lie so close, that one would think those spots were paved with them." Leguat and a group of Protestant refugees arrived on Rodrigues in 1691, but living in a land of giant tortoises had its drawbacks. Settlers had to build walls around their gardens to keep the tortoises from eating their crops.

Few historical records tally the number of tortoises taken by ships prior to the eighteenth century and the colonization of the Mascarene Islands. Usually, vessels simply pulled up to an uninhabited island, loaded tortoises until the hulls were full or the sailors exhausted from carrying them, and set sail again.

In 1671, one person wrote that the tortoises were so abundant that "one person could kill 1,200 a day, or to put it more strongly, as many as he liked." A typical ship's haul was a hundred or more animals. Waste was common, since there seemed to be tortoises without end. At times, only the highly prized liver was eaten, with the rest left to rot. About 500 tortoises were needed to render a half barrel of oil. To ensure a tortoise was worth slaughtering, sailors drilled a hole in the shell and stuck in a finger to check the fat. If it wasn't enough, they left the tortoise to die slowly of its wound.

As with the moa and the sea cow, humans not only consumed the species faster than it could breed, but they were extravagantly wasteful with an important resource. This was self-defeating, but sustainability remained a foreign concept.

As the main islands were settled in the 1700s, colonists developed a profitable industry out of selling tortoises to passing ships, which arrived more frequently than ever. Soon, by the mid-1700s, Mauritius and Réunion had used up all their tortoises. What to do? Exactly. Colonists shipped tortoises from Rodriques to Mauritius, and sales continued. On Rodrigues alone, one estimate is that 280,000 tortoises were harvested from 1732 to 1771.

The pressures on tortoise populations weren't just due to hungry sailors. Settlers ate giant tortoises themselves, they cleared land for plantations and cattle pastures, and they introduced a host of invasive species: rats, cats, dogs, goats, and pigs. Rats and feral pigs were especially damaging, since they ate tortoise eggs and hatchlings. Thus, destruction and fragmentation of tortoise habitat, and elimination of generations of young tortoises, helped drive these giants into a terminal decline.

By the 1800s, not a single Mascarene island had any more giant tortoises in the wild, so the nearby Seychelles entered the tortoise trade. From the 1770s until the 1830s, Seychelles colonists shipped tortoises to Mauritius until they'd emptied their beaches, and then colonists collected them from Aldabra. It was one big shell game.

Over a fifty-year period, up to about 1800, all five species of Mascarene Island giant tortoise went extinct. It's hard to pinpoint the exact dates because of all the mixing of tortoises among the islands. Plus, residents liked to keep giant tortoises as pets, confining them within the same walled gardens once built to keep them out.

For locals, a pet tortoise was a status symbol, like parking a vintage '57 Chevy on the front lawn. Tortoises were cared for until a relative got married, when the family pet became the centerpiece of the wedding feast. In this way, individuals of some species may have persisted a long time.

1835: Darwin, Evolution & the Galápagos

It is impossible to tell the story of the giant tortoise without mentioning Charles Darwin and the Galápagos. This book focuses on the Indian Ocean species, but what happened with these "other" giants played a role.

The Galápagos—880 miles west of South America and far from any trade route—were first encountered by explorers in the mid-sixteenth century, when they appeared on Spanish nautical charts as *ys de galapagos*, or "islands

The Dodo: Not Such a Stupid Bird

Mauritius is famous for two extinctions. The other is the dodo, the largest pigeon that ever lived. About 3 feet tall and weighing over 50 pounds, it couldn't fly, but it didn't need to. No mammals or predators lived on Mauritius, which had evolved into a kingdom for birds and giant tortoises. The dodo waddled like a fat, happy infant because it didn't have a care in the world.

That changed when European explorers discovered Mauritius. For reasons that remain unclear, people loved to hate this bird. No, it wasn't pretty. The dodo had a bulbous, crooked beak, a big butt, useless wings, and disappointing tail feathers. Writers delighted in the bird's ugliness, calling it one of "nature's mistakes," and everyone disparaged its tough, bitter taste.

But above all, the dodo seemed astonishingly stupid: you could walk right up to a dodo and clobber it to death, and the rest jumped in to save of the tortoises." The Galápagos are one of the earth's last remaining hot spots of biodiversity, but it's clear which animal made the biggest first impression.

However, for several hundred years, few sailors sought out this volcanic, dry archipelago. That changed in the nineteenth century, when British and American whalers used the Galápagos as a safe harbor while pursuing vast pods of sperm whales. About the only thing these sailors liked about the Galápagos was the menu, which featured a riotous abundance of fish, seals, and tasty shelled reptiles.

In 1835, young scientist Charles Darwin arrived during his six-year voyage of discovery on the *Beagle*. Until then, no naturalist had studied the Galápagos, and no one had ever studied the giant tortoise, either. For centuries, people in the Mascarenes had sold and eaten giant tortoise without ever pausing to think about the animal itself. Even Darwin partook while in the Galápagos, and he exclaimed, "Young Tortoises make capital soup."

As Darwin observed giant tortoises (and occasionally rode them) as they it, as if presenting themselves for strangling. Killing the dodo seemed to provide its own satisfaction.

Since then, we've learned a little about the innocence of island species. Dodos had never seen a cat, rat, or person and had no idea what they could do. No doubt, once they did, dodos regretted having given up flight so many eons ago, but it was too late. Dodos certainly learned to fear humans, but they couldn't escape them.

Europeans sailors quickly ate the dodo as an easy, if unpalatable meal until it was nearly gone, and the island's introduced cats, rats, dogs, pigs, and monkeys finished the job by eating the dodo's eggs. By the 1660s, the dodo was extinct, and few mourned its passing. We only remember the dodo today because it achieved a second life in popular culture— as the original icon of extinction itself.

beat well-worn paths and tended to their inscrutable prehistoric business, he marveled at their tameness, and that of every creature, writing, "The birds are Strangers to Man & think him as innocent as their countrymen the huge Tortoises." A sea captain wrote in 1825, "The birds and beasts do not get out of our way; the pelicans and sea-lions look in our faces as if we had no right to intrude on their solitude; the small birds are so tame that they hop upon our feet."

It's hard to imagine wild animals being so comfortable in our presence today. But during the age of exploration, this often happened with island species who'd never seen us before.

Both in the Galápagos and afterward, Darwin also noticed a curious thing: "that the different islands to a considerable extent are inhabited by a different set of beings. My attention was first called to this fact by the Vice-Governor, Mr. Lawson, declaring that the tortoises differed from the different islands, and that he could with certainty tell from which island any one was brought.... I never dreamed that islands, about 50 or 60 miles apart, and most of them in sight of each other, formed of precisely the same rocks, placed under a quite similar climate, rising to a nearly equal height, would have been differently tenanted."

This famous quote is universally cited as an early seed of the theory of evolution. In other words, Darwin realized that each Galápagos island had its own unique version of giant tortoise—and its own type of finch and mockingbird as well. We take this notion for granted today, but back then, this idea presented a real puzzle. Most scientists of that era believed that species were immutable, unchanging, each birthed once by God and remaining the same forever. If that was true, then how did giant tortoises in the Galápagos come to look so different from one another?

Darwin's answer revolutionized our understanding of life. He suggested that species do change. Living beings adapt to their environment in the ways they need to survive, and if conditions change—like, say, if a species happens to get swept away by a rogue wave and stranded on an unfamiliar desert island—they continue adapting as necessary. Thus, species *evolve*, both physically and behaviorally, generation by generation, at a pace too slow for the eye to witness.

As we now know, these changes are encoded in our genes, or our cells' internalized instructions. As genes change, animals are born changed, and so species must have been originally built to change. This idea is why Darwin's theory was considered so radical: it seemed to unseat God as the immutable, unerring creator. Darwin first described his theory of evolution in *The Origin of Species* in 1859. Unknowingly, the wise giant tortoise, as old a creature as exists, helped demonstrate to us the radical truth about the nature of life.

If Darwin had skipped the Galápagos, might the history of science have unfolded differently? It's an intriguing what-if. Weeks after leaving the Galápagos, Darwin visited the Mascarene Islands, whose giant tortoises were by then long gone, leaving Darwin none to notice.

Last Chance on Aldabra

And yet, in 1835, one species of Indian Ocean giant tortoise clung to life. It lived on the uninhabited coral atolls of Aldabra, and these tortoises would have been picked clean, too, if not for the dogged efforts of British zoologist Albert Gunther. In the 1870s, Gunther undertook history's first campaign to save an endangered species from extinction. Knowingly or not, conservationists have followed his example ever since.

Gunther worked for the zoological department of the British Museum, and he was the first scientist since Darwin to study the giant tortoise. In 1874, he learned that the Mauritian government intended to lease Aldabra to loggers, and Gunther knew, if that happened, the last remaining Indian Ocean tortoises were doomed to soup and steaks.

So Gunther drafted a petition and started a letter-writing campaign, but first he came up with a novel idea: a rescue operation to move as many Aldabran giant tortoises as possible to Mauritius, where they'd be protected within a new kind of outdoor preserve rather than caged in a zoo.

Next, Gunther drafted numerous high-profile scientists to co-sign his petition, including an elderly Charles Darwin. Gunther knew passion and science weren't likely to sway the Mauritian government, but the threat of public humiliation and scandal might. Gunther got the attention of the world's scientists, and by extension the world.

Gunther's plea is worth quoting, for it was one of the first times an animal was defended for its own sake, not for our desire to hunt it, use it, or eat it.

The rescue of these animals is recommended to the Colonial Government less on account of their utility… than on account of the great scientific interest attached to them. Beside a similar tortoise on the Galapagos islands (now also fast disappearing) the tortoise of the Mascarenes is the only surviving link reminding us of those still more gigantic forms that once inhabited the Continent of India in a past geological age.

This appeal worked, and in 1875, the Mauritian government declared the Aldabran giant tortoise a protected species. As often happens, this wasn't the *end* of the story. It was just the beginning of an excruciating, teeth-grinding journey into government bureaucracy, politics, industry, and public opinion. Here was another sobering lesson in conservation: Gunther devoted his life to saving the Aldabran giant tortoise, but it took so long he did not live to see it happen.

For twenty years, the 1875 declaration of the tortoise's protected status was nothing but a paper promise. Over the next two decades, new proposals arose to lease Aldabra to commercial operators, Gunther pursued more letter-writing campaigns, and Mauritius underwent regular changes in political leadership and attitude. The fate of the tortoise seesawed each time.

In 1895, Gunther won a mixed victory: though commercial harvesting of Aldabra's natural resources would finally be allowed, Gunther was able to get forty-two Aldabran giant tortoises moved to uninhabited Curieuse Island in the Seychelles. Hopefully, whatever happened on Aldabra, the species would survive in this new home.

Aging, his pen hand cramping, Gunther stepped back from tortoise conservation. In 1914, Gunther died, no doubt believing the Aldabran tortoise's relocation to Curieuse Island had saved the species. Sadly, it didn't. For reasons unknown, all those tortoises eventually died. However, commercial exploitation on Aldabra was never very profitable. In time, the developers quit, and the last handful of Aldabran giants, left alone, recovered all on their own.

Then, one last threat emerged. In 1965, Britain and the United States proposed building a joint military base on Aldabra, and once again, the scientific community united and rose up in protest. Led by the British Royal Society, they convinced the military to choose a different island for their base. In 1976, the Seychelles finally gained political independence, and one of their first official acts was to declare Aldabra a special reserve to protect the giant tortoise.

Today, over 100,000 giant tortoises live on Aldabra. In addition, Gunther's initial dream is finally being realized: Aldabran tortoises are being captive bred on Mauritius with plans to release them into the wild on *several* Mascarene islands. Test populations have been released on Round Island and Rodrigues, and if these are successful, they will be used to rewild Mauritius itself.

After that, who knows? Perhaps the giant tortoise could be restored in Madagascar, Africa, India, and all the other places where this benign elder once clipped the grass. ᴠ

NORTH
AMERICA

PASSENGER PIGEON: METEORS FROM HEAVEN

EXTINCTION: the last passenger pigeon, named Martha, died on September 1, 1914

One morning on leaving my wigwam I was startled by hearing a gurgling, rumbling sound, as though an army of horses laden with sleigh bells was advancing through the deep forests towards me... mixed with the rumbling of an approaching storm.

In 1850, Simon Pokagon, a Pottawatomie chief, described his unforgettable encounter in the Michigan woods:

While I gazed in wonder and astonishment, I beheld moving towards me in an unbroken front millions of pigeons, the first I had seen that season. They passed like a cloud through the branches of the big trees, through the underbrush and over the ground.... Statue-like I stood, half-concealed by cedar boughs. They fluttered all about me, lighting on my head and shoulders; gently I caught two in my hands and carefully concealed them under my blanket.

Like its fellow pigeon the dodo, the passenger pigeon is an icon of extinction, and its story defies belief, just as the bird itself defies imagining. It lived at extremes, and those who witnessed its frenetic life, its overwhelming numbers, and its terrible slaughter stumbled for words. Everyday language failed. How to convey the paradox that a single bird could be gentled inside your jacket, while a flock was a biblical storm that carpeted the sky for days on end?

In 1831, the great ornithologist John James Audubon wrote: "The air was literally filled with pigeons; the light of noonday was obscured as by an eclipse; the dung fell in spots, not unlike melting flakes of snow.... Pigeons were still passing in undiminished numbers, and continued to do so for three days in succession."

Once perhaps the most numerous bird species on Earth, the passenger pigeon was gone within the span of a few hundred years.

How could this happen?

The Great Wanderer

In a book about giants, why include a species that weighed less than a pound and was at best 16 inches long?

Good question.

Here's another: Is the size of an individual all that counts? What about the collective presence of the species? In North America, four out of ten birds were once passenger pigeons. Like bison, passenger pigeons lived and moved en masse, shaping and scarring the landscape with their passing.

A single bird was small, but they didn't live singly. They gathered by the millions, by the *billions*, in what we assume was an evolved strategy to keep their many predators from ever exhausting them.

A single flock defied counting. Some tried, using formulas that multiplied bird density by rate of speed by the approximate area of the flock by the time it took the flock to pass—but it was hopeless. Audubon once calculated a single flock to be over a billion birds; other flocks were calculated to be 2.2 billion and 3.7 billion. Was that every bird in existence, or were there other flocks like these? No one knew, and today few hazard to guess their totality. Collectively, they were too big to grasp.

Passenger pigeons formed aerial blankets over a mile wide and dozens, even hundreds, of miles long, and when they landed, they didn't just dominate the landscape; they became the landscape. It seems silly to call these "flocks," as if they were city pigeons descending on bread crumbs. A single nesting would have filled Manhattan a dozen times over; the largest nesting ever recorded would have covered every inch of Mauritius, the dodo's home. We need a new term. A plague of passenger pigeons? A monsoon? A scourge?

Without question, a giant.

Sleek and graceful, passenger pigeons were built for speed and could reach 60 miles per hour. They didn't slow down in the trees, either. Audubon said the passenger pigeon, when flying close by, "passes like a thought, and on trying to see it again, the eye searches in vain; the bird is gone."

In the sky? "I cannot describe to you the extreme beauty of their aerial evolutions, when a Hawk chanced to press upon the rear of a flock," Audubon wrote. "At once, like a torrent, and with a noise like thunder, they rushed into a compact mass.... They darted forward in undulating and angular lines, descended and swept close over the earth with inconceivable velocity, mounted perpendicularly so as to resemble a vast column, and, when high, were seen wheeling and twisting within their continued lines, which then resembled the coils of a gigantic serpent."

As Chief Pokagon wrote, "Never have my astonishment, wonder, and admiration been so stirred as when I have witnessed these birds drop from their course like meteors from heaven."

Passenger pigeons descended in a rolling wave that moved forward like a cyclone. As the lead birds landed, those behind passed over them to land, forming a continuous cylinder of motion, "its interior filling with flying leaves and grass," according to one witness.

When eating, passenger pigeons were gluttons. Like a boa, their mouths were elastic openings that could widen to swallow whole acorns, which were stored in a pouch in the throat, called a crop. Each bird filled the crop

The Pyrenean Ibex & Frozen Arks: Extinction Insurance

In 1999, farsighted scientists collected tissue from the last living Pyrenean ibex, also known as a bucardo, and preserved it in liquid nitrogen. If kept frozen at a cool minus 196°F, tissue samples can maintain viable DNA for thousands of years.

Unfortunately, this ibex died only months later (due to a falling tree branch), but scientists were ready: because of this preserved tissue, they could attempt to clone an extinct animal for the first time, using the same techniques that have been used successfully to clone living animals.

Cloning extinct animals is a spectacular challenge because, once an animal dies, its DNA immediately starts breaking up like an old brittle rope that falls to pieces. The longer an animal is dead, the more broken its DNA becomes, and the more pieces get lost. Cloning an extinct animal is like putting together an incomplete jigsaw puzzle that you finish by taking pieces from other puzzles (that is, living animals) and somehow fitting them into the holes.

in a panic, until it bulged almost as large as its body. If one was shot in this state, it sounded like a sack of marbles hitting the ground. For the passenger pigeon, the motto "You snooze, you lose" was an evolutionary adaption: millions of siblings eating at once meant gulping first and, over the next twelve hours, swallowing and digesting later.

After dispersing to eat, a pigeon flock reconvened in the evening to sleep, forming a gathering called a roost. A flock might occupy a roosting site for a day, maybe three, before migrating hundreds of miles to the next place with enough food to feed them all. What they left behind was devastation.

In 2003, the ibex cloning effort succeeded—for about seven minutes. A cloned bucardo kid was born (by a different species of goat), but it couldn't breath properly due to lung problems and quickly died (malformed lungs are a common problem with clones). In 2013, hopeful scientists began another, ongoing attempt to clone the Pyrenean ibex.

In the meantime, freezing tissue samples of endangered species has become a global mission. Called frozen arks, these growing collections of genetic material provide insurance against the day when these animals go extinct. In this way, frozen arks seek to preserve as much of the diversity of Earth's genetic inheritance as possible before it's lost through extinction.

Some of the largest facilities include the Frozen Ark at England's University of Nottingham, the San Diego Zoo's Frozen Zoo, the CryoBioBank at the Cincinnati Zoo, and the Cryo Collection of the American Museum of Natural History.

This frozen tissue isn't just raw material for cloning. Stem cells are created for use in medical research; collected sperm aides breeding programs; and eventually, each species' genome could be sequenced, thus revealing their biological blueprints.

When roosting, passenger pigeons literally sat on top of one another, overcrowding trees so badly that mature branches broke under their weight and young trees crumpled. All night, the sound of crashing limbs and screaming birds could be heard for miles. In 1845, an Ohio teenager described how they "bent the alders flat to the ground," and what looked like enormous "haystacks" in the dark "were only small elms or willows completely loaded down with live birds." Many birds died trying to sleep. It was crazy.

Further, as one observer wrote in 1759, "the ground below the trees where they had spent the night was entirely covered with their dung, which lay in great heaps." Watering the eyes with the ammonia tang of a commercial chicken farm, the inches-deep guano often killed many of the rent and broken trees afterward.

Yet this avian hurricane had surprising ecological benefits. Roosting sites opened up large patches of dense forest for new growth, and the dung eventually created extremely rich, fertile soil—as attested to by farmers. Further, pigeons dispersed seeds over thousands of miles, and their feeding impacted the types of trees that grew. In these ways, the passenger pigeon acted just like any megaherbivore: influencing the very character of the continent's forests and the habitats of many creatures.

Pigeons also gathered en masse to nest. Compared to the condensed chaos of a roosting, nestings were orderly, organized, spread-out affairs. A roosting crammed millions into a dozen acres (or up to 100 square miles), while large nestings ranged from 200 to over 800 square miles (occasionally, nestings were much smaller). Nesting areas were carefully shaped: longer than they were wide, they had interior "lanes" of bird-free forest, which allowed everyone easier access to food.

Nesting lasted only four to five weeks; passenger pigeons created the next generation with typical haste. In this way, they were the exact opposite of a slow-breeding giant species. Mating, nest building, and egg laying took three days. Like a great broom, the birds swept the forest floor clean of twigs to make nests, but these were "a crude affair," a Kerplunk-style crossing of sticks just sturdy enough to hold a single egg. Two weeks later, the egg hatched, and two weeks after that, all the parents rose at once, leaving their fat downy babies to figure out the flying thing on their own.

This abandonment is curious. Over the next few days, the babies dropped from their nests and toddled like drunkards until they got their wings working. In the meantime, predators had a field day eating baby pigeons. Why would adults leave their young unprotected? Some have speculated that they didn't always do this. Rather, it became a learned response to the disturbance of human hunting.

A Movable Feast in North America's Forests

Passenger pigeons flew fast, ate fast, bred fast, and were always on the move. As one journalist wrote in 1913, "They were pilgrims and strangers, the gypsies of birdom." Originally, they ranged across almost the entire North American continent, but within historic times, they primarily roamed the eastern half, and they rarely returned to the same place annually. Some areas saw the great flocks but once every dozen years.

This inspired the bird's scientific name: *Ectopistes migratorius*. The first word is Greek for "wanderer," and the second is Latin for "one that migrates." In New England, the Narragansett called it *wushko'wha'an*, or "the wanderer."

On the other hand, the Seneca called the passenger pigeon *jah'gowa*, meaning "big bread." True enough, this bird was food for everyone.

Pretty much every predator had its fill when passenger pigeons arrived: wolves, mountain lions, bears, hawks, owls, vultures, weasels, skunks, raccoons, and, of course, humans. As long as people have lived in North America, there is fossil evidence they dined on passenger pigeons. The oldest evidence dates back to possibly 16,000 years ago, though the largest quantities of bones date from AD 700 to 1000.

The passenger pigeon was a meal, not an appetizer. In the eastern United States, the white deer and the wild turkey were the most important game for native peoples, but the passenger pigeon was the second-most important bird and a critical food source. As an indication of its cultural importance, there were passenger pigeon dances, songs, and myths. In one Seneca myth, the passenger pigeon gives people life:

> The Spirits of men came upon the earth seeking incarnation, among the birds and animals, with an appeal, "Ho, Elder Brother, the children have no bodies." But they were unheeded, until the pigeon came and answered: "Your children shall have bodies; my bones shall be their bones, my flesh their flesh, my blood their blood, and they shall see with my eyes."

In one respect, passenger pigeons competed with humans for the same foods. The birds preferred mast, or nuts like acorns, beechnuts, chestnuts, and hazelnuts, and they loved maize, or ancestral corn. Then again, when the passenger pigeons arrived, they provided people with an even tastier feast.

This banquet was so abundant, and so unpredictable, that indigenous tribes typically dropped any feuds to enjoy it. When a nesting arrived, Native Americans would send around word to neighboring tribes, and all but the youngest and oldest would drop what they were doing and travel to that place, creating huge cooperative celebrations of hunting, eating, and play. These communal events continued into the eighteenth century.

Notably, many Native Americans prohibited killing adult birds at a nesting, and they waited until the babies, or squabs, were as fat as possible and almost ready to fly. Then they moved in and harvested the young. You couldn't really call it hunting, since any child with a stick could whack the flightless squabs off a nest. During roostings, Native Americans typically used nets to capture flying birds.

Thus, whenever and wherever passenger pigeons shadowed the earth, they provided an all-you-can-eat buffet to other creatures. According to fossil evidence, passenger pigeons lived in North America since at least 100,000 years ago, and their evolved survival strategy served it well: they outnumbered their enemies and kept moving. Despite the numerous birds that predators caught, the collective was too big to overcome. Even after humans first arrived, passenger pigeons thrived. But this meant the species only knew how to live as a winged city.

Like any strategy, this had a downside.

Pigeon Pie: Hunting for Fun, Food & Profit

The story of the passenger pigeon is part of the same story that includes the eastern elk, the bison, the wolf, and the grizzly bear, among other North American giants who were driven to extinction, or nearly so, over the last 400 years. This is, of course, the story of European colonization and the rise of our modern industrialized society.

Like everyone else, European settlers and colonists in the New World enjoyed the passenger pigeon. Farmers might curse the species as a virulent pest that gobbled sown grain before it could sprout, but mainly, as with Native Americans, Europeans greeted the arrival of the passenger pigeon with awe, celebration, festive hunting parties, and feasting.

Because the passenger pigeon was such a strong flyer, it had large breast muscles, and these made good eating. The list of cooking methods was exhaustive: the meat was stewed, fried, roasted, boiled, smoked, salted, cured, pickled, and preserved in spiced apple cider. Humble pigeon pie was a favorite, but gourmet restaurants served pigeon with foie gras and truffles. Squabs were rendered into oil, which was sold by the barrel, and feathers stuffed pillows and mattresses.

Equally inventive were hunting methods. Like Native Americans, Europeans employed nets and clubs, but they also used poles to knock down nests, they cut down entire pigeon-filled trees, and they set fire to trees, so that preroasted birds fell smoking to the ground. They burned pots of sulfur, whose fumes knocked the birds unconscious. And they used guns, which had the advantage of killing more than one bird at a shot. In 1664, a Frenchman said killing eight to twelve birds at a time was common, but pigeons so packed the air that, as unlikely as it sounds, "forty or forty-five can be killed with the single discharge of a gun."

To attract pigeons into net traps, hunters spread out food or they used living decoy birds. Some "Judas birds" were simply tethered to the ground. More disturbing were "stool pigeons," a term that originated with this practice. These pigeons had their eyes sewn shut and were tied to a perch or stool. As a flock flew over, the stool was toppled so the bird would flap wildly as if landing, ideally drawing the others.

Nor was pigeon hunting confined to the countryside. When great flocks clouded city skies, people in New York and Philadelphia stuck guns out of windows, or ran for the rooftops, and opened fire. When a flock passed Albany in the early 1800s, one woman said this inspired "a total relaxation from all employments, and a kind of drunken gayety, though it was rather slaughter than sport."

About the same time, Ontario tried to outlaw pigeon shooting within city limits—reasonably enough, for public safety—but even elected officials ignored the ban, leading someone to comment: "It was found that pigeons, flying within easy shot, were a temptation too strong for human virtue to withstand."

Clearly, a different era.

However, until the early 1800s, people hunted pigeons mostly for themselves. Few made money at it; they were merely having a good time and filling the pantry. That changed starting in the 1840s. The spread of the telegraph allowed for instant, long-distance communication of pigeon nestings, which attracted more people. The spread of railroads allowed for quick, bulk transport of pigeons, which otherwise spoiled in transit. And the explosive growth of cities provided attractive, large markets for sales. It was the classic equation of America's industrial revolution: mechanization increased volume, volume increased profits, and profits spurred a professional industry that quickly invented new ways to grow and make more money.

Thus, the professional pigeon hunter was born. In a few short decades, pigeon hunting transformed from a recreational local pastime to a ferocious, greed-driven slaughter whose intensity boggles the mind. If it wasn't also being repeated with America's bison, elk, grizzly, wolf, and waterfowl, we'd scarcely believe it.

Martha and the Last Giant Flocks

By the 1860s and 1870s, clear signs indicated the species was suffering. People noticed that the flocks were steadily abandoning the East Coast and only appearing farther west. This made sense: by then, the East Coast had the most people and the least forest, which had been replaced with pasture, field, and town. Habitat destruction certainly led to the passenger pigeon's decline, forcing it to gather in fewer places that were easier to reach.

"THE PASSENGER PIGEON LIVED AT EXTREMES, AND THOSE WHO WITNESSED ITS FRENETIC LIFE, ITS OVERWHELMING NUMBERS, AND ITS TERRIBLE SLAUGHTER STUMBLED FOR WORDS. EVERYDAY LANGUAGE FAILED."

Pigeons also abandoned their nests more often. They were more nervous and easily disturbed. That also made sense—hunters never left them alone—but it undermined breeding. Not only were passenger pigeons being killed on a scale they'd never experienced before, but those who survived weren't reproducing at the normal rate.

From 1870 to the early 1880s, the last giant nestings occurred. These were so singularly gigantic that they misled observers: surely, the passenger pigeon was doing fine if so many still existed. In reality, as various flocks were decimated, the survivors regrouped to restore their safety in numbers. Yet by always flocking in giant congregations, they only made themselves easier targets.

In 1871, the largest nesting ever recorded descended on Wisconsin; it covered 850 square miles and included an estimated 136 million nesting birds, plus squabs and those not nesting. Some researchers theorize this was no longer one of several such flocks, but possibly all the passenger pigeons that remained.

About a 100,000 people came, including 600 registered professional netters. One anonymous writer later described what it was like as everyone with a weapon opened fire at once:

> Imagine a thousand threshing machines running under full headway, accompanied by as many steamboats groaning off steam, with an equal number of... trains passing through covered bridges... and you possibly have a faint conception of the terrific roar following the monstrous black cloud of pigeons as they passed in rapid flight... a few feet before our faces... nearly on a level with the muzzles of our guns.... The slaughter was terrible beyond any description.

Netting, however, remained the most efficient method. Netters caught so many that they counted and sold them by the dozen or the barrel. A single netter could haul in 85 dozen, 110 dozen, even 300 dozen at once, or from 1,000 to 3,500 birds. Of course, once netted, the birds had to be killed by hand, one by one, typically by either clubbing or strangling.

After 1871, about nine more giant nestings followed, the largest in 1874 and two final ones in 1878. By this time, the professionals were far too successful for their own good: after each massive hunt, millions of pigeons flooded urban markets, prices collapsed, and barrels of birds went unsold and were thrown away.

Through the 1880s, passenger pigeon hunts continued, but the bird's population had collapsed; the massive flocks were never seen again, and each hunt became more thorough than the last. It's also assumed that, as flocks dwindled, they lost their numerical advantage over other animal predators. With such a mobile, migratory species, it's virtually impossible that humans killed every last one. Rather, the final small gatherings probably could not reproduce fast enough to overcome predation by wild carnivores.

In the 1890s, "last sightings" in states and regions accumulated steadily, and each ended the same way, with someone shooting the bird almost as a reflex. Was the bird really that delicious, or human virtue that weak? When a lone passenger pigeon appeared in a Chicago park in 1894, a stranger asked around for a gun, leading an observer to remark, "He had no soul above pigeon pie."

For a long time, it was believed that the last wild pigeon was killed by a fourteen-year-old boy in Ohio in 1900, but another bird was killed in 1902, and a small flock was observed in 1907 by none other than President Teddy Roosevelt, who was an avid birder.

After that, no more were seen in the wild, and only two passenger pigeons were known to exist. Named George and Martha (perhaps after the Washingtons), they lived in the Cincinnati Zoo. George died in 1910, and Martha died four years later, on September 1, 1914. As is frequently remarked, the most numerous bird species on Earth had been reduced to a single individual whose passing became one of the rare occasions when we know the exact moment of a species' extinction.

Even sadder is imagining Martha's loneliness and captivity. Passenger pigeons were built for neither solitude nor stillness.

Phoenix from the Ashes: De-extinction & Cloning

In 1947, naturalist Aldo Leopold wrote of the passenger pigeon, "Today the oaks still flaunt their burden at the sky, but the feathered lightning is no more."

Hold that thought.

In labs right now, scientists and researchers are trying to re-create that lightning.

Bringing the passenger pigeon back from extinction is the flagship project of Revive & Restore, run by the Long Now Foundation. The aim is for the first passenger pigeon chick to be born, or reborn, by 2025. If that goal is reached, Revive & Restore estimates that a self-sustaining population of wild passenger pigeons could be a reality by 2060.

That would be amazing, historic, unprecedented. However, this science fiction scenario raises a number of practical and philosophical questions.

First off, how? Unfortunately, the cloning methods that have already been proven to work with living animals won't work with extinct ones. In 1996, Dolly the sheep became the first cloned animal, and since then we've cloned pigs, horses, dogs, and deer, among others. In 2003, we even cloned the first *extinct* species, the Pyrenean ibex. But this was only possible because before the species went extinct in 2000, scientists collected and froze living cells from the last individual when it was still alive.

Another method has to be invented for the passenger pigeon. Right now, the most promising avenue is to cut-and-splice the DNA of the passenger pigeon's closest living relative, the band-tail pigeon, and mix it with synthesized passenger pigeon DNA. The passenger pigeon's genome has already been sequenced, so scientists could keep mixing DNA until they have a match. Then, they would inject this into a band-tailed pigeon embryo. This would create a creature that was a hybrid of the two species. Traditionally, this is called a chimera: in this case, it would be a band-tailed pigeon with the sperm or eggs (depending on the gender) of a passenger pigeon. This "chimera pigeon" would not be a passenger pigeon, but because its reproductive system matched a passenger pigeon's, the chimera would be able to give birth to one.

Once it did—hurray, de-extinction! Follow all that?

In truth, no one is certain this method will work. Even if scientists get the DNA right, species are more than genetics. They are behavior, and we have no living passenger pigeons for a comparison or model. Observers wonder: Will this new bird learn to act like a passenger pigeon even without any passenger pigeon parents? Without any passenger pigeon society? Once in the wild, will it adopt the same ecological role? What if nature is too changed for it to survive?

Further, once released, will this bird instantly be labeled an endangered species? Will it be patented, a creation that someone "owns"? If it causes trouble for us or other species—if it spreads disease, wrecks habitats, or threatens other animals—can we get rid of it or destroy it? If the birds flourish, and millions again fill the skies, can we eat them?

You get the picture. Profound and difficult questions confront us if we try to bring extinct species back. Or should I say "as we bring them back"? The stories of the passenger pigeon, the aurochs, the thylacine, and even the woolly mammoth may not be over just yet. ↘

NORTH
AMERICA

CALIFORNIA GRIZZLY: ELDER BROTHER, COUSIN, GREAT-GRANDFATHER

EXTINCTION: a North American subspecies of brown bear, the California Grizzly went extinct in 1922

Who doesn't have a bear story?

Bears of one kind or another encircle the Northern Hemisphere, and wherever they live, they are synonymous with wilderness. Any walk in the woods is improved when it runs through bear country, since any meeting with a bear—so long as you survive it—makes a story worth telling.

This is the story of one bear, the California grizzly, and of how people first learned to live with it until they decided to live without it.

Old Ephraim in the Real Wild West

Nicknamed Old Ephraim by European settlers, the North American grizzly is a type of brown bear. Today, the grizzly is the biggest bear in the world, and the biggest grizzlies live in Alaska's Kodiak Islands. However, in its day, the California grizzly was the biggest bear south of the Yukon.

But first, consider any bear: it eats like us, can move like us, can fight like us, can use its fingers like us, and under its fur, its body looks like ours. It's also smart, curious, and even at times a trickster.

Bears can stand on two legs, perfectly balanced, to walk, reach food, or fight, and they swing their sledgehammer paws like fists. Bears can sit, balanced on their haunches, paws free in order to delicately manipulate one or all five fingers, like a handful of dexterous chopsticks. A bear skeleton (except for the skull) resembles a human's, particularly the pair of bones in the forearms and lower legs, which allow twisting motions. A bear's feet flatten when it walks, leaving human-like footprints.

Bears are omnivores like us, with the widest diet of any animal. Of the California grizzly, naturalist John Muir wrote, "To him almost everything is food except granite." Grizzlies gorge happily on every plant, fruit, and root, on every kind and size of animal, on every nest and hive—honey, comb, bees, and all.

"Crunched and hashed," Muir continues, "down all go to his marvelous stomach and vanish as if cast into a fire. What digestion! A sheep or a wounded deer or a pig he eats warm, about as quickly as a boy eats a buttered muffin; or should the meat be a month old, it still is welcomed with tremendous relish. After so gross a meal as this, perhaps the next will be strawberries and clover, or raspberries with mushrooms and nuts, or puckery acorns and chokecherries."

Bears have binocular vision like us, and in California, they communed together to dine, vocalizing in conversational grunts, groans, coughs, and huffs. Bears are usually silent, and what we remember are their spine-shivering roars. But it's easy to imagine sitting and talking with a bear.

Is it any wonder that indigenous peoples thought the bear had once been our ancestor? Yet bears are not us, which makes them all the more remarkable.

The original bear was the size of a dog. This is fitting since bears evolved from the canid lineage over 20 million years ago. About 5 million years ago, *Ursus etruscus* split off, which gave rise to the European cave bear and, about 1.3 million years ago, to the brown bear (*Ursus arctos*), possibly in China.

The cave bear was a Pleistocene giant, weighing some 900 pounds, and it might have been the first bear humans ever met. Cro-Magnon painters certainly noticed it, and they included its portrait on France's Chauvet Cave walls.

By then, bears of all kinds were spread across the globe's northern half; even North Africa had the Atlas bear (which went extinct in the 1870s). Estimates of when the brown bear species crossed from Siberia into North America vary from 200,000 to 70,000 years ago. When they did, they came face-to-face with North America's legendary short-faced bear.

The short-faced bear averaged a ton, or 2,000 pounds, and it migrated to North America about 1.3 million years ago, establishing itself as perhaps the earth's largest mammalian terrestrial predator. An adult California grizzly averaged from 600 to 1,000 pounds, but huge individuals could reach a ton. Neither was a pushover, and both awaited humans when they strolled into North America about 14,000 years ago.

All we really know is the result of this clash of titans: grizzlies and humans survived; the short-faced bear did not. Whatever killed North America's Late Pleistocene megafauna, whatever did in the sabertooths, mammoths, mastodons, and ground sloths—however skilled early human hunters were—nothing unseated the grizzly.

Instead, people lived with this bear for the next 11,000 years. Maybe the grizzly was so adaptable, so resilient, so like us, we didn't have a choice.

Great-Great-Grandfather, "Sequoia of the Animals"

While all grizzlies are brown bears, only brown bears in North America are called grizzlies. The name refers to its often "grizzled" silver- or golden-tipped fur, though grizzly coats vary from cinnamon to burnt umber to gray and even black.

Yet grizzlies are also "grisly," as in terrifying. The grizzly is renowned as the most aggressive ursine species. Why so mad, brother bear? Some think that in the predator-mad octagon of North America, the grizzly learned to claw first and ask questions later.

"WHAT DIGESTION! A SHEEP OR A WOUNDED DEER OR A PIG HE EATS WARM, ABOUT AS QUICKLY AS A BOY EATS A BUTTERED MUFFIN; OR SHOULD THE MEAT BE A MONTH OLD, IT STILL IS WELCOMED WITH TREMENDOUS RELISH."

—JOHN MUIR

The grizzly spread throughout the entire western half of North America, from Alaska and the Arctic Circle all the way south into Mexico and east to the lip of the Great Plains. However, it thrived in California like nowhere else, becoming the biggest and perhaps the most abundant grizzly population. Year-round in the Golden State, life was so good, the food so plentiful, that most grizzlies didn't hibernate.

By the time the Spanish settled here in 1769, approximately 10,000 grizzlies lived in California (out of perhaps 100,000 in the continental United States), but the number could have been higher. Meanwhile, California held perhaps 130,000 native peoples.

If the grizzly was so tough and so mean, how did we coexist?

Carefully, and with a lot of respect.

For one thing, indigenous peoples didn't live in canyons known for grizzlies. Indians along the Klamath and Trinity Rivers built windowless houses out of plank boards with only a small round hole for a door. In winter, when grizzlies wandered by looking for food, this hole let people in but kept bears out.

Native tribes across North America venerated and feared grizzlies. They felt a familial connection, calling them "grandfather" and "great-great-grandfather," "chief's son," "elder brother," "cousin," and "little uncle."

Cherokee considered grizzlies ancestors who'd traded our hard human life for a bear's easy one; Pomo thought bad people remained on the earth as bears. Shasta said you could converse with bears, if you sat with them quietly, and Yavapi thought the only difference between us and them was that humans made fire. The Yosemite Indians named themselves after their word for grizzly.

For many tribes, in California and elsewhere, the grizzly was a totem animal, and bear shamans were the most powerful healers. Some believed shamans could transform into bears and smite enemies and that bear claws, worn around the neck, made you impervious to injury.

Tribes had bear ceremonies, rituals, and dances: to placate the bear, ask for protection, celebrate a harvest, and as puberty rites. Some prohibited hunting the grizzly and refused to eat its meat. Others hunted grizzlies, but not casually.

"The biggest man is scared of a grizzly," Sargent Sambo, a Shasta chief along the Klamath River, once said. "He will cry and tremble. Anyone who has had trouble with a grizzly will just bawl and cry. If you just hear one, it scares you to death. You may not know you are shaking until you light your pipe and your hand will just be shaking. Nothing else has that power."

The descendants of the mammoth hunters were tough people, but no creature in the landscape rivaled the grizzly. Later, John Muir captured this, calling the grizzly "the sequoia of the animals."

Grizzlies, in turn, learned to avoid people.

It's interesting, actually, even a paradox. As ferocious as grizzlies can be, they are also extraordinarily tolerant. They rarely attack people unless startled, provoked, or to protect a cub; perhaps some tribes didn't hunt them for this reason. If they can, grizzlies will avoid conflict by running away; if they can't or decide not to, they don't hold back. Each grizzly is different, with its own regal personality. Some are irascible and mean; some curiously playful; some so docile they willingly perform in shows. The grizzly is terrifying when it wants to be, but it can also put up with us like a benevolent elder.

For millennia, humans inserted themselves into the predator hierarchy of California's rich landscape. In the pecking order at an elk carcass, grizzlies asserted themselves first, it would seem, whether they, gray wolves, a jaguar, or a mountain lion made the kill. Bobcats, foxes, golden eagles, and smaller predators waited their turn, as did flocks of California condors.

But when clover bloomed, when acorns and blackberries ripened, herds of bears descended. When the bulbs of lilies and onions swelled, they tore up fields like rototillers. When salmon spawned, they flooded the rivers. Bears lived everywhere, eating what they wanted, when they wanted, without depending on any single thing.

That's probably one secret of this arrangement. Humans ate all these things, too, and were just as flexible. Whoever took a carcass or harvested acorns, more waited in the next valley. California's abundance fostered harmony.

Spaniards & Their Cattle

When Spanish explorers surveyed the coast in 1602, they found grizzlies scavenging a beached whale and fishing in the surf. With paws like these, who needs fishhooks?

However, the Spanish didn't settle California until the Portola expedition arrived in 1769. In the following decades, they built missions, presidios, and ranchos, and they filled the lowland meadows with grazing horses and domestic cattle.

For opportunistic grizzlies, this was manna from heaven.

In a short sprint, a grizzly can gallop as fast as a horse, but killing fleet, wary prey like elk requires endurance, and bears probably did this rarely. Catching a dopey ol' cow? All you need is a little trickery.

It sounds like a tall tale, but apparently it happened. Sometimes a grizzly would enter a pasture, lie on its back, and play with its paws. It'd tumble like a buffoon until some annoyed bull charged or a curious heifer nosed too close. Then the grizzly would rise like thunder and smack it down, killing with a single blow.

Even better, from the grizzly's perspective: the Spanish often raised cows only for their hides, slaughtering them in the fields and leaving the meat, which grizzlies scavenged with abandon. In Monterey, the capital of Spanish-governed Alta California, grizzlies arrived daily to kill cattle, and the Spanish couldn't stop them. Grizzlies thrived, even though the Spanish shot and poisoned them and steadily pushed them—and Native Americans—out of the prime coastal and lowland habitats where they'd always lived.

Until the mid-1800s, this settled into an awkward, new coexistence. The Spanish had a bear problem they couldn't fix, but with so many cattle and so much land, they mostly shrugged off the losses as the price of doing business.

Grizzlies, meanwhile, had to endure the first human foe who could get the better of them. Not because of guns, which were weak, muzzle-loading annoyances. But because of the lasso, or reata.

Spanish vaqueros developed an unparalleled skill with the reata. They proved it with the grizzly, whom vaqueros captured alive in order to use in their bear-and-bull fights. Like classic bullfights with matadors, these deadly animal-on-animal contests were a centuries-old Spanish tradition. They fit within the dramatic, ritualized pageantry of Spanish culture, in which whole towns would pray in church on Sunday morning, feast all afternoon, and later crowd the arena to cheer on these bloody shows.

Bear-and-bull fights became Alta California's signature entertainment during fiestas, saint's days, Easter, and town anniversaries. The earliest recorded contest was held in 1816 to celebrate the arrival of the territory's new governor, but informal, local ones had surely been held for decades.

First, you had to rope a grizzly, which depended tremendously on the bravery of your horse. From four to twelve mounted vaqueros would sur-round a bear, sometimes by first setting out a dead cow as bait. After provoking the bear to charge, vaqueros from behind would lasso a leg, but bears learned a neat trick: they'd stand, grab the rope, and pull it in, paw over paw—grizzlies aren't dumb. Stronger even than a straining horse, whose saddle was knotted to the rope, grizzlies injured and killed many a horse, and sometimes a rider, this way, unless another vaquero roped a second limb first.

Once two limbs were caught, vaqueros could pull in opposite directions, unbalancing the bear and catching it with more ropes until it was wrapped and tied.

In the ring, grizzlies faced the notoriously angry Spanish bull, a close descendent of the mighty aurochs. Yet the outcome was rarely in doubt. Grizzlies defeated bulls almost every time.

To keep the combatants in the ring, and to prompt them to fight, a long leather cord often connected them, tying a bear's back leg to a bull's foreleg. Grizzlies rarely attacked first. They waited for the bull to become enraged enough to charge, then the bear tackled it, sometimes biting its nose. Unless the bull gored the bear on the first strike and tossed the grizzly into the air, it was usually game over.

Holding the wounded bull to the ground, grizzlies waited for the bull to pant or scream, then they'd claw the exposed tongue and hold on to it until the bull collapsed. Sometimes, vaqueros shot bulls to end their agony.

It's hard to imagine cheering such a gruesome spectacle today. When American pioneers eventually migrated from the east and took California from the Spanish, they continued the bear-and-bull fights, but strictly as moneymaking amusements. Stripped of its cultural and community context, the event was widely condemned as sanctioned cruelty, and by 1860 it was outlawed across the state.

This didn't reflect any love for the grizzly. The Spanish caused the first real trouble the bear ever faced, but vaqueros weren't trying to rope the species to extinction. Instead, extinction became the goal of the next wave of human immigrants.

How to Hunt a Grizzly

Native tribes in California developed a number of clever methods for hunting grizzlies.

One was described by Sargent Sambo, a Shasta chief, in 1946. He said the Shasta would approach grizzlies in their den: "Reaching the den, a number of short, sharp stakes were driven into the ground in front of the opening, and then, as the bear came out and was engaging in tearing down and clearing out of the way this obstruction, he was shot under the neck."

Ethnographer Catherine Holt added, "Sometimes a man to show bravery would grab the dying grizzly by the ears and rub his head against the bear's forehead."

The Maidu tribe in northern California used more of a round-robin approach, almost like a game of tag. A group of four or five men would spread out and hide themselves not too far from a grizzly. Then one man would approach the bear and shoot it with an arrow. As the enraged bear charged, the man would run toward the place where another hunter was hiding.

As researcher Roland Dixon wrote in 1905, "Slipping behind the tree or rock, the first hunter would stop; and the fresh runner would instantly jump out, and run toward the place where another man was concealed."

Meanwhile, the first runner would continue to shoot arrows at the bear, and this game continued with the third, fourth, and fifth man.

"Thus each hunter had time to rest," Dixon wrote, "and to shoot several arrows, while the other men were taking the attention of the bear. By thus changing off, they tried to tire out the bear, and fill his body full of arrows, until he finally succumbed. It was always, however, dangerous sport, and not infrequently several of the hunters were killed."

The Horrible Bear: Gold, Rifles & Progress

What's in a name? Does it matter if we call the grizzly a grizzly, a North American brown bear, great-grandfather, or *Ursus arctos horribilis*?

In 1815, scientist George Ord used the Latin name *Ursus horribilis*, "horrible bear," to distinguish North America's species of brown bear, and this seemed to cement the bear's "grisly" reputation in its scientific name. However, in 1851, scientists realized that all brown bears worldwide are closely related, despite their confusing differences in size, coat, and habitat. So today all brown bears in Eurasia and North America share the same genus name, *Ursus arctos*, and subspecies are distinguished by a third name. The North American brown bear is now *Ursus arctos horribilis*.

North America does possess a few other recognized subspecies of brown bear—including Alaska's Kodiak bear (*Ursus arctos middendorffi*) and the extinct California brown bear (*Ursus arctos californicus*). But these distinctions—and the sometimes heated debates about brown bear taxonomy that have led to all this renaming and reclassifying—didn't really mean anything to America's nineteenth-century settlers, except that they agreed that brown bears in the United States were "horrible."

And yet, in 1846, when California announced its independence from Spain, it did so under the emblem of a California grizzly and became known as "the bear flag republic." In 1849, a bear silhouette became an official part of California's state seal. Thus, Californians embraced the "horrible" grizzly as a symbol even as they put every effort into exterminating the living animal.

In 1848, two things sealed the California grizzly's fate: gold was discovered in California, and the breech-loading, repeating Sharps rifle was invented. In the name of progress, to get at the gold, in order to tame the wild west for the benefit of pioneers, merchants, farmers, and the burgeoning United States republic, the grizzly had to go, and people now had the means to do it. In contrast to the Spanish, Americans had zero tolerance for large predators, which famously included gray wolves, jaguars, mountain lions, and coyotes.

Grizzly hunters, Sharps rifles in hand, relished their profession. Nothing brought more glory than killing grizzlies, and in the exaggerated tales of mountaineers, grizzlies always towered as the scariest, biggest giants who ever lived. No doubt, enraged brown bears must have loomed quite large; they were legendary for how many bullets they could take. Shot once, twice, three times, grizzlies often just kept coming. Like vaqueros throwing reatas as fast as they could, a grizzly hunter must have prayed continually for the next bullet to stop the bear.

Newly minted Californians couldn't have been more grateful. Grizzlies scared the stuffing out of them. By the 1850s, grizzlies didn't just steal livestock of all kinds; they decimated and trampled fields of corn and wheat overnight. They wandered into San Francisco; herds gathered near Napa and Sacramento. A school once closed to keep children from being attacked while walking to and from school. A newspaper man once opined that grizzlies made "the rearing of cattle utterly impossible." Modern life isn't a picnic with the grizzly around.

In California, bear bounties arose in the 1870s, along with a market for bear meat and bear "robes." This provided further financial incentives for slaughter. By the late 1880s, California grizzlies steadily vanished from one region after another. The southern Sierra Nevada became their last stronghold, and the last reported California grizzly was killed in 1922.

The horrible bear worried Californians no more.

Garbage Bears & Rewilding Yellowstone

For over a century, this same thing was repeated wherever grizzlies lived across the West. From 1890 to 1979, grizzlies were exterminated in Texas, North Dakota, Utah, Manitoba, Oregon, Saskatchewan, New Mexico, Arizona, Mexico, and Colorado. In the continental United States, 99 percent of grizzlies were lost, along with a quarter of their original range in Canada.

Only the California grizzly subspecies went extinct; the North American grizzly, though virtually extinguished in the continental United States, remained abundant in northern Canada and Alaska.

In continental America, one place that protected and preserved grizzlies was Yellowstone National Park, which was established in 1872. As grizzlies disappeared elsewhere, a small population survived here. By the mid-twentieth century, they had become a bona fide wildlife attraction, since this was one of the last places in the lower forty-eight where you could still find them.

Enterprising park rangers even created an entertaining grizzly theater every night: they set up lights and bleacher seats at the park dump, sorted the park's edible trash—its apple cores and chicken bones—onto tables, and invited the public to watch as the grizzlies arrived like clockwork for an evening meal. Sometimes seventy or eighty bears would show up, along with hundreds of people snapping photos.

In time, these "garbage bears" became controversial, and Yellowstone ended the practice in 1971. For one thing, the grizzlies came to rely on this food, which wasn't healthy for them. For another, they were getting a little *too* comfortable near people. When three people were injured by grizzlies in Yellowstone in the late 1960s—and after two women were killed by grizzlies in Glacier National Park in 1967—rangers realized grizzlies needed to find their own food.

Today, about 150 grizzlies live within Yellowstone, part of about 675 to 840 that live in the Greater Yellowstone Ecosystem. Further, since 1997, Yellowstone has been part of a historic effort to rewild the spine of the Rocky Mountains, which extends into Canada. Called the Yellowstone to Yukon Conservation Initiative, or Y2Y, this effort has also adopted the grizzly as its symbol.

The guiding vision of Y2Y is summarized in the phrase "cores, corridors, and carnivores." That is, its aim is to create links, or natural corridors, through which all wildlife—but especially megafauna and top predators like grizzlies and gray wolves—can travel between existing core conservation areas, from Yellowstone in the south all the way into Canada's Northwest Territories. This monumental, ongoing project seeks to link 2,000 miles of terrain, making it one of the largest such efforts in the world. As small, previously isolated populations of megafauna become connected—allowing them to breed together—they will become healthier and more resilient, and these keystone species can better fulfill their evolved ecological functions.

Similarly, some hope to one day reintroduce North American grizzlies into California's Sierra Nevada. This won't bring the California grizzly back to life, but it would restore an essential character, one that has always defined and shaped California's wilderness.

Climate Change & Polar Bears

There is one final coda to the grizzly story, and it involves the polar bear.

As you probably know, global warming is melting the glacial ice sheets in the Arctic, which are home to the polar bear. In 2008, primarily because their hunting habitat is melting out from underneath them, polar bears were listed as threatened under the US Endangered Species Act. They are the first species to be listed as threatened almost solely because of climate change.

The polar bear is about the same size as the Kodiak bear, and so it also vies for the title of world's largest bear. What you might not know is that grizzlies and polar bears are also the most closely related of all bear species. Apparently, some time from 200,000 to perhaps only 10,000 years ago, some grizzlies migrated north, their brown fur turned white, and they became polar bears.

Today, these "kissing cousins" are increasingly being reunited. As climate change shrinks Arctic habitat, polar bears are occasionally meeting grizzly bears as they both scavenge the same whale carcasses along Arctic coasts. To the surprise of biologists, some of these meetings have led to mating and successful wild hybrid offspring. One such polar bear–grizzly hybrid was killed by a hunter in 2006 in Canada. While these hybrids have occurred in captivity before, that was always considered artificial, a product of unnatural confinement. In the wild, polar bears and grizzlies usually fight.

Perhaps not always, or not always anymore.

This probably isn't happening very often, but if this crossbreeding continues, it could one day lead to a new bear species, which scientists will have to name and fit into their taxonomy.

But the bears don't care what we call them. Survival is the only thing that counts. ᔦ

AUSTRALIA: A LOST CONTINENT

Like Madagascar and New Zealand, Australia is one of those odd cases that makes us realize that the way things are isn't necessarily the way things *have* to be. Other evolutionary paths are possible; life is *extremely* flexible. For 40 million years, wildlife on this isolated continent unfolded differently from anywhere else on Earth, turning the prehistoric land Down Under into a veritable Alice's Wonderland of the illogical, the bizarre, and the unlikely.

Our arrival, unfortunately, shattered that world. The impact of the first human visitors was as devastating as a meteor strike. Every animal larger than 220 pounds vanished, and over half of those between 22 and 220 pounds was lost. In the Late Pleistocene, no continent comes close to matching the decimation of Australia's giant species.

Perhaps strangest of all, we can find precious little evidence of how, why, or even when this all happened.

Humans almost certainly were the main cause for extinctions, but it's a case built on circumstantial evidence that wouldn't hold up in a court of law.

Mammoth Marsupials & Killer Kangaroos

It would be worth building a time machine just to see the faces of the first people to sail to Australia.

Many mammals didn't run—they bounded and hopped—and every animal looked off-kilter, like half-finished escapees from H.G. Wells's novel *The Island of Doctor Moreau*. Take reproductive systems. Two species—the echidna, a bumbling ball of spines, and the semiaquatic, duck-billed platypus—laid eggs like reptiles but suckled young like mammals. They were (and are) among the last survivors of an extraordinarily old mammalian branch called monotremes, which predates every other living mammal species.

Meanwhile, the rest of Australia's mammals had their reproductive systems turned inside out: instead of giving birth to fully developed babies, they grew fetuses in an external pouch. Bouncing marsupials carrying children in satchels crowded this jaw-dropping landscape.

That wasn't all. A 6-foot, 400-pound wombat, the largest that ever lived, burrowed underground, creating prairie-dog towns of mogul-size hills. There were 400-pound horned turtles, a 400-pound giant flightless bird (similar to New Zealand's moa), and a 200-pound snake. The scariest predator was the toothsome goanna, a 1-ton lizard literally as big as an allosaurus. Other deadly predators included the "marsupial lion," a leopard-size carnivore, and the thylacine, a wolf-shaped beast with tiger stripes.

The largest marsupial herbivores were downright ugly: Palorchestes resembled a 1-ton ground sloth, but with massive claws on massive arms and a long nose that drooped like Snuffleupagus. The biggest animals, the diprotodons, were 2-ton, woolly, giant-headed browsers with hippo-like bodies and tree-trunk legs. A sort of rhino, zygomaturus had extended cheekbones wider than its face was long.

The real gobsmackers were the kangaroos. Over a hundred species bounced in every ecological niche and habitat. Some lived in the trees, and the short-faced giants were carnivores. Perhaps twice as big as today's kangaroos, and standing up to 7 feet tall (and maybe even taller), procoptodon was the biggest: it had a potbelly, a blunt square face, powerful arms, and a pair of dagger-like claws on each hand. Two smaller carnivorous kangaroos were the size of wolves and moved like rabbits.

Australia's "golden age" of giant mammals, as paleontologist Tim Flannery has called it, was defined by this spectacular abundance of kangaroo species. But for humans from Eurasia, the place must have been a true head-scratcher. Where were all the "normal" animals—the placental mammals—like big cats, grazing ungulates, wolves, bears? What the heck happened here?

It's no quip to say evolution happened. Australia became an isolated, continent-size island about 40 million years ago, and in that time, marsupial mammals flourished like nowhere else. Meanwhile, placental mammals either died off or never arrived. Australia became another unique evolutionary experiment, one populated by its own cast of characters.

Flannery theorizes that Australia's resource-poor environment particularly favored marsupials, who seem designed for maximum energy efficiency. Marsupials didn't evolve to have large brains like placental mammals (big brains use a lot of energy!), and in Australia, marsupials coevolved in mutually cooperative ways that conserved the environment's available nutrients. Plus, hopping is actually much more energy efficient than running, but you need a strong, sturdy pelvis to withstand the strain. Placental mammals need a flexible pelvis to birth larger, fully developed babies, but marsupials don't, since their young are the size of jelly beans when born.

Australia's marsupials sometimes resembled placental mammals due to convergent evolution, or the process by which different species evolve to look similar because they occupy similar ecological niches. In essence, Australia's ancient marsupials often looked sort of like rhinos, hippos, lions, and wolves because they were equivalent large herbivores and top predators—but they didn't look *exactly* the same because the raw materials differed, as did Australia itself.

Overkill in the Land Down Under

Humans from Southeast Asia most likely arrived in Australia between 45,000 and 48,000 years ago, but it's possible they arrived as early as 62,000 years ago. Australia's giant animals, meanwhile, started disappearing around 45,000 to 46,000 years ago, and this wave of extinctions ended by at least 35,000 years ago.

Thus, if the dates are right, Australia was the first continent to experience mass extinctions of giant species in the Late Pleistocene, and this occurred long before the start of the last ice age, which began around 30,000 years ago. Ergo, this wasn't a weather-related catastrophe. Humans caused the extinctions.

But the dates may not be right. Radiocarbon dating gets increasingly inaccurate past 30,000 years, and it's unreliable beyond 50,000 years. Plus, older fossils are more easily "contaminated" by younger sediments, resulting in false dates, and this is a particular problem in Australia's arid, eroded landscapes.

Not only that, but we have yet to find any reliable, confirmed archaeological evidence of ancestral human hunting in Australia. Zilch, nada. There is no smoking spear, as it were. If humans exterminated all these animals, they did it so fast and efficiently that they left behind no evidence of killing or cooking.

This proposal that early humans always hunted the largest species first and kept hunting them until they were extinct is called overkill, and some use this theory to explain the Late Pleistocene extinctions on every continent—not as the sole cause, but as the primary one. However, this theory is controversial: some say humans can't have eliminated so many giant species across continents. If they had, we'd find more evidence.

Overkill theorists respond in three ways. First, wherever humans traveled, we know hunting happened; the evidence might be waiting to be discovered. Second, especially in Australia, it's no coincidence that all the species that humans would target as food would suddenly expire the very moment humans arrived. And third, when you crunch the numbers, you find that, given a millennia, even a moderate amount of hunting by a relatively few people could lead to widespread extinctions of slow-breeding giants.

In Australia, hunting impacts were probably magnified because Aboriginal peoples used fire to clear and reshape the land, and the continent's already fragile ecosystems may have collapsed more easily, thus accelerating extinctions.

Further, other evidence seems to show that only after Australia's big herbivores were gone and no longer "managing" the landscape did that landscape transform into what we know today. This means that habitat change didn't kill Australia's giants. Instead, after the giants went extinct, Australia's landscape seemed to have burned to a crisp and become re-covered in dry-adapted plants, so that what had been central forests were replaced by the desert known as the Outback.

In the end, over sixty species went extinct, including all the largest animals. Only two kangaroo species escaped the carnage: the gray kangaroo and the red kangaroo, which is today the largest animal in Australia at about 190 pounds. The largest remaining predator—besides humans—was the thylacine, which went extinct in Australia about 3,500 years ago, not long after the arrival of the dingo.

Island Hopping

Those who support the overkill theory often point to islands as the most dramatic examples of what ancient humans could do in a short time. Australia suffered the first mass extinction of its giants, but long after the Pleistocene and the last ice age ended (about 12,000 years ago), extinction waves kept occurring every time humans discovered a new island.

For instance, humans arrived on Cyprus about 11,000 years ago, and its largest species—its dwarf hippos and elephants—soon vanished.

Humans arrived on Cuba about 6,000 years ago, and its ground sloths, giant rodents, and flightless owls disappeared over the next 1,200 years.

Humans settled Polynesia beginning about 3,500 years ago, and clusters of extinctions followed in their wake, especially of bird species.

In the modern era, people finally reached New Zealand, Madagascar, and the Mascarene Islands—and you know what happened from the stories in this book.

None of these extinctions were due to climate change. Another theory is that, in a few cases, native island species might have suffered an epidemic or hyperdisease, much the same way indigenous peoples in the Americas were decimated by smallpox and other diseases brought by the first Europeans. However, we don't know of any disease that would affect animals this way, and certainly none that would affect mostly large animals.

Instead, what we've seen is that when skilled human hunters show up—unannounced and uninvited—many species don't recognize them as predators and they can't cope with this unfamiliar threat. Even dominant, dangerous giants can at first be innocent of the danger we pose. If this has been true on islands in historic times, it's possible it occurred in each new place where Cro-Magnons arrived. ⤻

AUSTRALIA

TASMANIA   NEW ZEALAND

THYLACINE: THE GREAT GHOST TIGER

EXTINCTION: the last known thylacine died in Hobart Zoo on September 7, 1936

The thylacine was a curious creature. The first Europeans to encounter it weren't sure what to make of it. People called it a tiger, a hyena, and a wolf, but it was none of those things.

The thylacine also inspired a curious amount of fear. Few species besides the wolf have been so demonized, persecuted, and scapegoated for crimes it did not commit. We convinced ourselves that our lives would be better off without this animal, and then we made sure that happened.

Most of all, though, thylacines were themselves curious. They showed wolf-like smarts, a social nature, and a tolerance of us, so much so that some thylacines made willing, friendly pets.

Imagine: What if we hadn't driven the thylacine to the grave? We might have found ourselves with another domestic companion—not a dog, but something curiously like one.

Not Tiger, Hyena, or Wolf: A Marsupial

When Europeans first settled Tasmania in the nineteenth century, they called the thylacine a "Tasmanian tiger," a "zebra wolf," and a "hyena opossum," among other fanciful names, but in fact the species was then the world's largest living marsupial carnivore.

What exactly is *that*?

In essence, a meat-eating mammal who raises young in a pouch.

Or to be more exact: placental mammals nurture fetuses in the womb, where they are fed by a placenta, and they give birth to fully developed babies. Marsupial mammals have no placenta, and so after a short one-month pregnancy, they give birth to blind, tiny, relatively undeveloped offspring, called joeys, who crawl directly into the mother's pouch, where they nurse until they develop into juveniles.

Marsupial pouches vary among species. The thylacine (*Thylacinus cynocephalus*) had a backward-opening pouch (like an opossum, and the opposite of a kangaroo) and typically birthed two to four babies at a time. After about three months, thylacine joeys would begin leaving the pouch and return to nurse. Eventually, young thylacines were also fed solid food in the same fashion as wolves and dogs—the mother regurgitated the food.

In all of Earth's history, marsupial carnivores are rare, and the only place they ever dominated was in Australia, New Guinea, and Tasmania. By the historical era, the two largest that remained were the thylacine and the Tasmanian devil (about the size of a squat Jack Russell terrier), and they existed solely on Tasmania.

In size and shape, the thylacine was somewhere between a dalmatian and a medium-size wolf. A mature adult weighed 50 to 75 pounds and was about 4 feet long, plus a 2-foot tail. Side by side, the skulls of a thylacine and a wolf look almost exactly alike, except for differences in their teeth. Yet when the thylacine yawned, what you noticed was how its narrow wolfish mouth gaped much wider than you'd like.

This was an animal who knew how to bite. Then there were those dark racing stripes: a baker's dozen rippled across the short tawny fur of the thylacine's lower back, much like a tiger or zebra. The stripes may have been camouflage, or for individual identification, or to announce to nearby wallabies and kangaroos: *I'm here, start running*. Meanwhile, its strong, thick, stiff tail resembled that of neither a wolf nor a tiger, but it was as emotionally expressive as a canine's.

Scientists have speculated that the tail helped thylacines swim, kept them balanced during a chase, or even hampered their running ability. In truth, we still struggle to understand even the basics, particularly the thylacine's behavior and abilities. It was never formally studied when alive, and popular accounts vary wildly. Some said it was fast and agile, swiftly chasing prey on all fours, and some said it was an awkward runner with a strange loping stride, almost hopping on its back legs like a kangaroo.

What did the thylacine sound like? Some said it was almost mute, but many others described its angry "coughing bark," along with a range of other sounds it's impossible to hear again, since no one recorded them.

How did thylacines hunt? We know they preferred wallaby and kangaroo almost exclusively. Yet some describe individuals relentlessly pursuing prey until they collapsed from exhaustion; others saw small family units hunting cooperatively, and sometimes strategically startling prey into a waiting ambush. Some said the thylacine's home range was a couple of square miles; others, hundreds of square miles.

Family dynamics are also somewhat mysterious. One zoo curator said that female thylacines "had extremely strong maternal instincts." But we don't know if the father lived with the family unit or not. Observed differences in hunting styles and "home ranges" might relate to shifting pack dynamics. Perhaps individual adult males hunted by chasing and roamed widely, while female-led family packs of five or six related thylacines hunted cooperatively and stuck to a small territory. Or perhaps family packs included both parents, and roaming individuals were unmated male "teenagers."

Conflicts and discrepancies aside, one reason we can't always take early European accounts at face value is that people often disparaged the thylacine as inferior. Their accounts exaggerate supposed "defects" to make the case that it was an ill-conceived species, which justified its extermination. Today we're forced to read between the lines to try to understand the truth about this animal.

Once Upon a Time in Australia

What we do know is that thylacines were so different from placental mammals that, as naturalist Errol Fuller has written, "humans bear a closer relationship to whales than thylacines do to dogs."

Of course, thylacines *look* so much like canines, and we look so unlike whales, that this seems impossible, but it's another example of convergent evolution and of how life adapts to its environment. Marsupial and placental mammals have operating systems as different as Apple and Microsoft, but as we've seen with the moa, the elephant bird, and the Steller's sea cow, habitats and ecosystem dynamics make the animal as much as the other way around.

In this case, the premise of the question is easily reversed: why is it that wolves look so much like thylacines? As a species, the modern thylacine was actually older than the modern wolf.

It's just hard to say how old. Australia's fossil record is extremely spotty. The Thylacinidae family evolved in Australia some 30 million years ago, and the modern thylacine evolved some 4 to 8 million years ago. Quite successful and very adaptable, the thylacine spread across the entire continent and lived in just about every environment, from hot deserts and cold mountains to wet forests.

After humans arrived in Australia over 46,000 years ago, nearly all of Australia's megafauna went extinct (see page 132), leaving the thylacine as Australia's largest mammalian carnivore, the world's largest marsupial carnivore, and the lord of its domain. After that, the thylacine somehow survived over 40,000 years of coexistence with humans in Australia only to give up the ghost about 3,500 years ago—when all of a sudden the thylacine (along with the Tasmanian devil) got toppled from its throne and went extinct on mainland Australia and New Guinea.

For decades, the accepted theory was that the thylacine's abrupt disappearance on Australia was due to the dog, or, more specifically, the dingo. Between 3,500 and 6,000 years ago, Aboriginal peoples brought the domestic dog to Australia, which got loose, went feral, and became the dingo.

"FEAR OF THE THYLACINE BECAME NEARLY HYSTERICAL, ITS REPUTATION TERRIFYING. SOME SAID IT HAD A VAMPIRE-LIKE PREFERENCE FOR BLOOD, AND THAT IT KILLED TO DRINK RATHER THAN EAT."

Since the thylacine hadn't competed with a similar-size predator for millions of years, perhaps it got outclassed by a better one. This fit the once-popular scientific notion that placental mammals are inherently superior to marsupial ones.

Today, both ideas are mostly dismissed. Prehistoric Australia is evidence that, under the right conditions, marsupials can dominate and succeed as well as placentals. And there is no evidence that the dingo charged into the Outback and took the thylacine's top-predator crown, mano a mano. Ample evidence exists that dogs were almost universally scared of thylacines, who had no problem dispatching a canine or two. Nor did people witness wild dogs threatening the thylacine in Tasmania in the nineteenth century.

However, the arrival of the dingo clearly disrupted the existing balance somehow and in ways that were bad news for the thylacine. It may be that Aborigines, now with packs of dogs to help, actively hunted the thylacine like never before, or perhaps they hunted wallabies and kangaroos like never before and took the thylacine's prey. As this happened, perhaps the thylacine couldn't adapt by eating other types of prey or expand its diet to become omnivorous. Or, perhaps most likely of all, maybe the thylacine had been in a long, slow decline due to long-term competition with humans and habitat destruction—and so it was near extinction on Australia anyway, and the impact of the dingo became the last straw.

Whatever the case, no dingoes ever reached Tasmania. The island separated from Australia about 12,000 years ago, before the dingo arrived, and by some stroke of luck, no Aborigines traveling to Tasmania ever brought a dog. Whether that made the difference or not, the thylacine flourished on the island until Britain chose it for a new penal colony in 1803.

Bounty Hunters in Van Diemen's Land

What we know about the thylacine on Tasmania before the British arrived is that it lived across the entire island, it may have numbered about 5,000, and it had a benign relationship with the Aborigines. Tasmania's indigenous peoples did not eat it, fear it, or persecute it, and they lived in all the same places and had a similar population of about 5,000. Did humans and thylacines coexist in the same way in Australia millennia before? Perhaps, but Tasmania alone shows that humans could live peacefully with this predator.

Dutch explorer Abel Tasman first sighted Tasmania in 1642; he called it Van Diemen's Land to honor his voyage's sponsor. In the late 1700s, various European explorers visited briefly, including Captain Cook in 1777. Then in 1803, the British established the first European settlement in Tasmania, in what's now called Hobart Town.

The British plan was to send to Tasmania their worst convicts and political prisoners, who would harvest timber and wool to ship back to England. This ill-advised and ill-fated idea ran into trouble immediately. Ultimately, it spelled doom for both the Aborigines and the thylacine.

Within months, Tasmania's Aborigines violently attacked the colonists, making it clear that they would resist this attempt by the British to occupy and take over their home. This sparked a long-running war that was punctuated by periodic and ruthless British massacres of the indigenous peoples. By 1828, the colonial authorities declared martial law and established a bounty for dead Aborigines: they would pay five pounds for an adult Tasmanian and two pounds for a child. By 1847, this tragic, brutal war ended. Only 47 Tasmanians remained, and they agreed to relocate peacefully to Flinders Island, where they lived the remainder of their lives. The last Tasmanian Aborigine died in 1876.

Even as the conflict with the Aborigines began, the British outpost grappled with its own problems: their convicts kept escaping to become free-ranging outlaws, and they were constantly on the brink of starvation, as the land wasn't very good for agriculture. British authorities armed convicts to hunt kangaroo in order to eat, and for two decades, Van Diemen's Land was part "wild west" frontier, part war zone, and part horrific penal colony.

Then, in 1826, the Van Diemen's Land Company started sheep farming in Tasmania. The prospects were poor—the climate was too cold for sheep, the land uncleared, the grasses provided bad fodder, and lawlessness abounded—but Mother England imagined great profits. By 1830, over a million sheep roamed the north, but each year thousands of sheep died due to cold, starvation, and predation, primarily by wild dogs and possibly Tasmanian devils.

Rather than admit the truth—that raising sheep in Tasmania was simply a bad idea and would probably never make money—the company chose a scapegoat: they blamed most of their losses on the thylacine, which officials called a ruthless "sheep killer." Since the thylacine looked like a wolf, it was an easy sell. Here was another rapacious predator hungering for livestock. In 1830, the first of several thylacine bounties were enacted, which encouraged hunters to eliminate this "vermin" and supposed obstacle to progress and profits.

It's Happened Before:
The Five Other Mass Extinctions

In the grand scheme—that is, over the 3.8-billion-year history of life on Earth—the Late Pleistocene extinctions are no big deal. Many similar, moderate extinction waves have happened before. Scientists are concerned today because our current extinction crisis is on pace to match five previous "mass extinctions" that stand out as the most deadly. That is why it's been dubbed the sixth extinction.

The five mass extinctions define the ends of these geological periods:

1. Ordovician, 440 million years ago
2. Devonian, 365 million years ago
3. Permian, 245 million years ago
4. Triassic, 210 million years ago
5. Cretaceous, 65 million years ago

As biologist Edward O. Wilson wrote, these events are like "a hurricane to a summer squall" compared to others.

The Permian extinction was the worst. From 77 to 96 percent of marine animal species died (marine animals being easiest to count), and if land

---

The company's own records have since revealed the extent of its lie. From 1830 to the 1850s, thylacines accounted for a handful of sheep deaths a year; at some stations, only one a year. Of the hundreds of sheep lost to predation annually, one estimate is that thylacines accounted for less than 7 percent. Further, accounts of thylacines preying on pigs, cattle, horses, and goats are virtually nonexistent. It's surprising, perhaps, but the evidence is that the thylacine hardly ever preyed on domestic animals.

Yet fear of the thylacine became nearly hysterical, and its reputation species matched this, the earth very nearly wiped the slate clean.

For the first four mass extinctions, climate change due to shifting continental landmasses was probably the primary cause. The Cretaceous extinctions were caused by a meteor striking the earth, along with massive volcanic eruptions.

As everyone knows, the dinosaurs went extinct after that meteor strike, and yet a batch of tiny mammals survived. Both had evolved together starting around the same time, some 200 million years ago, but only dinosaurs dominated until that unlucky catastrophe. Without it, they might rule still.

As paleontologist David Jablonski said, "Mass extinctions change the rules of evolution. When one strikes, it's not necessarily the most fit that survive; often it's the most fortunate."

Indeed, scientists calculate that since life began, 99 percent of all species have gone extinct. The planet has never held more diversity than it does today, but that's still only 1 percent of all the species that have ever existed.

Further, species diversity after a mass extinction takes a long time to recover. After the Ordovician, Devonian, and Cretaceous extinctions, it was 20 to 30 million years before diversity reached previous levels. After the combined Permian/Triassic extinction, it took 100 million years.

Mammals were fortunate once, but that's no guarantee next time.

terrifying. Some said it had a vampire-like preference for blood, and that it killed to drink rather than eat. As crazy as this sounds, this vampire folklore may have misinterpreted a real tendency: many carnivores, including thylacines, eat the "best parts" first, such as the liver, heart, and other organs, along with vascular tissue, or veins and arteries, which are highly nutritious for a carnivore. Also, similar to big cats and wolves, thylacines killed with a gaping bite to the throat. Seeing a thylacine at work can't have been pretty.

For Victorian-era settlers, fear of the thylacine also embodied a generalized fear of wilderness itself, which was regarded as the opposite of everything that made us human. People saw supernatural monsters like werewolves in every brooding forest. Once the thylacine was branded as evil, people needed no further excuse to kill it. Even one was an affront to civilization. And for decades, people killed thylacines with a missionary zeal.

By the dawn of the twentieth century, thylacine bounty hunting in Tasmania was a lucrative, widely practiced profession. From 1888 to 1909, records show that 2,184 thylacines were presented for bounty rewards, typically one pound per adult. A bounty was paid by the government, another by the Van Diemen's company, and hunters were also paid by local farmers. Enterprising hunters could get paid multiple times for the same carcass.

Then, after decades of steady declines, the thylacine population suddenly crashed. In 1909, only two thylacines were presented for the official government bounty, and the program ended. At this point, the writing was on the wall. Yet it's fair to wonder, could things have turned out differently?

Vampire on a Leash

Only one Aboriginal myth about the thylacine has been preserved. In this story, Palana, the son of a god, is attacked by Tarner, "the big boomer kangaroo." Though a god himself, Palana is only a boy, and he's soon in mortal trouble. Palana calls for help, and the only animal who responds is a thylacine pup.

The pup attacks Tarner, biting him on the throat. Tarner uses all his strength to remove the pup, but the pup won't let go. Eventually, Tarner is killed, and he crashes to the ground, knocking Palana and the pup unconscious.

Palana's father eventually finds them and nurses them back to health. Having survived this battle, Palana crosses the threshold into manhood, while the pup is ever after to be respected as "Wurrawana Corinna, the Great Ghost Tiger." Palana then gives the thylacine his stripes, so that all will know him from now on.

Indigenous peoples often identified with top predators, even when they also competed with, hunted, and feared those predators. This story doesn't mean Aborigines treated living thylacines as genuine companions. However, this "Great Ghost Tiger" sure sounds an awful lot like a faithful dog, and his story is a far cry from the villainous one that Europeans told.

Did it have any basis in reality?

Maybe. From 1826 to 1851, twenty-two individual thylacines are known to have been kept as pets by Europeans, and there were probably more. Ronald Gunn kept three over the years, and in 1851 he wrote, "My living Thylacine is becoming tamer: it seems far from being a vicious animal at its worst, and the name Tiger or Hyaena gives a most unjust idea of its fierceness."

Thylacines would bond closely with their main human caregiver and otherwise react suspiciously and aggressively with strangers, growling as they approached. In this, they were better watchdogs than dogs. Like wolves, thylacines seemed to have a hierarchical social structure that would accept humans as a leader. Zookeepers noticed this, too: captive thylacines tended to develop close, affectionate bonds with a single keeper and be indifferent or hostile to others.

Most amazing of all, thylacines accepted being walked on a leash—what vampire does that! Multiple accounts describe thylacines acting "as tame as pet dogs" while following someone on a lead. If it can be believed, one man transformed a snared thylacine into a cooperative companion in a single afternoon. A certain William Cotton caught a thylacine and, instead of killing it, put around its neck a noose attached to a 5-foot pole and walked him into the nearest town 4 miles away. To quote one account: "He had great trouble to get the animal to travel, but after going a few hundred yards the animal started to act just like as if it was a dog, and followed along beside him for the rest of the way to Swansea with the least of trouble."

Many stories were told of wild thylacines trailing people closely for no other apparent reason than curiosity. Thylacines didn't stalk people, and they almost never attacked people except when they themselves were being

attacked. Rather, thylacines seemed naturally inquisitive about us. That is a rare quality in wild animals, who tend to ignore us if they don't already fear us.

The wolf is one of few others to show this curiosity—and look how that turned out. Our lives would be immeasurably impoverished without the dedicated companionship of the dog. What if we'd also developed a marsupial companion with tiger stripes? Australia's Aborigines eventually brought their own dog and never found out. In Tasmania, a few people welcomed thylacines into their homes and discovered they didn't live up to their demonic reputation after all.

Victorian-era Zoos: Come See the Thylacine!

Victorian attitudes toward nature were nothing if not contradictory. Wilderness gave people the heebie-jeebies, but they loved seeing wild exotic creatures in zoos and menageries. Similarly, nineteenth-century scientists were driven to understand and preserve the earth's flora and fauna, but they somehow didn't mind denuding a landscape to get specimens for their collections. At times, "collecting in the name of science" reached massive scales, and it actively imperiled certain species and ecosystems. This happened with giant tortoises in the Galápagos and with many neon-feathered island bird species.

Sometimes, zoos help give endangered species their only shot at survival, but for the thylacine, zoos inadvertently helped spur the animal's demise.

From the mid-1800s onward, zoos around the world paid dearly to have captive thylacines shipped to them. This exotic beast really drew crowds. Thylacines appeared in Washington, DC, New York, Berlin, Sydney, Melbourne, and particularly London, which always kept a good supply on hand.

Unfortunately, as zookeepers learned, thylacines wouldn't breed in captivity. As years passed, the only way to keep them on display was to capture more. This became urgent as the threat of extinction loomed, and it led to a curious circumstance. Zoos would pay Tasmanian bounty hunters more for a living thylacine than the government paid for a dead one, but the result was the same: thylacines were removed from the wild.

In 1909, the same year the official bounty program ended, the government paid one pound for an adult thylacine, but zoos paid about seven pounds. In 1926, the London Zoo paid 150 pounds for what turned out to be the last living thylacine ever purchased.

Further, capturing a thylacine alive was difficult. Snares were painful for the animal; an untold number were injured and died trying to escape. This didn't bother the hunter, who collected a bounty either way, but how did this make sense to science? How was capturing thylacines conserving the species?

Even at the time, people called attention to this contradiction, but no one acted until it was too late. From the 1910s, efforts arose to create a thylacine sanctuary on Tasmania, but business and government interests successfully opposed this until 1930, when a partial ban on hunting passed. Finally, in 1936, the species was given full protection, and uninhabited Maria Island was eventually set aside for the release of captured thylacines.

It's still waiting.

That same year, on September 7, 1936, the last known thylacine died in Hobart Zoo. Just like Martha, the passenger pigeon, the thylacine is another rare species whose last living individual we held in our hands.

Ghost in the Outback

Even in a situation this clear-cut, extinction is a complex mix of factors. Habitat loss, the loss of prey species, invasive species (such as rats, cats, dogs, and foxes), and even perhaps disease also impacted the thylacine. However, human persecution was the primary cause.

It's fair to say that collective regret and guilt run deep. An entire marsupial family was lost. Nothing like the thylacine exists anymore, and there's a strong desire to discover thylacines still living in some remote corner. Cryptozoologists make a good living off supposed thylacine sightings. Even in 2012, a well-circulated video, which was quickly proven to be a hoax, claimed to show a hunched thylacine padding across Tasmania.

To see video of a real thylacine, seek out historic zoo footage from the 1930s, which can be found online (see page 261).

Yet we can't entirely dismiss the possibility that thylacines persisted long after we declared them gone. Some think the thylacine may have survived in Australia into the 1800s, and earnest claims of actual signs and sightings on Tasmania continued into the 1960s. For instance, in 1966, a mummified thylacine was found, which was either 4,500 years old or months old, depending on whom you believe.

Part of the problem is that thylacine paw prints and scat closely resemble a dog's, and a dingo itself can resemble a thylacine at a distance. As with alleged moa sightings, it's easy to see what you want to see.

Finally, in 1999, the Australian Museum announced it would try to clone the thylacine, but to date it has yet to finish sequencing the thylacine's genome. Science is not quite ready to resurrect this predator.

Maria Island isn't the only place awaiting the thylacine's return. Australia is, too. Currently, the dingo is Australia's largest mammalian carnivore, and it's simply inadequate for the role of top predator. Large kangaroos often imbalance and overrun Australia's ecosystems. If the Great Ghost Tiger ever returned, perhaps things would be different. ↴

LIONS: LONG LIVE THE KING

EXTINCTION: the Cape lion was declared extinct in 1865; the Barbary lion is believed to have gone extinct in the 1960s

---

Movie about to start? The husky roar of the MGM lion gets our attention.

That roar has held our attention for what seems like forever. Ever since modern humans evolved, that terrifying sound has filled our ears, rolling like thunder across the grassy African plains.

Lions ruled our birthplace, so it's fitting that they became our ultimate symbol of royalty. Male lions, sitting erect, flamboyant mane announcing their presence, guard their pride and their territory, and with their powerful voices they warn anyone who edges too close, intimidating others without even rising from their haunches.

How appropriate, then, that we invariably choose lions to guard our cultural monuments: protecting the entrances to the New York Public Library and Beijing's Forbidden City, flying over Venice's St. Mark's Square, posing at the base of London's Nelson's Column.

The lion is the original king, and the lion pride was our original example of how a top predator behaves. Coevolving in the same environment, early humans may have learned a few lessons from the lion about how to be a carnivore, how to establish territory, how to hunt large prey. And it may be that only after Cro-Magnon peoples had learned these lessons well enough that they walked out of Africa to announce a new king.

Our genes say we descended from great apes, but our behavior is marked with a lion's paw.

The Lion King Roars

The earliest discovered ancestral lion fossils are in Africa, and they are only 3.5 million years old. This is odd considering what an ancient, large, and dominant species the lion is. The *Panthera* genus, which includes lions, tigers, leopards, jaguars, and possibly the snow leopard, split off from other ancestral cats some 10.8 million years ago.

Earlier than that, over 15 million years ago, sabertooth cats diverged from the branch that led to today's felines, which makes sabertooths only very distant relations to modern cats. Yet by then several adaptions of tooth, eye, and claw defined felids, making each and every one a force to reckon with.

All carnivores have sharp teeth, but a cat's canines became exceptionally long and vicious. A male lion's canines are 3 inches long, rounded conical shivs capable of stabbing the toughest hide, then holding, cutting, and tearing. Sabertooths took this to extremes; their canines flattened like curved sabers and extended up to 11 inches long. Unlike wolves and bears, cats don't have teeth for grinding bone; they are flesh eaters only.

Cats are also famous for their tremendous eyesight. They hunt by chasing and developed excellent binocular vision. Since they hunt both day and night, their eyes evolved to handle the extremes of light. Their night vision is possible because of a reflective layer that causes light to bounce twice through the retina; this layer is what causes a cat's "eye shine." During the day, to protect their eyes from too much sun, cats developed a slit pupil. The narrowness of the slit varies among species; a lion's pupils are the most oval.

What really sets cats apart, though, are their retractable claws. The claws of other carnivores may be bigger, but they get dull and broken. Retractable claws stay razor sharp, making them uniquely dangerous weapons capable of grabbing and holding prey. A cat's claws retract naturally; only when cats flex do the claws emerge, closing like a fistful of daggers.

"THE 'GREAT ROARING CATS,' AS THEY'RE CALLED, HAVE UNIQUE VOICE BOXES THAT SEEM TO HAVE DEVELOPED SOLELY TO SCARE THE LIVING DAYLIGHTS OUT OF COMPETITORS AND PREY. FOR *PANTHERA*, INTIMIDATION IS AN EVOLUTIONARY STRATEGY."

The *Panthera* genus is further distinguished from other felines by its roar. The "great roaring cats," as they're called, have unique voice boxes that seem to have developed solely to scare the living daylights out of competitors and prey. For *Panthera*, intimidation is an evolutionary strategy. A lion's roar can reach 114 decibels, equivalent to a jet airplane taking off, and it can be heard for 5 miles.

Today, lions have one further trait that makes them unique among cat species. They alone prefer to live together. All cats *can* be social—but like our famously diffident house cat, most species suffer the company of others only occasionally and not for long. They are solitary hunters leading mostly solitary lives.

Lions, however, form family-centered prides and hunt strategically in groups. This works well in Africa's wide-open savannas, and prehistoric humans, aspiring to be more than ape-like gatherers, found success as hunters using similar methods. Could this be coincidence, or did we self-consciously emulate the lion? As with the wolf, ancient human society and lion society show affinities that may be a lasting heritage of coevolving in similar landscapes as similar predators.

Lion prides are fascinating, complex, and dynamic, and a few things stand out. One is that, ironically, there is no anointed "king" or "queen." Lions do not follow a rigid social hierarchy, in which one or two lions are always deferred to and others are relegated to "the bottom." Social position is constantly negotiated. At a kill, each lion will and must compete with the others for a share, no matter their gender or size, even cubs. Pride leadership is loose and flexible; smaller groups within the pride will split off and remerge continually, and who follows whom can change daily.

Lion prides are famously matriarchal. Each has an enduring, stable core of related females who work communally, doing most of the hunting and the raising of cubs, and they are most often the leaders. These lionesses are sisters, mothers, daughters, and granddaughters. Among themselves they form a cooperative, friendly unit, but they do not allow strange females to join.

Adult males, meanwhile, join prides for only a short time, a few months to a few years. When male cubs reach maturity, they are usually driven from the pride. These nomadic males then roam alone or form small "bands of brothers," looking for prides to take over; such turnover happens regularly. An adult male's main job is defending the pride's territory, to ensure the availability of prey and to protect the cubs.

From what we know, prehistoric human groups also formed family-centered tribes that were possibly matriarchal, with flexible social hierarchies and a division of labor. Tribes claimed and defended territory to ensure access to its resources, and they used group hunting to kill the largest prey.

These hunts required strategy, and the flanking maneuvers and coordinated attacks of a lion hunt are a master class: provoking prey into ambushes, using terrain to close off escape routes.

However, humans also did something that lions, curiously, rarely do. Humans followed the migratory herds of wildebeest, buffalo, and gazelle, while lions usually remain in their established territories. One reason lions don't follow the herds is because of their cubs, who can't walk far or fast. Human babies can't either, and that's what's interesting.

Some propose that one reason humans developed the ability to walk on two legs was to pursue large migratory prey. Once humans were bipedal, their arms were free to pick up their children and carry them wherever they wanted to go.

In Europe: Cave Lions & Cave Paintings

At least 900,000 years ago, the modern lion (*Panthera leo*) spread from Africa to Europe and then prowled into Asia and the Americas. Along the way, it evolved into various subspecies (possibly full species) that grew even larger than the original. Today, male African lions average 375 to 420 pounds, with some individuals topping 550 pounds, making it the second-largest living cat species after tigers.

The European "cave lion" was bigger, and the American lion was bigger still. These cats may have reached 600 to 770 pounds. Only South America's gigantic sabertooth *Smilodon populator*, which reached 880 pounds, outweighed them.

In other words, when traveling Cro-Magnons, babes in arms, arrived in Europe at least 40,000 years ago, they encountered the biggest lions they'd ever faced, and cats only got worse after that.

The European cave lion is long gone, winking out in southern Europe about 2,000 years ago. Despite its name, it probably did not live in caves; that's just where archaeologists have found their bones. Also, it may have been maneless. Since fur doesn't preserve like fossils, how do we know?

We found the paleolithic cave paintings Cro-Magnons left behind.

This ancient graffiti litters France and Spain, where over a dozen sites date from perhaps 36,000 to 10,000 years ago. Drawings of lions appear in most of these caves, but Chauvet Cave in France is unique. The walls of Chauvet hold over seventy lions, more than in all the other caves combined, and one section, called the Lion Panel, depicts a pride of a dozen stalking a collection of ancient European megafauna, including rhinos and a mammoth.

None of the lions have manes. It could be that all are females, but some seem clearly male except for missing their signature hairstyle. This doesn't seem like a mistake. In other ways, such as the stippled black dots representing whiskers, the drawings are quite accurate.

They are also remarkably, unmistakably beautiful. That also doesn't seem like an accident. Re-created from memory—assuming lions and rhinos weren't lounging in the cave with the artists—the drawings seem designed to evoke emotion, wonder, awe. Whatever the drawings meant—and we know they were important, for they are too skilled and deliberate to have been made casually—we recognize them as art.

The Chauvet lions gaze with obvious intensity at their prey, and we feel the same intensity in the gaze of the painter. This tells us that—no matter how hard lions made our lives, no matter how often they took our kills—we watched, we learned, we admired.

In Egypt & the Middle East: Sekhmet & the Royal Hunt

And we trembled.

In ancient Egypt and the Middle East about 5,000 years ago, when this region was birthing human civilization, lions were a plague. They helped themselves to cattle along the Nile, killed us, and inspired fear everywhere.

Naturally, everyone venerated the lion as a god. What else could lions be? They were clearly nature's supreme predator, and in our myths, religions, and folklore, lions came to represent supreme supernatural power.

At one time or another, all top predators have received this star treatment, including wolves, bears, tigers, leopards, sharks, and so on. Cultures often imagine that humans are descended from these great creatures, for we want to identify ourselves with their power. Yet these ideas get tangled up in our heads and get expressed in the strangest ways.

Consider the hybrids: the Sphinx was a riddle-spouting half-lion, half-woman; a chimera was a fire-breathing lion with a goat coming out of its back and a snake for a tail; a griffin was an eagle-headed lion; and in Mesopotamia, Anzu was a lion-headed eagle. In ancient India, Narasimha was a lion-headed god with a man's body who was known as the Great Protector. And in ancient Egypt, Sekhmet was one of the greatest gods of all—a lion, usually with a woman's body, whose breath formed the desert.

The cult of Sekhmet dominated Egypt for thousands of years. She was the goddess of war who slaughtered enemies with a lion's mercilessness, but she was also the goddess of healing, since that same ferocity could stop all evil and sickness. Sekhmet was wildness incarnate, a goddess who once almost destroyed humanity, and ancient Egyptians held a huge annual festival to placate her.

With a crazy, violent lion goddess in charge, hunting actual lions must have been a no-no, right? Wrong. Lions themselves were not protected by this deity. We know because inscriptions in Egyptian tombs document the lion-hunting prowess of the pharaohs.

This is another common theme: our veneration of top predators often makes them even more desirable as hunting trophies. Our admiration and respect rarely benefits the animal. Even in Greek myth, as the first of his twelve labors, Hercules had to kill the Nemean lion, who had an impenetrable hide.

In the tomb of King Tutankhamun, who ruled from 1332 to 1323 BC, a chest shows the young pharaoh hunting lions with a bow and arrow. The tomb of another Egyptian pharaoh boasts that he killed 102 lions. In nearby Assyria, palaces were adorned with stone bas-reliefs showing kings killing lions as they are released from cages; this method of hunting kept the king from real danger. Ashurnasirpal II (883–859 BC) claimed to kill fifteen lions as well as thirty elephants. But no one topped Assyrian king Tiglath-Pileser (1115–1077BC), who allegedly killed 920 lions, 800 from a chariot and 120 on foot.

Living lions were chained before Assyrian palaces as guardians even as Assyrian rulers became heroes and won glory by hunting them. This schizo-phrenic attitude reached its peak a few centuries later in Rome.

In Rome: The Arena

By 186 BC, Roman rulers were collecting fierce predators and giant animals from around the world to put on display. Over time, these included elephants, rhinos, apes, leopards, bears, tigers, hippos, and, of course, lions. By the first century BC, rulers were upping the drama by staging arena "hunts" as entertainment. Throughout history, hunting top predators and dangerous prey like aurochs has often been reserved for royalty, but the Roman rulers enhanced their status and reputation by turning this idea on its head.

Maned male lions were often considered the principle attraction. Since the European cave lion was by then extinct, and probably maneless, Romans captured lions in Africa, Syria, and Mesopotamia and brought them to Italy.

Julius Caesar (100–44 BC) once ordered the slaughter of 400 lions in a single show, and Pompey the Great (106–48 BC) did the same with 500 to 600 lions, finishing the day with a battle between elephants. Augustus (63 BC–AD 14), the first ruler of the Roman Empire, is said to have used over a thousand gladiators to kill over 3,500 animals during the course of his reign.

These shows were, needless to say, a huge success, and over seventy am-phitheaters were built across the Roman Empire, with the greatest being the Colosseum in Rome, which could hold 50,000 people and was com-pleted in AD 80.

Sabertooth Cats: Long in the Tooth

Sabertooth cats once dominated the world, and it's easy to see why. Just look at those teeth.

A sabertooth's upper canines reached 11 inches long, with about 6 inches protruding over the lower lip. For a sense of what this meant, hold a ruler across your body: those teeth would have pierced right through you.

With ridiculous weapons like that, the real puzzle is why sabertooth cats ever declined. It defies logic. Sabertooths first evolved over 15 million years ago, and a wealth of sabertooth species eventually spread across every continent. Then, about 1.5 million years ago, they died out in Africa. And about 500,000 years ago, they disappeared from Eurasia. And by 10,000 years ago, they were gone from North and South America.

Only one of these disappearances, the last, coincides with the Late Pleistocene ice age and the migration of humans as big-game hunters. Elsewhere, other causes must have been at work, and sabertooths are a good example of why a single cause rarely applies to all extinctions everywhere.

Not that scientists haven't tried. For a long time, many proposed that a sabertooth's quintessential attribute must have become a liability. Perhaps those long teeth broke too easily, or maybe they hampered eating, and sabertooths became too specialized for their own good. However, no ill-conceived species lasts for over 13 million years.

Still, those teeth—so long and narrow and perfect for slicing—would have been prone to damage if they hit bone. Paleontologist Alan Turner theorizes that these curving fangs were built to deliver a vicious "shearing bite" to the soft belly or throat as prey was held immobile by the cat's inescapable claws. To kill, a sabertooth's gape stretched 30 percent wider than a lion's, and to eat, the cat used a set of protruding front incisors, which extended past the giant canines, to take small bites.

What we also can't explain is why, after coexisting in Africa for at least 2 million years, the continent's sabertooths disappeared while Africa's modern lions persisted.

Lions had smaller teeth, but perhaps they had a mightier roar.

Spectators to the three-day opening witnessed a genuine massacre: among the 8,000 animals slain were ostriches, deer, giraffe, aurochs, crocodiles, lions, and many more. The animals were kept caged beneath the Colosseum and starved until showtime, when the cages rose on lifts to the center of the arena. Drums pounded, trumpets blared, and the crowd roared as the animals were loosed. Sometimes the animals attacked one other, and sometimes gladiators with spears and tridents gave chase, play-acting a deadly hunt.

For over four centuries, the Roman "circuses" sanctioned an inconceivable level of cruelty, which notoriously included mock battles in which slaves, Christians, and other people were killed. The Roman need for large animals, however, is credited with emptying whole regions of their most charismatic species. By AD 325, the gladiator battles were outlawed, but the theater of killing animals continued for another century.

By 414, the Roman Empire was having trouble finding lions for its shows, and it passed a law to regulate the hunting and commercial trade of lions. Whether or not any Roman citizen was still bothered by wild lions, the law felt the need to reassure the public that they could defend themselves. It said, in part, "We allow everyone the right to kill lions, and We permit no one at any time to fear malicious prosecution therefor, for the safety of Our provincials necessarily shall take precedence over Our amusements."

This law was too little too late on several counts: the amusements ended soon after this, followed closely by the fall of the Roman Empire.

The arena spectacles are shocking and heartbreaking to imagine. It's hard to grasp how the Romans were even able to get 500 lions in one place, much less killing them in a day. *Did* people find this amusing?

The Roman spectacle was designed to humble and humiliate the greatest predator. Caged and controlled, the lion did what *we* wanted and suffered at *our* whim, which inflated our ego. If we did not regard the lion with awe, its death would hold no power, but the Roman spectacle became a bloody parody of a wild encounter, one that sacrificed awe for entertainment.

In North & South Africa: Extinctions & Extirpations

Despite the ravenous Roman appetite for lions, many countries in the Middle East had at least a few wild lions into the nineteenth century. Palestine lost its lions in the twelfth century, but Assyria (now Iraq), Turkey, and Syria did not lose their lions until the late 1800s. The last lion in Iran was reportedly seen in 1944.

In South Africa, the Cape lion was one of the largest modern lions, estimated to weigh over 500 pounds. It had a luxurious, strikingly black mane that extended along the belly.

The Dutch first arrived in South Africa in the seventeenth century, and the British took over and settled South Africa beginning in the early nineteenth century. As settlers do, they converted the countryside into farms and ranches and relentlessly hunted wild predators as pests. By the 1850s, the Cape lion was all but gone, and the last recorded shooting of one was in 1865.

The Cape lion also declined because of the steady loss of its habitat and prey—such as the quagga, a gorgeous chocolate-brown zebra that was driven to extinction in South Africa around the same time. Today, parts of South Africa are almost a mirror image of Iowa, with crops neatly rowed as far as the eye can see. The region's once great migratory animals, like wildebeest and bontebok, couldn't be restored even if we wanted them back, and they exist now only in fenced protected parks.

North Africa was the home of the Barbary lion. This subspecies was as big or bigger than the Cape lion and sported the greatest mane of any species. This dark, thick, shaggy coat covered half its body, extending along the back as well as the belly. The dramatic, gigantic Barbary lion was the quintessential lion of the Roman arena.

The Barbary lion was also a favorite in medieval European menageries. When England's Henry III established the first royal menagerie in 1235 in the Tower of London, Barbary lions were a featured attraction. Barbary lions were also given as gifts among European rulers.

As in South Africa, hunting, habitat loss, and loss of prey caused the steady disappearance of North Africa's lion. Beginning in the sixteenth century, and for the next 300 years, the Barbary lion retreated from Egypt, Libya, Algeria, and then Tunisia. By the 1900s, they lived only in Morocco's rugged Atlas Mountains. These mountains had also been the last holdout of the Atlas bear, which went extinct in the 1870s. The only species of bear native to Africa, the Atlas bear was another headline predator in Rome's spectacles.

For a long time, it was believed the last wild Barbary lion was killed in Morocco in 1922, but recent research has uncovered "last sightings" in Morocco and Algeria from 1948 and 1956, respectively. Since these were not "last shootings," it's possible the Barbary lion lived into the 1960s.

Further, Barbary lions were so popular in royal menageries and zoos that several claim to still possess pure captive-bred specimens. Morocco's Rabat Zoo says it has thirty-five Barbary lions, who are supposedly descendants of wild-born lions once owned by sultans and kings. However, these lions have become so inbred that their lineages are hard to untangle, and in any case, scientists don't have a full Barbary lion genome to compare them to. The Barbary lion bones and taxidermied skins that currently exist in museums are too old to provide a complete genetic profile.

If scientists confirm that Barbary lions still exist in captivity, they could be restored in North Africa. Or, there's another possibility. Genetic tests have discovered that the last remaining Asiatic lions in India's Gir Forest National Park are very closely related to the Barbary lion. North Africa's Barbary lions were most likely the colonizers who migrated to the Middle East and India.

Asiatic lions themselves live on the edge of extinction. They are currently the most endangered species of lion, with just over 500 remaining in the Gir forest. Using Asiatic lions to rewild North Africa would expand lion habitat and help preserve that species. Conservationists are also considering crossbreeding Asiatic lions with Morocco's captive lions. A more genetically diverse, Barbary lion hybrid might have the best chance to survive in the wild unmanaged by us.

After all, a lion in a cage doesn't do the world any good.

In the Serengeti: Living with Lions

The earliest hominid fossils have been found in East Africa. Thus, the modern human species rose to its feet in a setting that resembled Tanzania's Serengeti National Park. *Serengeti* comes from a Maasai word meaning "the place where the land runs forever." Or, as one of the first Europeans to visit wrote in 1907, "And all this a sea of grass, grass, grass, grass, and grass. One looks around and sees only grass and sky."

And animals. Everywhere countless animals. Today, Serengeti National Park contains possibly the largest population of African lions, about 3,000, in addition to Africa's full cast of characters: vast herds of wildebeest, zebra, Thomson's gazelle, and impala, plus African elephants, African buffaloes, black rhinos, giraffes, leopards, cheetahs, hyenas, and Nile crocodiles.

The Serengeti preserves a healthy biodiversity of Africa's original megafauna, who reflect the complete, complex dynamics of predators, prey, and landscape. For eons, the Serengeti's biodiversity has remained virtually unchanged, except for us.

Humans don't live in the Serengeti anymore, which is ironic, since humans are one of the Serengeti's original top predators. By removing ourselves, we have actually decreased the Serengeti's biodiversity by a species. For millions of years, nomadic hunter-gatherers were an integral part of Africa's landscape, which is why most scientists think that humans *didn't* cause any megafauna extinctions on this continent 40,000 years ago, as we did elsewhere. We took so long to become a top predator that other animals in Africa had time to adjust to us as a threat.

Today, we are a threat. This is why, when Serengeti National Park was founded in 1951, the people who had been living there—including the Maasai, who established themselves in the Serengeti in the 1700s—were forced to relocate outside park boundaries. In Africa, India, and Asia, this has happened many times: indigenous and traditional peoples have often been forced to move, and sometimes to abandon their lifestyles, when wildlife preserves are established. In 1972, the same thing happened to the Maldharis in India when Gir Forest National Park was created to preserve the Asiatic lion. This is always controversial, since it raises difficult questions of fairness and coexistence.

The Maasai are seminomadic pastoralists, herding cattle as their livelihood, and they have coexisted with the Serengeti's lions for centuries. They have always had to guard against lions to defend their herds, and they have always hunted lions as a cultural practice: as a rite of passage for young men, as a test of bravery and prowess. Among Maasai in Kenya, tradition said to be a chief you had to kill a lion.

Without question, the traditional Maasai hunt requires unthinkable bravery. In a primal test of courage, a single warrior with a spear and shield must start a fight to the death with a roaring male lion in his territory, the open plain.

The Maasai do not live the same lives that ancestral humans did, but could this lion-hunting ritual be that old? Is this what our ancestors did to prove to themselves that they had finally become the lion's rival? And is this what we've been doing ever since, in every society in every age, from Egyptian pharoahs to Roman gladiators, from British colonists to modern-day big-game hunters—proving ourselves by killing the king of beasts?

If we want to keep the lion, we can't afford to prove ourselves like this anymore. There are simply too many of us and too few lions. In total, Africa contains over a billion people—with perhaps a million Maasai in Tanzania and Kenya—and fewer than 20,000 lions.

The Maasai themselves are changing. To help preserve lions, most Maasai no longer practice solo hunts, and even ritual group hunts are limited. In Kenya, to select a chief, they now compete using their traditional "jumping dance," the *adumu*, rather than hunt lions.

Preserving lions will take much more than that, but it's an inspiring idea. Instead of killing, dance. ⤳

NORTH
AMERICA

RED WOLF: DOG OF THE WOODS

EXTINCTION: the red wolf became extinct in the wild in 1980

The red wolf is a surreal, epic story of near death, resurrection, and conservation, but let's clear up one thing first: the red wolf lives. It's one of two, and possibly three, recognized wolf species in the United States. The other is the gray wolf, and the eastern wolf might be a third.

These notes of doubt—"possibly," "might be"—shadow the red wolf's story from beginning to end. Some say the red wolf itself once comprised three subspecies, two of which are extinct—one in 1917 and one in 1970—while others say there has only ever been one red wolf species.

In 1980, the species was about to go extinct, and biologists jumped in and did something they'd never done before: they deliberately removed every last known red wolf from the wild in order to *save* the species. That is, scientists knowingly caused a wild extinction in order to prevent the ultimate extinction. This effort was controversial then, and it's controversial now.

Why? In part because no one knew if it would work. In part because wolves are still so feared that some people resist any effort to restore this top predator. In part because we can't agree on what the red wolf is. And finally, because without our meddling, the red wolf would probably breed itself out of existence in a New York minute.

How to Define a Species

In order to tell the red wolf's story, we must confront a problem that this book has successfully avoided until now: there is no single, universally accepted way to define a species.

That seems impossible, but it's true.

Species may seem self-evident—a bear is a bear, and a wolf is a wolf—but distinguishing one species from another can involve a certain amount of art. It sometimes requires a judgment call. Species are not fixed units, like atoms in a periodic table. The fundamental fact of evolution is that life is always, incrementally changing (thank you, Darwin and giant tortoises!). Because of that, all living beings exist along an ever-shifting continuum. Marking a section of that continuum and calling it a "red wolf" requires interpretation.

Species distinctions are not arbitrary, but boundaries can be fuzzy. Bears and wolves are fundamentally different, but in the far distant past, they once shared a common ancestor, the original canid. At some point, at many points, over millions of years, some of those original canids evolved to become wolf-like, while others became bear-like. Then those ancestral wolf species kept changing until they became today's modern wolf, which we further divide into more wolf species across the globe.

The question always is, how much difference, and what kind of difference, qualifies an animal to be called its own species?

The main approach uses the "biological species concept." This says, according to biologist Edward O. Wilson, that "a species is a population whose members are able to interbreed freely under natural conditions." In other words, if animals willingly mate in the wild, we can consider them members of the same species. After all, making children is the most direct connection there is—two beings merging their genetic heritage.

This approach is imperfect. It works best for animals, less so for plants, and not at all for bacteria. It implies something very important: if animals *don't* interbreed, even if they can, then they will inevitably, over time, become too different to mate. They become "closed gene pools," Wilson says.

For example, bears and wolves have been different for so long they can't crossbreed anymore, but lions and tigers still can. When they do, they create hybrid animals we call ligers or tigons (depending on who is male and who is female). But lions and tigers still aren't considered the same species because they only interbreed in captivity; in the wild, as far as we know, they never do.

Lions and tigers are also considered different species because they are physically different, they behave differently, and they live in different places. Biology, behavior, and geography are also important criteria for distinguishing species.

Finally, there are genes. Scientists relate and divide species based on their genetic lineages, on who descended from whom—no matter how different animals may look, how far apart they live, or if they could or do breed. Fifty years ago, based mostly on geography and looks, North American wolves were split into over twenty species, but today, modern genetic studies have led scientists to lump all those wolf populations into only two or three species.

So, when it comes to categorizing species, which is more important: whether animals mate in the wild, how they look and behave, or what their genes tell us? Sometimes, this evidence conflicts.

Is a Red Wolf Still a Red Wolf If It's a Hybrid?

Which brings us back to the red wolf.

To conserve a species, and even to decide if an animal is distinct enough to require conservation, we need to know what it is and how many there are. We need to define the species, or subspecies, and then count them. Knowing what an animal is shapes our efforts to conserve it, and success itself is often measured by counting: if we have more of that species than when we started, hurray—success!

But what if an animal isn't a distinct species because it's actually a hybrid? Or what if a species, even if it's not a hybrid, is doing everything it can to become one? How are we supposed to conserve it then? That is the central dilemma of the red wolf.

"SPECIES MAY SEEM SELF-EVIDENT—A BEAR IS A BEAR, AND A WOLF IS A WOLF—BUT DISTINGUISHING ONE SPECIES FROM ANOTHER CAN INVOLVE A CERTAIN AMOUNT OF ART. IT SOMETIMES REQUIRES A JUDGMENT CALL. SPECIES ARE NOT FIXED UNITS, LIKE ATOMS IN A PERIODIC TABLE."

By 1970, the red wolf was on the verge of extinction. It once occupied the entire southeastern United States, but by then only a few hundred remained in east Texas and Louisiana. As scientists studied them, they soon realized that not only were red wolves breeding rampantly with coyotes, but most of the remaining "red wolves" were actually hybrids.

Normally, wolves attack coyotes, so scientists wondered, why was this wolf species mating with them? Most felt it was the desperate act of a dying species. Red wolves weren't living "under natural conditions." Persecution, habitat loss, and disease were driving the last handful of red wolves to breed with the numerous coyotes surrounding them, since red wolves couldn't find enough of their own species to breed with.

If biologists didn't do something fast, this "hybrid swarm" would leave nothing but mixed-breed canids, neither this nor that. So they proposed a radical plan: capture all the remaining pure red wolves, making the species go extinct in the wild; breed a new population of red wolves in captivity; and then reintroduce them into their original range, far away from coyotes.

To do that, scientists had to distinguish true red wolves from hybrids or the plan would be pointless. This proved maddening. From 1973 to 1980, 400 animals were captured, apparently all that remained of the red wolf.

However, using mostly vocalizations and skull x-rays, only fourteen were judged to be true red wolves and used in the captive-breeding program.

So far so good, but then some researchers said, wait, what if the red wolf isn't a distinct species at all but is actually itself a hybrid? After all, the red wolf looks exactly like a cross between a gray wolf and a coyote. Red wolf males range from 55 to 85 pounds, smaller than gray wolves, but twice as large as coyotes. They are lanky, with long legs and long ears. Their fur isn't glowing auburn like a red fox, but dusky, black-speckled cedar … like a coyote. This would explain why red wolves are so hard to tell apart from coyotes.

Genetic studies in the 1990s only added to the confusion. The genetic evidence is tangled; red wolves and coyotes seem to share certain types of genes, but who originally gave these genes to whom and when?

Today, the mystery of the red wolf's origins is unresolved, despite ongoing genetic studies. Three theories, each now mostly discarded, have been that the red wolf is an ancient species that is completely separate from the North American gray wolf; that the red wolf is actually a subspecies of gray wolf; and that it is a gray wolf-coyote hybrid that probably resulted when these animals crossbred in the wild only a few hundred years ago.

However, the Red Wolf Recovery Program believes in a fourth possibility, one that has increasingly been supported by recent research: that red wolves, eastern wolves, and coyotes share a common lineage, one that split from gray wolves about a million years ago, and then split from one another about 300,000 to 150,000 years ago.

The origin of eastern wolves has also been long debated. Eastern wolves were once considered a subspecies of gray wolf, but recent genetics studies seem to show that they are distinct from gray wolves, and so are a possible third North American wolf species. However, they are so closely related to red wolves that these two might really be a single species.

What's interesting is that eastern wolves, like red wolves, are known to crossbreed with coyotes in the wild (thus creating completely different hybrids), but as far as we know, gray wolves *never* mate with coyotes. What might be happening is that when the ranges of red wolves and eastern wolves overlap with coyotes, these canid species freely mate because they didn't separate from one another all that long ago—not unlike grizzly bears and polar bears.

Yes, this can be hard to follow, and in the end, it can leave us wondering, does it really matter what we call the red wolf?

Sometimes, for the animal, it can mean life or death. How we categorize and define an animal affects how we count that animal, whether we consider it a unique population worth saving, and whether it qualifies for protection under the Endangered Species Act (which was passed in 1973). Especially for wolves, taxonomic distinctions often spark angry political debates over whether certain regional wolf populations deserve protection.

Without question, if not for the Endangered Species Act, the red wolf, whatever it is, would be six feet under by now.

Silencing the Howling Woods

When European settlers arrived on America's East Coast in the 1600s, wolves of some kind howled in the woods. That was all people needed to hear. In 1630, the Pilgrims of the Massachusetts Bay Colony taxed livestock to pay for the first wolf bounty, and for the next three centuries, humans greeted North American wolves with nothing but death.

"When we were all asleep in the Beginning of the Night, we were awaken'd with the dismall'st and most hideous Noise that ever pierc'd my Ears," surveyor John Lawson wrote while camping in the Carolinas in 1700. "Our Indian Pilot (who knew these parts well) acquainted us that it was customary to hear such Musick along the Swamp-Side, there being endless Numbers of Panthers, Tygers, Wolves, and other Beasts of Prey... making their frightful Ditty."

By then, Europe had been waging a war on the wolf for over a thousand years, and settlers brought that war to America without thinking twice. For the most part, they didn't bother to sort out the casualties: if it was a predator, they killed it. Even scientists were indifferent, doing little (until the 1960s) except bestowing the red wolf with a Latin name, *Canis rufus*.

Credit for recognizing this southeastern wolf as a distinct species falls to naturalist William Bartram, who in the late 1700s noted that the Florida population was entirely black. Yet southeastern wolves were unimpressive compared to their larger, fiercer European and North American gray wolf cousins, and they mostly inspired disdain. Lawson called red wolves the "dog of the woods."

By 1700, New England was free of wolves, and in 1748, North Carolina enacted its first wolf bounty: ten shillings a scalp. Throughout the 1800s, bounties flowed west with the pioneers, arising in Iowa, the Oregon Territories, Washington, Montana, Arizona, and so on. Methods of killing were macabre, ruthless, and indiscriminate.

The most effective and destructive was poison. Beginning in the 1750s, settlers left strychnine-laced carcasses for wolves everywhere. This killed wolves in bunches, as well as any scavenger that took the bait or fed on the dead wolves. But people were nothing if not creative. They used leg-hold traps, rifle traps, hunting dogs, guns, and sticks. They infected wolves with mange and set them loose to infect others, wired their jaws shut so they'd starve, and used dynamite to blow wolf dens to smithereens.

The extermination of America's wolves is an oft-told tale. It included all wolves and goes beyond the red wolf's story. However, one dynamic of that tragic period had a unique impact on the red wolf. As wolves were eliminated in state after state, as agriculture, roads, and towns disrupted predator habitats, and as human hunting eliminated prey like bison and deer, the western coyote started migrating east, filling in the abandoned niches where the wolf used to dominate as the top canid predator.

By 1930, you could barely find a wolf anywhere in the continental United States. By the 1940s, none lived east of the Mississippi River. Yet already, by the 1900s, western coyotes were breeding with the beleaguered group of red wolves hiding in the Texas-Louisiana swamps. At that time, coyotes were unknown in the eastern United States; they wouldn't cross the Mississippi River until the 1960s. When they did, they heard birdsong, but no howling wolves.

Today, the coyote is considered one of the world's most adaptable predators. It is uniquely tolerant of people, even infiltrating city parks. This flexibility is also demonstrated by how quickly it will occupy a wolf's abandoned territory and how willingly it interbreeds with America's eastern wolf species. This openness and adaptability are now the biggest threat to the red wolf.

Evolution, Coexistence & Fear

If the evolution of the red wolf remains mysterious, wolves we know well. They are the most widespread mammal in the Northern Hemisphere, as successful a predator as has ever existed. They live in every terrain except tropical forests. They feast on all sizes of prey, from mice to moose and, once upon a time, perhaps even mammoth.

Humans have always lived with wolves. As with every top predator, this hasn't been easy. The real question, the one all wolf reintroduction programs must confront, is why do people hate the wolf so passionately. As many have noted, these feelings fly in the face of the historical record, which shows that feral dogs are far more dangerous to livestock and people than wolves. Yet the vision of a forest filled with wolves can evoke an almost hysterical dread.

We didn't always react this way.

Wolf-like canids have only been around for about 3 million years, but the canid branch goes back 20 million years, to when canines split from felines. Once early wolves evolved, they migrated extensively, leaving versions of themselves on every northern continent. It's believed that wolves migrated in and out of North America several times: the red wolf, gray wolf, and dire wolf may all represent separate recolonizations of the hemisphere.

The gray wolf evolved about a million years ago, and the dire wolf appeared in North and South America about 300,000 years ago. Though equivalent in build, the dire wolf was bulkier, with a massive head and giant teeth—as *Game of Thrones* has made famous, it was the most formidable wolf ever. The first humans in North America had to contend with both species until, for reasons unknown, the dire wolf expired about 8,000 years ago.

By then, the wolf had already bequeathed us the domestic dog, which evolved from wolves anywhere from 32,000 to 14,000 years ago. This domestication event, the first ever, probably happened in several places, and it indicates how closely humans and wolves coexisted for centuries, probably millennia. Domesticating a top predator must have been a revelation—and it could only have occurred if humans cared for wolves, enfolding them into human life, until tameness and a fondness for us became a genetic trait. Domestication would never have happened if all we'd ever done was hunt and kill wolves.

As an interesting aside, since then, people have regularly bred dogs with wolves to create the opposite: stronger, wilder human companions. Alaskans have used such crosses as sled dogs, and Plains Indians used them as draft animals. However, wolf-dog hybrids can be dangerous predators with no fear of humans. Ironically, more of these captive hybrids live in the United States today than wild wolves, with 300,000 wolf-dogs and counting.

Native American cultures almost uniformly regarded the wolf as an intelligent, spiritually powerful animal. The wolf was both revered and feared, honored and hunted. Some regarded the wolf as kin, but all recognized the parallels between human and wolf society. The wolf pack resembled human tribes and had similar hierarchies; wolves strategized group hunts for the same prey; wolf parents remained together as devoted mates; wolves communally nurtured their young and their elders; wolves grieved their dead; and wolves were curious, quick students of nature.

In myth, anyway, some wolves even became famous for nurturing humans. Romulus and Remus, founders of Rome, were nursed by a she-wolf, and stories of wolf-raised children were once legion in India—as immortalized in Rudyard Kipling's *Jungle Book* stories.

So what happened?

Agriculture and domestic livestock, for one thing. About 10,000 years ago, humans domesticated sheep and pigs, and eventually cattle. Humans and wolves had always competed for large prey, but humans didn't raise elk. They didn't own them. Wild prey was fair game for all predators. However, domestic livestock became one of the earliest forms of wealth, and a wolf who took a cow impoverished the farmer. Once humans had an investment to protect, wolves became an enemy.

This is the pragmatic explanation, and it's often still raised today; any shepherding culture has a practical reason to dislike the wolf. However, hatred of the wolf seems to have arisen in the Middle Ages when the Christian church used the wolf as a symbol of evil, villainy, deceit, and greed. If the aim of civilization was to tame wilderness for the good of human society, the goal of religion was to tame inner wildness to save one's soul for eternity. The wolf became shorthand for both. In medieval Europe, the werewolf wasn't a mythical, cheesy horror-movie staple or a romantic lead; it was a real demon whose bite turned you into a monster from the inside out.

For all these reasons, from the ninth century onward, peoples across Europe and Asia tried to exterminate the wolf. This took longer, and was less thorough, than in North America: wolves first disappeared in Britain in the 1500s, and north and central Europe weren't wolf-free until the late 1800s. Meanwhile, eastern Europe, Russia, India, and Asia never eradicated all their wolves, though the species declined everywhere.

In America in the 1970s, the biologists of the Red Wolf Recovery Project chose the Albermale Peninsula in North Carolina as the best site to eventually reintroduce their captive-bred red wolves. Yet they knew that releasing the animal was going to be easy compared to getting people to accept a wolf in their midst.

Ranchers hadn't heard a wolf howl in North Carolina since 1905. What was going to happen when they did?

Reintroducing a Predator
& the Trouble with Hybrids

In the 1980s, the red wolf program embarked on a reeducation campaign to ease the public's fears and address their concerns: once red wolves were released into the Alligator River National Wildlife Refuge, no fence would contain them. Towns, ranches, roads, schools—human society was interwoven, if sparsely, on the peninsula, among a hodgepodge of federal and state lands. If a red wolf threatened a person or a sheep, could you kill it? If you hit one with a car, or accidentally shot one while legally hunting, would you be arrested?

After all, it's a federal crime to harm an endangered species.

In 1982, Congress amended the Endangered Species Act to create a new status. The released red wolves would be called a "nonessential experimental" population, rather than labeled "endangered." The released wolves would be considered expendable. People could protect themselves and their property, and live their normal lives, without risking arrest if a red wolf was harmed. Indeed, this "nonessential" status proved key to winning cooperation from locals, and it's been used successfully for other predator reintroductions since then.

But once again, the red wolf entered semantic limbo. Was the species important or "nonessential"? Endangered or "experimental"? This linguistic no-man's-land eventually created more trouble for the red wolf.

Another key to winning local support was the recapture collar. Each released wolf would wear a telemetry collar that tracked its position and could be remotely triggered to inject an anesthetic. This device helped convince the public that field biologists could manage these wild predators once set free. Today, collars use GPS.

Finally, in September 1987, the first pair of captive-bred red wolves were released. They had spent the previous six months in an outdoor holding pen getting acclimated to the peninsula. This way, they'd be less likely to bolt for Texas, or wherever they thought was home. This strategy, too, was successful.

Trophic Cascades: Gray Wolves in Yellowstone

The reintroduction of gray wolves to Yellowstone National Park is one of the greatest success stories in wildlife conservation.

Given the gray wolf's history of persecution, their return to the American West is nothing less than a "miracle," according to naturalist Thane Maynard, who cautions that "it took decades of work and educating and arguing and explaining for that crazy combination of Western conservationists, ranchers, federal biologists, and dreamers to succeed."

Gray wolves were eradicated in Yellowstone in 1926, and seventy years later, in 1995 and 1996, thirty-one gray wolves from western Canada were released into the park. Today, 400 to 450 wolves live in the Greater Yellowstone Ecosystem, and about ninety-five wolves live within Yellowstone National Park itself.

In truth, the conservation plan was pretty simple: "They largely need to be left alone," writes Mike Phillips, who ran the Yellowstone gray wolf program from 1994 to 1997. "You give wolves a big landscape with something to eat, they're going to do just fine."

What conservationists didn't know was what impact the wolves would have on the landscape and other wildlife. When a habitat loses a top predator, it can cause a "trophic cascade," or a widespread negative ripple effect among many species. Without wolves, Yellowstone's ecosystem had become unbalanced, but would restoring the wolf, all by itself, fix anything?

It has, and much more dramatically than conservationists predicted. For instance, today, wolf kills provide more carrion for other scavengers, which helps grizzlies, coyotes, and eagles. Wolves keep deer and elk populations in check, and change their feeding habits, which has allowed riverside aspens, cottonwoods, and willows to flourish again. Long-missing beavers have returned, and their dams improve habitat for waterfowl and fish. Healthy riparian forests have attracted more songbirds and even improved the Yellowstone River, since more trees mean less erosion.

To what degree gray wolves are *primarily* responsible for all these changes is difficult to measure. Ecosystems are extremely complex, and other factors are certainly at work. Nevertheless, an unmistakable "virtuous circle" of healthy changes is occurring now that Yellowstone has its wolf back.

Restoring this species, adding wolves to the world rather than subtracting them, qualified as a conservation miracle.

Over the next seven years, sixty-three wolves were released. Except for an identity crisis and a forced extinction, all they had to do now was overcome the same challenges facing most top predators: fragmented habitats, lack of prey, too many cars, too many people, pollution, hunting, and all the rest.

Field biologists didn't name released wolves because it was too painful when they died. Success was measured by how many wolves sired pups in the wild; about one-fifth did. With each generation, the wolves got warier around people, and public complaints lessened. By 1999, sixty-four wild litters had been born, but there was a growing problem.

Eleven of those litters were confirmed or suspected red wolf–coyote hybrids.

Faster than anyone expected, coyotes had migrated into North Carolina and infiltrated Albemarle Peninsula. In 1983, a few coyotes were known in the west of the state, but by 1998, they were everywhere. And the red wolf, still struggling to establish itself, was crossbreeding with them all over again.

In more ways than one, this jeopardized everything. If another hybrid swarm swamped the red wolf's genes, the red wolf as a species would disappear, flushing away all the work to preserve it—voiding the program and the Endangered Species Act's protections.

Biologists made a painful decision: to preserve the species, they would kill the hybrid wolves and somehow eliminate coyotes from Albemarle Peninsula. This near impossible task meant assessing the DNA and tracking the matings of every single red wolf. It meant trapping, killing, and sterilizing coyotes to create coyote-free zones. It meant micromanaging this species as intensely as any in history.

But it worked. By 2007, biologists had developed new field techniques and DNA tracking, and they had successfully beaten back both coyotes and hybrids, so that they could say, with pinpoint accuracy, that the wild red wolf gene pool had recovered to 96 percent red wolf and only 4 percent coyote. And that little bit of coyote is now considered healthy, since it guards against the risk of inbreeding. (Coyotes themselves, meanwhile, are about 20 percent wolf.)

By saving the red wolf from extinction—again!—the Red Wolf Recovery Program won the 2007 North American Conservation Award, the highest honor a conservationist can get. Today, from 75 to over 100 red wolves live in the wild, and a captive-breeding population of 175 to 200 animals is maintained in dozens of zoos and facilities.

The red wolf's human caretakers are justifiably proud, but most of all, they love the red wolf. This is a little secret about scientists and biologists: they care deeply about the animals they study and conserve. They desire what most of us desire, to meet and know wild animals in the wild.

And sometimes, they howl. Among their educational programming, the Alligator River park rangers conduct "Howling Safaris" so the public can hear what they've been missing all these years. Biologists have been known to let loose themselves. As one field biologist told Jane Goodall: "You never forget the first time a wild wolf responds to your howls, offered into the dark night."

Into the Future: Will Evolution End the Species?

In a fairy tale, the story would end here. But the reality of the red wolf's predicament is that it may always need human help. Since this is expensive, continuous, hands-on work, people wonder, how long can we keep this up?

Not everyone is happy to see the red wolf. In 1991, when researchers first suggested that the red wolf might be a gray wolf–coyote hybrid, the American Sheep Industry Association petitioned to have the red wolf removed from the Endangered Species List. Today, because wild red wolves remain a "nonessential experimental population," the state of North Carolina refuses to acknowledge their protected status on state lands, and it wants the conservation program shut down.

The Albemarle Peninsula is hardly pristine wilderness, and this limits how many red wolves can live there. Further, it's shallow. In a hundred years, if global warming causes seas to rise 2 feet or more, much of the red wolf's current home might be underwater.

Biologists are eager to find other homes for the red wolf, but nothing has been successful so far. From 1992 to 1998, a reintroduction of red wolves in Great Smoky Mountains National Park failed. Precious little southeast wilderness remains that is large enough to hold wolves.

Southeast ecosystems need red wolves. The successful reintroductions of gray wolves in Yellowstone and Idaho demonstrate the positive impacts that wolves can have on ecosystems, as well as how resilient wolves can be when they have the room they need.

Then again, some argue that all the Southeast really needs is a top predator who acts like a wolf. They suggest that red wolves should be allowed to breed with coyotes—if that's what they are doing on their own, and if the resulting wild animal is healthy and self-sufficient, able both to kill deer and to tolerate human society. This type of animal would benefit crowded Southeast ecosystems the most, and it would respect the stunning evolutionary process that keeps trying to unfold before our eyes.

As professor Paul Wilson has said, red wolf–coyote hybrids "are the canids that have been selected *for* in a human-modified landscape."

If staying separate doesn't matter to red wolves or coyotes, why does it matter to us?

Even Darwin recognized that evolution would never satisfy our desire to label and categorize. He called species distinctions "trying to define the indefinable," and he dismissed "the vain search for the undiscovered and undiscoverable essence" of a species.

Accepting a hybrid would be bittersweet. It would mean losing a species to gain one. Looking ahead, we may face many such crossroads in the future. ᷦ

DISCOVERING THE NEW WORLD: THE AMERICAS

Oddly enough, the most controversial of all the Late Pleistocene extinctions is also the most recent: the one that occurred in North and South America. So many dates and so much evidence is disputed and argued over, it's easier to list what scientists agree on rather than what they don't. So here goes.

Humans from Siberia arrived in the Americas by some route by at least 14,000 years ago (probably by walking over the Bering land bridge).

About 13,200 years ago, Clovis peoples in North America developed a massive 6-inch spearhead and killed some number of mammoths and megaherbivores with it.

By 11,000 years ago, most of the megafauna in North and South America were gone.

When did the first humans actually get to the Americas, and how?

Maybe, some speculate, they used boats and sailed down the coast. Or maybe, since glaciers advanced and briefly retreated even during the ice age, small groups raced across the Bering land bridge whenever a warmer, spring-like weather pattern opened a route. Right now, we simply don't have enough evidence to say for sure.

We also can't confirm whether the continent's megafauna were flourishing by 14,000 years ago, or if they were already on the verge of extinction due to ice age climate change. There's some evidence of humans hunting large animals in the Americas, but not much, and the reason could be that there just weren't many giants left to hunt by the time we got there. However, scientists do agree on one more thing: North and South America once contained a diversity of megafauna that equaled the splendor of Africa.

Big Animals, Big Spear

In North America, the richness of giant species included both woolly mammoths and Columbian mammoths, the biggest of all. There were mastodons, 6,000-pound giant ground sloths, long-horned bison, buffalo, stag-moose, musk ox, dire wolves, camels, horses, grizzlies, 8-foot-long modern lions, jaguars, and cougars.

Sabertooth cats, the iconic top predator of the Pleistocene, sank their formidable canines into animals from Canada to Patagonia. Various sabertooth species dominated the Americas, a fact immortalized by the 1,200 or so *Smilodon fatalis* and *Homotherium* sabertooths who got stuck, and fossilized, in Los Angeles' La Brea tar pits. South America boasted the largest species, *Smilodon populator* (meaning "he who brings devastation"), which may have weighed 880 pounds, making it the biggest cat ever.

Then there was the short-faced bear, which weighed a ton and stood 11 feet tall. Scientists argue whether it was a relatively benign vegetarian or the continent's most powerful predator and the largest land carnivore in history. If so, even a sabertooth couldn't have stopped a short-faced bear from scavenging its kills, and humans stood no chance. Perhaps the 6-inch Clovis spear was developed to keep this beast away as much as to kill mammoths. Or perhaps humans weren't even able to migrate south of Alaska until the short-face bear had already died out from other causes.

When they did, the first humans to reach South America surely lowered their spears in amazement. Like Australia, South America evolved for millions of years as an island continent, then it connected to North America about 3.5 million years ago. As a result, its megafauna embodied yet another alternate evolutionary track, one full of marsupials and odd creatures that defy easy comparisons. Four-ton gomphotheres were like elephants, macrauchenids were like camels, and toxodonts were like hippo-rhinos in need of orthodontia. Glyptodonts were like Volkswagen Beetles: 2-ton mammals ambling beneath a helmet-shaped carapace and dragging an armored tail.

South America had two of the world's largest species of ground sloths; *Megatherium* reached elephantine proportions and may have been the largest bipedal mammal. A slightly smaller species of ground sloth burrowed, leaving us with 6-foot-wide tunnels to gape at.

Then, with the same swiftness that defined Australia, most of the giants in the Americas disappeared. Dating these extinctions is also controversial. Some occurred before humans arrived, but most went extinct afterward. In North America, they happened over a very short time period: 69 percent of megafauna, or 37 of 54 species over 100 pounds, went extinct between 13,500 and 12,500 years ago.

In South America, extinctions continued until about 8,000 years ago. We have no accurate count of species losses, but 80 percent of genera were lost. However, on both continents, nearly all of the largest species went extinct: all the sabertooth cats, lions, glyptodonts, ground sloths, dire wolves, camels, horses, mammoths, mastodons, and short-faced bears.

Today, the largest animal in South America is the endangered Baird's tapir, which can reach 660 pounds. North America retained a greater handful of megafauna, such as grizzlies, bison, moose, elk, caribou, and gray wolves. These impressive animals dominated the wilderness where Native Americans made their home. This coexistence wasn't without conflict, but extinctions of large animals ceased as people and wildlife reached a self-sustaining equilibrium that lasted until Europeans arrived, hot on the heels of Christopher Columbus.

A New Type of Predator Takes Charge

When we consider what happened in the Late Pleistocene, we know that Cro-Magnons and ancestral peoples didn't mean to cause extinctions. They were simply surviving and adapting. From a human perspective, changes among wildlife would probably have been so gradual that people wouldn't have noticed. From one human generation to the next, as centuries turned into millennia, life would have seemed virtually unchanged. Without writing, could *we* remember what the world was like 500, even 200, years ago?

Only from our modern perspective can we see how much life transformed across the globe. Only on a geological timescale do the Late Pleistocene megafauna extinctions appear "sudden" and cataclysmic.

And we still aren't entirely sure what happened, despite digging up fossils, dating carbon, and tracking ancient weather patterns for over 200 years. Circumstances clearly differed on each continent, since the results in each place were so different: there were very few extinctions of giants in Africa, a moderate number in Eurasia, a majority in North America, and the near total annihilation of large species in Australia and South America.

If there was a single cause—such as either from human hunting or from ice age–driven climate change—then extinctions would have unfolded more consistently everywhere.

We've learned a *few* things, however. One is that, when they occur to-gether, habitat change and human impacts make a deadly combination. As one factor makes species more vulnerable, the other can easily prove fatal. This lesson speaks directly to us, since both threaten many species today.

Another is that the speed or rate of change can make all the difference in survival. Animals in Africa had the longest time to adapt to human hunt-ing; they coevolved with us and survived the best. Species in Australia and the Americas, who'd never even seen an ape before, seemed least able to cope with our sudden appearance. The same is true for habitat change: with enough time, animals can migrate and find more ideal habitats or even adjust their diet.

But just as importantly, in the 10,000 years or so since the Pleistocene ended, humans have changed the rules of the game. Our creative minds have kept inventing new ways to make our lives better: domestic animals, agriculture, the wheel, books, government, pie. The human population has exploded, and we continue changing with a speed unknown in Earth's history—not physically, but culturally. To adapt, evolve, and thrive, we are no longer bound by the pace and limits of genetic change. If we need wings, we build wings. If we need bigger brains, we build computers.

Nor do the interdependent dynamics of the food web constrain our numbers or limit our menu. Humans no longer coexist with other ani-mals as equals within particular ecosystems. Rather, we adapt habitats to fulfill our needs, and we determine which animals live in them, since our creativity gives us strength and dominance no other animal can match. We've learned how to hurry evolution along, thumbing our noses at the constraints every other species lives within.

Yet the extinction crisis is driving home that this has a downside. We may not need to live in any one particular ecosystem, but we need a healthy planet, and the earth requires a healthy biodiversity of all types of species. No animal, no matter how dominant, can live beyond nature's rules, not even us.

When we consider the age of megafauna in the Late Pleistocene, we realize that Alfred Russel Wallace was right. Our lives are better off without having to contend with woolly mammoths, sabertooth cats, short-faced bears, carnivorous kangaroos, and 1-ton goannas.

But a world without any giants? No one wants that. As it turns out, we need them. ⤳

ASIA

TIGERS: THE PERFECT PREDATOR

EXTINCTION: the Bali tiger was declared extinct in 1938, the Caspian tiger in the 1950s, and the Javan tiger in the 1980s

---

When Rudyard Kipling needed a villain for his Mowgli stories in *The Jungle Book*—about a lost man-cub raised by wolves in India—it was a no-brainer: Shere Khan, the tiger, wants Mowgli as his prey. This breaks the "law of the jungle"—which is not to kill humans, since that drives humans to exact revenge on all predators—but Shere Kahn doesn't care.

In nineteenth-century India, when Kipling wrote his story, this was not fiction. Tigers regularly killed people, and people relentlessly hunted tigers. In that era, across all of Asia, tigers were a constant threat.

Even today, no animal is more feared because no animal is more likely to stalk us. Tigers are the quintessential "man-eater," and their presence, often unseen, electrifies the forest. You walk alive to every movement, every rustle, every sound, praying *not* to see a tiger because, by then, it might be too late...

Living with Tigers

Coexistence with tigers has never been easy. Our relationship has been long and deadly, and our feelings extremely complex. Today, the dilemma boils down to this:

Tigers are the most imperiled big cat species on earth. Of the nine recognized subspecies, three are extinct, one is extinct in the wild, and the

"TIGERS ARE THE MOST IMPERILED BIG CAT SPECIES ON EARTH. OF THE NINE RECOGNIZED SUBSPECIES, THREE ARE EXTINCT, ONE IS EXTINCT IN THE WILD, AND THE OTHER FIVE ARE CONSIDERED ENDANGERED, THREE CRITICALLY."

other five are considered endangered, three critically. The most abundant subspecies, India's Bengal tiger—and Shere Khan's inspiration—numbers from 1,700 to 2,500, while, overall, from 3,800 to 5,200 wild tigers remain in the entire world. That isn't enough to fill the average minor-league baseball stadium.

Tigers evolved to become a nearly perfect predator, but their survival now depends on us—so, how badly do we want this man-eater around?

First of all, tigers (*Panthera tigris*) are the largest living cats, though lions are a close second. Among tigers, the biggest subspecies is either India's Bengal tiger or Siberia's Amur tiger. Take your pick. For both, adult males average from 440 to 570 pounds, but individual Amur tigers can be exceptional. The largest on record was 847 pounds. The tiger's size and strength allow it to kill prey five times its own weight—making humans easy pickings.

Their mesmerizing coats—ragged black stripes, each as unique as a fingerprint, brushed over shades of autumnal orange and reddish amber, with white accenting their eyes, cheeks, lips, and belly—only stand out in cement cages. Nestled in dense foliage among dappled shadows, tigers are expertly camouflaged, their tigery outlines obscured. Walking on their toes, as all cats do, they move silently despite massive paws.

Tigers typically hunt alone from dusk to dawn, so that darkness also hides their presence, and they rely on surprise. They don't pounce until they're close, about 50 to 100 feet away, and then they explode in an agile, furious rush. If they miss, they won't chase prey much farther than the length of a football field, so there's that.

Still, predation is a dangerous business. Tigers can be seriously injured by large horned prey like water buffalo and gaur. Tigers don't always win, and researchers have variously estimated their hunting success rate from 5 to 50 percent. The low end might seem pathetic, but researchers admit they're guessing. Very few witness a wild tiger in the act of killing who isn't on the receiving end.

The *Panthera* genus evolved 10.8 million years ago, and the earliest tiger fossils are 2 million years old. However, the modern tiger's direct ancestor emerged some 73,000 years ago, when what's been called "the largest known explosive volcanic event on Earth" occurred in Sumatra. The ensuing "volcanic winter" almost wiped out all tigers, but a few survived and spread across Asia, from the Indian subcontinent north to frigid Siberia, filling pretty much every forest in the Far East.

Only India is blessed with both of Earth's largest cats. Otherwise, tigers and lions live separately, one mostly solitary, one largely social, each recognized as a "king." Yet despite their differences in appearance and behavior, lions and tigers have nearly identical skeletons. In fact, all big cats are closely related on the inside, and tigers even share 95 percent of their genome with the domestic feline.

Hey, if it ain't broke...

Tigers are such effective, superior predators that some wonder why they don't eat humans more often. Preserves today are surrounded by people, and tigers have oodles of chances to attack us, far more than they take advantage of. Nor has every country with tigers been plagued with man-eaters. Historically, Iran, Sumatra, Bali, and Thailand, among others, have had very few. Tigers have certainly earned their deadly reputation, no question—some calculate they've killed more people than any other large carnivore—but as it turns out, that's a bit misleading.

A certain collection of circumstances seems to define places with tiger problems: there's a shortage of natural prey, tiger habitat has shrunk and been disrupted, livestock graze in or next to tiger habitat, and too many people crowd the tiger's doorstep. Even then, the tigers who most often prey on people tend to be desperate. They are females with hungry cubs and old, injured, or infirm tigers who can't kill large wild prey or compete with healthy tigers.

Even the fictional Shere Khan is "the Lame One," frustrated by a bad leg and able to kill only domestic cattle. In reality, park rangers in India have called tigers "on the whole very good-tempered." Further, people who live near protected tiger reserves don't always protect themselves as well as they might. More than a few people have been ambushed while walking alone along forest trails at dusk.

In other words, people are also partly responsible for the tiger's bad reputation. Not every tiger seeks us out. Some do, but mostly tigers can't avoid us. We take their natural prey, invade their homes, parade livestock under their noses, and then wonder why the world's top predator can be so hard to live with.

India: Man-Eaters & Project Tiger

Tigers are an enduring reminder that humans were once, and can still be, prey. Despite this, human societies have rarely, if ever, hated this species. Farmers and industry may disparage tigers as pests, but cultural awe and respect remain undiminished. We shower tigers with admiration and symbolically identify ourselves with the tiger's ferocity, intelligence, and dominance.

The earliest depictions are cave paintings in India, which go back 8,000 years. In Hinduism, the goddess Durga is often shown riding a tiger, which symbolizes unlimited power, as she protects the virtuous and slays both demons and the evil forces within—such as hatred, selfishness, and prejudice. In modern times, the tiger became the national emblem of six countries.

In India, the tiger was considered the most prized hunting trophy. As with the lion, this expressed a strange sort of respect; nothing ever provides more glory than hunting the ultimate hunter. Paintings from the sixteenth and seventeenth centuries depict elaborate royal hunts. Hunting was a rite of passage for young princes and a source of legitimacy for maharajas and kings. Some thought slaying 109 tigers was a lucky number. But you know people: two maharajas became famous for killing a thousand tigers, thus multiplying their luck.

Slaying tigers as a form of pest control only grew throughout the nineteenth century, and with good reason. In 1822, in a single Indian district, tigers killed 20,000 head of cattle along with 550 people. Across India in 1877, tigers killed nearly 800 people. On average from 1902 to 1910, tigers killed 851 people annually, and in 1922, they outdid themselves, killing 1,603 people.

The common estimate is that the world contained 100,000 tigers by the turn of the twentieth century, yet this may be undercounting. An Indian historian also calculated that from 1875 to 1925 at least 80,000 tigers were killed in India alone. Kipling published *The Jungle Book* in 1894, in the middle of this madness.

If this was a war, the tiger lost, and its disappearance was noted. In 1912, India passed a wildlife protection act that regulated tiger hunting. In theory, you weren't supposed to kill a tiger without a permit, unless you were the viceroy, or you hunted a man-eater or cattle-killer. For decades, no one paid any attention to this.

Then in 1968, someone did the math and realized that India had legally exported 3,000 tiger skins while issuing only 500 hunting permits. That amounted to 2,500 illegally killed tigers. When people tried to estimate the number of tigers left in India, they came up with only about 2,000 to 2,500. Another year like 1968, and India's tigers would be finished.

So India banned tiger hunting, and in 1973, faced with losing its iconic species, its symbolic heart and soul, India enacted a groundbreaking initiative called Project Tiger. Still considered the world's most comprehensive tiger conservation effort, the project's centerpiece was the creation of nine tiger reserves, which soon expanded to fifteen, then nineteen, and today totals forty-two. When it was launched, Prime Minister Indira Gandhi said,

"The tiger does not exist in isolation. It is at the apex of a large and complex biotope. Its habitat… must first be inviolate."

This wise, lofty strategy met with immediate success. By 1984, tigers seemed to have doubled their numbers, reaching perhaps 4,000. Project Tiger showed that protecting tigers, their prey, and enough space is all tigers need. The ultimate hunter is very resilient.

India metaphorically wiped its brow. The nation had saved the tiger. India patted itself on the back, raised a toast, relaxed, and over the next ten years, in a stunning reversal, let complacency, corruption, and neglect undo all that hard work.

Through the late 1980s and early 1990s, even though tiger populations actually started to decline, India kept publishing optimistic, higher tiger counts. It papered over a problem it didn't understand and didn't want to acknowledge.

That problem burst into the open in 1993. Investigators discovered Tibetan refugees in Delhi with a huge cache of illegally poached skins and bones from tigers and leopards. All the feline pieces and parts added up to some eighty dead cats, and this was clearly just the tip of the iceberg.

The skins made sense. Until the 1980s, that's why poachers usually killed tigers, for blankets, rugs, coats, hats—for predator fashion. But what did they want *bones* for?

Oh, the smugglers said in effect, those are going to China to make medicine.

Indonesia: Tiger Islands in a Sea of People

This shouldn't have been a surprise, but the world was stunned by this shocking threat to tigers. Yet for millennia, China had used tiger parts in traditional Chinese medicine, and local markets across Southeast Asia openly sold tiger parts and tiger-bone products to feed these ancient cultural prescriptions for good health.

However, before addressing China and the threat to tigers from poaching, let's first discuss the three tiger species native to Indonesia. Two of these species were already extinct by 1993, and the tiger's plight in Indonesia exemplifies the complexities of living with tigers in our modern world. Regardless of poaching, tigers won't survive if we don't solve these issues of everyday coexistence.

As far back as a million years ago, tigers colonized the Indonesian islands closest to mainland Asia, such as Borneo, Sumatra, Java, and Bali. They did so, most likely, by walking. During ice ages, when sea levels dropped, land bridges emerged to connect these islands. Wildlife sauntered across many times. However, after the last ice age, rising sea levels restored these islands, and marooned tigers evolved until each island held its own subspecies.

One interesting adaption was that Indonesia's tigers became smaller than those on the mainland. They suffered island dwarfism like the ancient hippos on Madagascar. The Bali tiger was the smallest tiger. An adult male didn't weigh more than 300 pounds and was about 8 feet from the nose to the tip of the tale; Bengal tigers are about twice as heavy and up to 10 feet long.

Borneo's tigers, a scientifically unnamed species, disappeared over 200 years ago. Bali tigers lasted until 1938, but their life in this tropical paradise was never easy. Minuscule Bali held no large prey. After World War I, as European settlers and colonists cut down Bali's forests and hunted its tigers, the end came quickly.

Java, meanwhile, is twenty-two times bigger than Bali and positively hummed with tigers through the nineteenth century. Yet eventually the same thing happened. As the human population exploded, people converted forests into agriculture and ranches, and they shot and poisoned the tiger as a pest. The tiger retreated to ever-more-remote forests, but on an island, you can't retreat forever.

From 1915 to 1975, the human population on Java grew from about 28 million to 85 million, and 92 percent of Java's original forest disappeared. Even though dozens of nature reserves were established, none was large enough to support a tiger's needs. Considering everything, it's surprising Javan tigers lasted as long as they did. The last sightings were in the late 1970s, and extinction likely occurred in the 1980s.

Today, the only Indonesian island with any tigers left is Sumatra. About the size of California, Sumatra also still has rhinos, but both species hang by a thread. From 1970 to the 1990s, Sumatran tigers decreased by half, from about 1,000 to maybe 500, and today about 300 tigers are scattered in small pockets across the island. This decline in tigers exactly mirrored, in reverse, the increase in people: the island doubled its human population from 1970 to 1995, from 20 million to 40 million, and today it holds over 50 million people.

Can Sumatra reverse the trend and find a way for its 50 million citizens to coexist with its 300 wild tigers? Sumatra is trying. In particular, three national parks enclose vast stretches of diverse, pristine wilderness that can support healthy tiger populations. Whether they will depends on how well Sumatra defends those parks from poachers and industry.

Keeping out poachers is easier said than done. By definition, it means preventing illegal tiger hunting, but it also means slowing or halting what's called the "bush meat trade." Poor Sumatrans sometimes make a living by hunting and selling wild boar and sambar deer, which is cheaper than raising pigs and cattle. Hungry families also hunt wild game for their own table, but all of this decreases the tiger's main prey. Tigers faced with starvation, in turn, are more likely to take livestock, thus increasing tiger-human conflicts, which up to now have been rare on Sumatra.

In addition, those living next to tiger preserves are impacted the most. They are more often killed by wild tigers, and they tend to be poorer people for whom the loss of a single cow is an economic tragedy. Then again, for a small population of tigers, the loss of one tiger is a tragedy. Thus, tackling issues of social justice—compensating people for losses, decreasing poverty in general, increasing employment—would help Sumatra save its tigers. People are less likely to retaliate against tigers, or eat a tiger's prey, if they aren't living on the edge.

Sumatra also has to keep its industry from chewing up the island's last remaining wilderness. No tropical country except Brazil has lost more forest than Sumatra in the last twenty-five years. This is mainly because Sumatra's economy depends on commercial agriculture, which produces coffee, paper, rubber, and especially palm oil. Often simply called vegetable oil, it is the world's most popular oil, and Sumatra is the world's largest producer. We all use it.

Commercial plantations have already fragmented the countryside so badly that tigers can only survive in protected preserves. Sumatra would like to increase agricultural production, but that means cutting down more forest. Deforestation, meanwhile, has led to massive wildfires with devastating consequences for everyone, people and wildlife alike.

From one angle, tiger conservation is simple: tigers just need space, food, and freedom from hunting. Yet providing that in today's world is deeply complicated. It involves sacrifices, tradeoffs, and the political and cultural will to make it happen. Even if people never poached tigers again, coexistence with tigers will remain a tricky balancing act of competing needs and impacts.

It's true on Sumatra and everywhere: Earth's greatest predator must now eke out a living within "forest islands" that are steadily shrinking due to a rising tide of people.

A Tiger Cure: Traditional Chinese Medicine & Poaching

Unfortunately, poaching remains a very serious problem. According to one calculation, the worldwide black market in illegal wildlife is a $20 billion industry. It affects tigers, rhinos, elephants, and many exotic, endangered species. As India discovered in 1993, even when nations make endangered species conservation a high priority, illegal poaching can undermine everything.

Today, the illegal poaching of tigers and rhinos largely serves China's ancient cultural practices of traditional Chinese medicine (TCM), as well as other similar traditions across Asia.

The techniques of traditional Chinese medicine go back at least 4,000 years, though the earliest known recipes using tiger bone date to about 1,500 years ago. TCM combines a mystical or spiritual approach to healing along with physical exercise, diet, and natural potions and remedies. It is based on Taoism and Eastern beliefs about the essential connections between mind, body, spirit, and health.

Other Asian countries, such as Korea, Vietnam, and Japan, have similar but distinct traditional medicines, and many people around the world, particularly in the United States, also incorporate TCM into their daily lives. To make their natural medicines, TCM practitioners use a total of perhaps 12,000 ingredients, mostly plants and minerals, but China's wild apothecary includes over 1,500 animals.

This is to emphasize that TCM and similar traditions are widespread and diverse. Practices vary considerably. Not everyone uses the same methods, nor do practitioners themselves agree about the effectiveness of every ingredient.

That said, the tiger is often considered one of the most potent ingredients, and for some people it is considered essential and is the most desired (along with the rhino). In a literal way, people ingest the tiger's power and strength. As conservationist Steve Winter writes: "Nearly every part, from nose to tail—eyes, whiskers, brains, flesh, blood, genitals, organs—is used to treat a lengthy list of maladies. Tiger parts are believed to heal the liver and kidneys and are used to treat epilepsy, baldness, inflammation, possession by evil demons, toothaches, malaria, hydrophobia, skin diseases, nightmares, laziness, fevers, and headaches."

Many in the West disparage and dismiss traditional Chinese medicine, which operates on very different philosophical principles than modern Western medicine. There can be deep cultural conflicts and disagreements over whether TCM practices work as effective medicine. But ultimately, when it comes to the fate of endangered species, the point isn't debating whether these animals make for genuine cures.

Rather, it's convincing TCM practitioners that preserving endangered species in the wild is what's *most* important, even if it means giving up certain medicines or using alternative ingredients. Many conservationists regard changing attitudes in this way as one of the keys to ending poaching and preserving wild tigers and rhinos.

China: "King of the Hundred Beasts"

What's ironic is that no culture loves and exalts the tiger more than China. If anything, China's history with the tiger is even older than India's.

An ancient Chinese epithet for the tiger is the King of the Hundred Beasts. The tiger was considered a living force of nature and a conscious spiritual presence, which village priests and leaders tried to appease and appeal to for mercy. Tiger talismans, with the Chinese character for "king" etched in their foreheads, were believed to ward off evil. As far back as Chinese folklore, art, and literature go, the regal tiger stalks.

This love of the tiger arose even though tigers have been legendary as man-eaters throughout China's history. One researcher accessed village records in four southern China provinces dating back 1,900 years and tallied a *minimum* of 10,000 tiger-related injuries and deaths. Significantly, the peak years of tiger-human conflict all coincide with periods of explosive population growth in southern China.

As a fourteenth-century Chinese poem called "Ballad of a Ferocious Tiger" says,

How fierce indeed a tiger, yet all still rejoice
If only it keeps to its swaggering far off in the mountains' depths.

Historically, several subspecies of tiger have lived within China's borders, such as the Amur tiger and the Caspian tiger (which is the third subspecies to go extinct, in the 1950s). However, the South China tiger is the only one to live solely in China, and it's the nation's iconic species.

By 1958, perhaps 4,000 South China tigers remained, but that year Chairman Mao Zedong launched an "antipest" campaign against the tiger and instituted a bounty. By 1982, fewer than 200 South China tigers remained, and TCM practitioners started looking beyond China's borders for tigers to use in medicine. Over the next decade, poachers feeding the TCM market hunted tigers in Siberia, Thailand, Malaysia, Indonesia, and India, as India learned in 1993.

All of this was illegal. All international trade in tiger parts was banned in 1975 by the Convention on International Trade in Endangered Species, or CITES, which is run by the United Nations. However, CITES can't directly enforce this ban. Each nation must police its own borders to stop any illegal wildlife trade.

In 1986, all the world's tigers were classified as endangered. Since, clearly, the supply of wild tigers was rapidly dwindling and was no longer enough to satisfy TCM practitioners, China raised the idea in 1992 that perhaps CITES would legalize the sale and use of tiger parts from *farmed* tigers—that is, tigers born and raised entirely in captivity.

The world went nuts. Harvest tigers like *cattle*? In the face of worldwide protests, China withdrew this proposal. Then it did a complete about-face: in 1993—the same year that the tiger poachers in Delhi were caught—China banned all domestic use of tiger parts in traditional Chinese medicine.

China's domestic ban was total. Tiger bone was removed as an approved ingredient in TCM, factories stopped making tiger-bone medicine, and tiger-bone stockpiles were sealed. Since then, China's ban has been used as a model for other Asian countries with similar practices.

China was universally praised for this powerful act of tiger protection, but you can't halt ancestral cultural practices with a pen stroke. Following this ban, China's market for tiger-bone products declined sharply, but it has never dried up. To try to change minds, some leaders of traditional Chinese medicine have implored TCM practitioners not to use tiger-bone products, and they have proposed substitutions for tiger that they consider equally effective as medicine. In 2006, the Dalai Lama successfully convinced many Tibetans not to wear tiger fur or use tiger products. So far this hasn't been enough.

Nor has making tiger products illegal. If there's enough money in it, someone will always risk arrest, injury, and even death to kill a wild tiger. In 2013, a tiger was calculated to be worth $100,000 in China's black market. For impoverished locals living near tiger reserves, even one percent of that profit is incentive enough to poach tigers. And organized poachers function just like organized crime. Paradoxically, they actually make *more* money as tigers become more endangered and harder to get, since each can be valued astronomically.

Further, China has acted ambivalently toward its own ban. After 1993, tiger farms in China multiplied rapidly, and today, China has about 200 tiger farms containing well over 5,000 captive-bred tigers—which is more than all the world's *wild* tigers. Two enormous Chinese facilities house over 1,000 tigers each. What do these facilities need with so many tigers? Legally, China allows breeding captive tigers only for entertainment and conservation. Yet tiger farms breed far more animals than they could ever use for either purpose, and farms are continually accused of secretly harvesting their tigers and selling them on the black market.

In 2007, as a response to this, CITES amended its international ban on tiger parts to specifically outlaw farmed, captive-bred tigers. The fear is that if captive-bred tigers are sold legally, this will increase demand—which will increase illegal poaching of wild tigers. Also, in a legal market, it would be impossible to distinguish legal from illegal tiger parts, and the ban on wild tigers would be impossible to enforce.

China's tiger farms are obviously banking that someday soon China will end its domestic ban. If that day comes, these farms will dominate the market in tiger parts and make a killing.

However, China may not end its ban. China loves the tiger and is actually trying to bring its own tiger back.

Reintroducing the South China Tiger

The South China tiger hasn't been seen outside a cage for twenty-five years, and most consider the subspecies extinct in the wild. About seventy South China tigers live in captivity, all bred from six wild tigers that were captured before 1970.

In 2002, China initiated a rewilding program that hopes to release eventually some of these captive-bred South China tigers. All rewilding projects face huge hurdles, and the biggest one here is, where to put a tiger? There exists no suitable, sizable patch of true wilderness left in southern China,

Pleistocene Park: Restoring
Mammoths & the Mammoth Steppe

Since the 1990s, Russian ecologist Sergey Zimov has been trying to re-create the Pleistocene from scratch by rewilding a small patch of Siberia. One day, not only will "Pleistocene Park" host all sorts of endangered megafauna like the Siberian tiger, but it could be home to the resurrected woolly mammoth—should scientists eventually bring this extinct behemoth back to life.

Yet unlike the fictional *Jurrasic Park*, this is no theme park. This isn't being built for tourists. Zimov's main goal is to combat climate change.

His theory goes like this: in the Pleistocene, when Siberia was crowded with megaherbivores, the collective impact of all that grazing and all that poop maintained an ecosystem that we call the mammoth steppe, a type of Arctic grassland. Once those Pleistocene giants went extinct, the mammoth steppe transformed into the forested, mossy, frozen tundra we know today.

The problem now is that the tundra is melting. The mammoth steppe grasslands originally stored massive amounts of carbon in the soil—and as the tundra melts, those vast quantities of carbon are being released back

which is one of the most densely populated regions on the globe. Farms would need to be converted back to forest, people relocated, and large prey reintroduced to create a place where wild tigers might thrive.

The captive South China tigers also suffer from inbreeding. They are no longer very healthy themselves. One possibility is to crossbreed the South China tigers with Indochine tigers to increase their genetic diversity. Not only are these subspecies closely related and geographic neighbors, but the genetic profile of the captive South China tigers seems to indicate some crossbreeding has already occurred. Ideally, China would like to preserve pure South China tigers, but a more genetically robust hybrid tiger might have the best chance to survive on its own.

Indeed, in the 1990s in the United States, the Florida panther was into the air. Increased carbon gas, as you may know, is one of the main spurs for global warming.

If Zimov is correct—if ice age megafauna were responsible for creating the mammoth steppe ecosystem—then repopulating Siberia with mega-herbivores could bring the mammoth steppe back, which would help keep all that carbon in the ground.

Right now, Pleistocene Park is small. About 10 square miles hold modest populations of five large herbivores: moose, Yakutian horse, musk ox, reindeer, and wisent. As soon as he can, Zimov wants to build tremendous herds of these cold-adapted species and also add wild Bactrian camel, yak, wapiti, saiga antelope, and wood bison, along with the Siberian tiger.

The keystone species, though, is the woolly mammoth, whose de-extinction is a signature effort of the Long Now Foundation. As cofounder Stewart Brand has said, "We're bringing back the mammoth to restore the steppe in the Arctic. One or two mammoths is not a success. A hundred thousand mammoths is a success."

Imagine that.

brought back from the edge of extinction by crossbreeding the last individuals with Texas cougars.

Today, tigers worldwide live in only 7 percent of their historic range, which—not unlike dismembering an animal for its parts—has itself been chopped up into sometimes unworkable "islands" that can't function as self-sustaining wholes. Tigers need more space than most animals—it should be said, for our own good—but the countries with wild tigers are inconveniently crowded. Between them, India and China house and feed a third of humanity.

Thus, if China, of all nations, could increase tiger habitat even a little, and restore one lost wild species, it would be another conservation miracle. It would give the tiger one more distant mountain where we might gladly admire its swaggering self. ⤳

CHINA

YANGTZE
RIVER

SHANGHAI

BAIJI: GODDESS OF THE YANGTZE

EXTINCTION: Qi Qi, the last known baiji, died in 2002; the species was declared extinct in 2007

It's easy to love dolphins. They are playful, smart, social, and friendly. They top the short list of animals—along with apes, elephants, us, and a few others—who clearly display self-awareness. They are legendary for their occasional life-saving actions—rescuing humans from drowning and even from shark attacks. They are so intelligent and emotionally sensitive, they help us in dolphin-assisted therapy.

Who would ever want to hurt a dolphin?

No one, really. We've always felt a special connection. Take away our hands and put us in the sea, and what do we imagine we'd turn into? Dolphins. That's how the ancient Greeks explained the ocean-going bottlenose dolphin. And that's how the ancient Chinese explained the baiji, the freshwater river dolphin who dove under and around their sampans in the mighty Yangtze River.

But then, you know how this story is going to end. The baiji would not be in this book, otherwise. Of all the tales of extinction here, this one might be the most heartbreaking because we never meant to harm the baiji.

We loved the baiji, but it wasn't enough.

Birth of the Yangtze Goddess

For thousands of years, the baiji was considered the Goddess of the Yangtze and revered as a gentle, kind presence who helped people by predicting the weather. Many refused to hunt or eat baiji out of honor and respect. Folktales about the baiji were once told up and down the Yangtze River, and many of its origin myths have the same tragic premise.

A young maiden is being ferried across the river to be sold into slavery or forced into marriage. In one version, she is already a captive, while in another her scheming stepfather tricks her into making the crossing. Either way, halfway across, the man is overcome with lust and attacks the maiden, so to save herself, she jumps into the river and drowns.

However, because of her pure spirit, the girl transforms into a white dolphin, the baiji. Meanwhile, a storm erupts and the man falls overboard, whereupon he transforms into a dark "river pig," or the Yangtze finless porpoise.

Other stories have remarkably similar endings, with drowned daughters or women becoming dolphins and impure, imperfect men becoming porpoises. Sure, these stories might be sharp critiques of gender relations in ancient China, but they also imply that these water-living mammals possess human-like consciousness. If the baiji wasn't originally human, how else to explain its stunningly human-like nature: giving birth to live young and nursing like humans, "standing" in the water, socializing, whistling in apparent conversation, even flashing that winning smile?

As we've seen, humans often closely identify with the largest species, and one way we "explained" the baiji's obvious intelligence was to imagine they were once us.

Actually, baiji are older than us. The Lipotidae family (of which baiji were the last living member) evolved some 20 million years ago, and the Hominidae family, which eventually led to modern humans, didn't arise until some 5 million years later.

Some river dolphins are older even than marine dolphins and porpoises. Ocean-going cetaceans branched off about 10 million years ago, making them half the age of baiji, and marine dolphins are adolescents compared to India's freshwater Ganges River dolphins, which are about 30 million years old. Like giant tortoises, river dolphins are among Earth's handful of "living fossils," species so ancient we want them to stop driving before they hurt someone.

Since most river dolphins are virtually blind, they shouldn't be driving, anyway. Most of the world's big rivers are muddy highways, and river dolphins are famous for their tiny eyes and poor sight. River dolphins compensate with highly developed echolocation or sonar; they "see" through sound with such accuracy that they could, literally, find a needle in a haystack. If the haystack were underwater.

The baiji's eyes were positioned higher on the head than those of most other dolphins, to make best use of the feeble sunlight trickling through the Yangtze murk. Want a gross fact to impress your friends? A baiji fetus began with its eyes in a "normal" position, but they traveled upward as the fetus developed.

River dolphins are physically different from marine dolphins in other ways. They have long, narrow snouts filled with sharp, tiny teeth, low dorsal fins, rounded pectoral fins, and extremely flexible necks. The baiji was not wholly white, as legend suggests: it was whitish on the bottom and a more common light gray or gray-blue on top. The baiji was 7.5 to 8 feet long and weighed from 300 to 500 pounds.

Several species of river dolphin can move between fresh- and saltwater, but the baiji did not. The baiji lived in the Yangtze alone, ranging from the lower Three Gorges region all the way southeast to where the river empties into the East China Sea. It also traveled into various tributaries and occupied both Dongting and Poyang Lakes. We can only speculate how many baiji lived when the species flourished. Top predators always number the fewest, and baiji may never have totaled more than 5,000 or 6,000.

Room to Live: Biodiversity & SAR

What is biodiversity, and why is it important? Usually measured by counting, biodiversity is more than a numbers game. It's a dynamic. Biodiversity is what results when life interacts to form a self-sustaining whole.

Biodiversity is defined in several important ways. Scientists look at genetic diversity, population size, and the total number of species and of types of species within an ecosystem.

Genetic diversity makes for a healthy animal population. When it's lacking—such as when a critically endangered species is down to its last individuals—inbreeding can cause inherited genetic problems and disease.

Yet any small population, even if it's genetically diverse, is at risk of being extinguished due to everyday or random events, like drought, forest fires, predation, annual birth rate fluctuations, and so on. As a population declines, as with the passenger pigeon and the baiji, it reaches a threshold below which it can't recover on its own.

Meanwhile, stable ecosystems typically have multiple species spread among a full range of types, creating a balanced food web. For instance, if a habitat has only one top predator, the loss of that species could undermine

Giants of the Long River

The Yangtze River has changed a great deal since humans first settled along it. It was originally, and in many ways still is, one of the greatest natural wonders of the world. Starting in Tibet, it tumbles for 3,915 miles, making it the earth's third-longest river after the Amazon and the Nile. Called the Amazon of the East, the Yangtze was once the Amazon's equal in terms of biodiversity and ecological importance. The baiji was neither the largest nor the strangest creature ever to inhabit these waters; eye-popping species once abounded. Today, the Chinese treasure the Yangtze's beauty and wilderness, even if that wilderness is a shadow of its former self.

the entire ecosystem, while the extinction of one among several similar prey species might have minimal effect.

When it comes to biodiversity, more is often better, but what allows for biodiversity in the first place is space. As scientists have learned, ecosystems have limited "carrying capacities." Each can hold only so many beings and so many species, and when habitat shrinks or grows, the number of species inevitably does, too.

A reliable formula can even predict by how much. Called the species-area relationship, or SAR, this calculation (expressed as the formula $S = CA^z$) boils down to this: every tenfold increase in area doubles the number of species. Conversely, as biologist Edward O. Wilson writes, "Every tenfold *decrease* in area cuts the number of species in half."

In other words, if a 10,000-square-mile habitat can hold 300 species, then a similar 1,000-square-mile habitat will hold only 150 species, and vice versa.

Thus, whenever we shrink or expand habitats, we are in effect deciding how many species have room to live.

In this, size always matters.

What is the river like now? Imagine taking the populations, cities, industry, and agriculture of California, Japan, and Bangladesh and slathering them along the river course, from the Three Gorges Dam to Shanghai, and you'd come close. The middle and lower parts of the Yangtze River, the baiji's original territory, are some of the dirtiest, noisiest, busiest, most crowded places on Earth. Over 400 million people, a third of China, live in the Yangtze basin, and for millennia, the river has been the agricultural, economic, and industrial heart of China. The fertile Yangtze delta provides the bulk of China's rice and fish, and a series of hydroelectric dams provide power.

In many ways, the Yangtze River made modern China, and to the Chinese, it is simply "the Long River"—in the same way New Yorkers call Manhattan "the City." Nothing else compares.

Given the Yangtze's two identities, the baiji's extinction is easily understood. When this many people and this much wildlife try to coexist in one place, something has to give. Invariably, it's giant species. The baiji was the river's first declared extinction in modern times, but it wasn't the first giant to be driven from the Yangtze, and it's unlikely to be the last.

The Chinese paddlefish may already be extinct. The last one caught was in 2007. Before that, it hadn't been seen since 2003. Averaging 12 feet long and about 550 pounds, it's a tough fish to miss. Legendary individuals have reached twice that size, making the Chinese paddlefish one of the largest freshwater fishes in the world. Because of its ridiculously long snout, it's sometimes called an elephant fish, but its nose is more like a stiff beaver tail brim over a cavernous mouth.

A rival for the title of "Yangtze's largest fish" is the Chinese sturgeon. Armored like a medieval knight, ranging from 7 to 16 feet long, and weighing 450 to 1,100 pounds, sturgeon are the Yangtze's oldest resident. They've been returning from the sea to breed in this river for 140 million years. *That's* a living fossil. The Chinese consider the sturgeon a national treasure, and it's so endangered some call it the "panda of the river." Thankfully, captive-breeding programs have proven very successful.

The Chinese alligator and the Yangtze giant softshell turtle are two other large, critically endangered species. Chinese alligators can reach 7 feet and 100 pounds, while turtles are half the length and twice the weight—big enough to make them the world's largest freshwater turtle. Both species are also virtually extinct in the wild, yet while alligators breed well in captivity, the turtles can't quite get the hang of it.

What about the "river pig"? Undeserving of its unflattering nickname, the Yangtze finless porpoise is dark gray, with a bulbous forehead, a stubby face, and no dorsal fin to speak of, but it has the sleek, elegant body of cetaceans everywhere. A mature adult typically reaches 6.5 feet long and 100 pounds. Sometimes gathering in groups of up to fifty, this is the world's only freshwater porpoise, and with only about 1,200 remaining, it is now so endangered it's considered the "second baiji."

Dense forests once blanketed the middle and lower Yangtze, and these hosted a wide range of large land mammals: tigers, elephants, rhinos, and more. As the forests disappeared, so did the giants. China's great symbol of conservation, the giant panda, is today confined to the Yangtze's upper reaches. Vast flocks of regal migrating waterbirds—including the endangered Siberian crane—still winter on Poyang Lake, but the impact of Three Gorges Dam may upset their habitat and force many to leave.

In short, the Yangtze River is itself giant, and it once bristled with giant species. Each has a tale like the baiji.

A River of Noise, a Thousand Cuts

The Western world did not know of the baiji until 1914, when seventeen-year-old Charles Hoy shot one with a rifle. The son of a school principal, Charles was on a duck hunt near Dongting Lake, and several baiji were "in shallow water working up the mud in their search for fish," wrote Charles, adding that, when shot, the animal "gave a cry like that of a water-buffalo calf."

In a famous photo, Charles posed over his catch. He later declared baiji meat to be "excellent" and "quite tender," and then he sold the skull and part of the spine to the US National Museum of Natural History, which in 1918 declared the dolphin a "new" species and gave it a Latin name, *Lipotes vexillifer*.

Charles was not the first person to eat baiji. Local Chinese venerated the dolphin, but they were practical and often poor. Since at least 200 BC, Chinese hunted baiji for lamp oil and medicine and occasionally for food, though not everyone liked the taste. Some locals even considered the baiji a pest, since it competed with them for fish.

Whatever impact this had on the species, one date stands out as a turning point: 1949. That year the Chinese Communist Party came to power and, led by Mao Zedong, created the People's Republic of China. Almost immediately, Mao inaugurated the Great Leap Forward. This was his plan to turn China's society of rural peasants and farmers into a modern, industrial nation almost overnight.

Mao once declared, "Man must conquer nature," and his policies aimed to do just that. Farmers stopped tending crops to forge steel. Along the Yangtze, people migrated en masse to the cities, cut down forests, raised factories, and built dams to harness the river's power. All this change, however, was too much too fast, and it led to famines that killed tens of millions of people, particularly in the early 1960s.

As a result, as a Hong Kong journalist once said, "the goddess of the Yangtze became lunch."

Impoverished locals were faced with a bitter choice, which one Yangtze River fisherman expressed eloquently in the 1990s: "Back in the sixties we needed to eat…. It didn't matter that we had once called them goddesses. We didn't care…. Yangtze fishermen have good hearts, you know. We love this river. We love the fish. We love the dolphin and we revere her. But back then—back then it was very different. It was very difficult. Mao did some terrible things. We had to eat. We thought we had no choice. It was the dolphins, or it was our children. Which would you choose?"

From the 1950s onward, in addition to this increased hunting, the baiji's life was made infinitely worse by three things: fishing methods, pollution, and ship traffic.

Two types of indiscriminate fishing often killed baiji accidentally. Gill nets were set up near shore, and baiji would get their long beaks stuck in the nets and drown. Even worse were rolling hook long lines, or rolling hook trawls. The length of a football field, these lines were covered with a thousand close-set barbs and left to tumble along the river bottom, snagging whatever was unlucky enough to get caught. The hooks, some 8 inches long, would rake the skin of a baiji, who either became too tangled to escape or often died later from the wounds.

"LIKE GIANT TORTOISES, RIVER DOLPHINS ARE AMONG EARTH'S HANDFUL OF 'LIVING FOSSILS,' SPECIES SO ANCIENT WE WANT THEM TO STOP DRIVING BEFORE THEY HURT SOMEONE."

The Yangtze River also became filled with ever-greater amounts of untreated waste and deadly chemicals from the factories, refineries, power plants, and cities sprouting along it. This included many of the worst pollutants, like mercury, cadmium, cyanide, and PCBs, which we now know can trigger cancer, organ damage, and physical deformities in fish and river mammals.

Finally, the growing human population and increased manufacturing meant that shipping on the Yangtze grew exponentially. One estimate is that, in 1949, perhaps 500 ships operated on the Yangtze; by the 1980s, tens of thousands of ships, including the largest freight vessels, were moving millions of tons of cargo each year.

People noticed that baiji were not very good at avoiding these ships. As baiji numbers declined, boat collisions became a leading cause of death. From our perspective, this didn't make sense. A dolphin's echolocation is more accurate than sight.

In 1988, author Douglas Adams (of *The Hitchhiker's Guide to the Galaxy* fame) visited China as part of a nature program on elusive, endangered animals. Unable to spot a Yangtze river dolphin, Adams decided to lower a microphone into the river to hear what a baiji hears. He was surprised that "instead of hearing the roar of each individual ship's propeller, what we heard was a sustained shrieking blast of pure white noise, in which nothing could be distinguished at all."

Water conducts sound extremely well. People and their machines were creating so much noise that it had turned the Yangtze into a horrifying echo chamber. The baiji couldn't hear, and so they couldn't see, and in their confusion they were running directly into ships and their propellers.

Adams is one of the funniest writers around. If you need proof, read *Last Chance to See*, his book on the baiji and other endangered animals. But here his sense of humor faltered:

> I realised with the vividness of shock that somewhere beneath or around me there were intelligent animals whose perceptive universe we could scarcely begin to imagine, living in a seething, poisoned, deafening world, and that their lives were probably passed in continual bewilderment, hunger, pain, and fear.

Qi Qi & Baiji Beer

Beginning in the 1980s, China tried to save the baiji. China assigned the river dolphin its highest conservation status: First Order of Protected Animals. It banned catching baiji and eventually banned rolling hook lines. China created protected areas along the Yangtze with reduced boat traffic and fishing. It also tried to start a captive-breeding program and a special dolphin reserve just off the river. As the baiji's plight caught the attention of the world, it became an icon of conservation.

Rescue efforts started in January 1980, when the most famous river dolphin in China's history was accidentally caught by a fisherman at Dongting

Lake. Dubbed Qi Qi (pronounced *chee chee*), this male baiji was badly injured by rolling hook lines, and he was transferred immediately to Wuhan, where the just formed River Dolphin Research Group kept him in a holding tank and treated his injuries. Miraculously, Qi Qi survived, even though at first researchers were so clueless they tried to feed him vegetables and apples rather than fresh fish.

As China's first captive baiji, Qi Qi soon became a national celebrity, one who would star in a real-world, dolphin version of *The Bachelor*. For two decades, all of China rooted for Qi Qi to hand a rose to some lucky female and start the world's first captive-breeding population of river dolphins.

It did not go well. Three dolphins were captured in 1981, but two died within weeks, and a third, a male named Rong Rong, lived for only a year. In 1986, a male and a female were captured together. Within months, the male died, and the female, Zhen Zhen, was moved to Qi Qi's tank. Scientists soon realized Zhen Zhen was too young to breed, and though she lived another two and a half years, she died before reaching sexual maturity.

Meanwhile, Qi Qi kept circling his tank.

The town of Tongling was selected to host a permanent baiji reserve in a separate channel off the overpolluted, overfished, noisy Yangtze itself. Tongling embraced the baiji with open arms. Anticipating a tsunami of baiji tourism, the town quickly branded everything: baiji beer, a baiji hotel, baiji cola, baiji toilet paper, and even baiji bentonite, a mining product.

Trouble was, the baiji never came. Except for the tenacious Qi Qi, captive baiji had an upsetting habit of dying. Also, another competing baiji reserve was developed by the Wuhan researchers. Wuhan thought its reserve was better than Tongling's, and this seemed to epitomize the efforts to save the baiji: scientists barely understood the species, and they couldn't agree on how to care for it. Doubt and confusion kept people from acting faster or more effectively.

Through the 1980s and 1990s, regular surveys scoured the river for baiji, whose population estimates kept dropping. In 1981, researchers estimated there were about 400 baiji; in 1986, 300; in 1990, 200; in 1996, fewer than 100; and by 1999, an estimated 13.

Plus Qi Qi, who was getting a little high-strung waiting for a mate.

His last chance was in 1996. In December 1995, an adult female baiji was captured (after a decade of failed attempts) and placed in the Wuhan reserve. Six months later, however, dithering researchers still hadn't transferred Qi Qi for his long-anticipated rendezvous, and the female baiji was found dead.

No more wild baiji were captured after that, and in 2002, Qi Qi died, apparently of old age and diabetes. For over twenty-two years, Qi Qi had charmed the world, and his funeral was broadcast on China's national TV. Unknowingly, people mourned not just the end of an individual, but the end of a species.

In 2006, baiji expert Samuel Turvey and an international group of researchers surveyed the Yangtze River one last time. They found no dolphins, and afterward, the species was declared extinct. Qi Qi was the last known living baiji. Some people still hope that within the river's wide, brown waters a few dolphins may live unseen, but with each passing year it's less likely.

The baiji's birthplace, the Yangtze River, can't support them anymore.

River Dolphins Around the World

The baiji was not the world's only species of river dolphin. At least eight other species are recognized today, though most are threatened by a similar collection of impacts: accidental deaths from indiscriminate fishing methods; direct hunting; overfishing; dams that fragment habitat; pollution; boat collisions; and the constant pressure of living in confined rivers with too many people.

As a result, scientists now consider them a useful ecological measuring stick. A healthy river dolphin population means a healthy river. The two go hand in hand.

Generally speaking, river dolphins come in two types. Obligate river dolphins live exclusively in freshwater rivers. Facultative river dolphins live along coastal areas and migrate back and forth from river to sea. That said, any marine dolphin species can survive in freshwater. Bottlenose dolphins occasionally travel up the Thames and Seine Rivers.

Not counting the baiji, there are three species of facultative river dolphins and five species of obligate river dolphins, and they live among three regions: India, Asia, and Central and South America. The two most endangered species are the Yangtze finless porpoise and the Irrawaddy, which lives in Southeast Asia rivers like the Mekong River.

The most famous is the Amazon pink river dolphin (also called a boto or bufeo), who sports a bubble-gum-pink belly. Though typically light steel gray on top, it can be almost wholly pink or even shade to white. It is the largest river dolphin species—averaging 350 pounds and 8.5 feet long—and also the most abundant and least threatened. They range widely in the Amazon River and other river basins along northern South America.

Interestingly, the Amazon pink river dolphin has inspired its own myth of human transformation. Legends say the bufeo can transform into a handsome, elegantly dressed gentleman who woos young women and leads them to an underwater "dolphin city." This myth apparently explains the parentage of children with unknown fathers: that rogue the bufeo did it.

Sounds cute and harmless, but in Amazonian communities it's long spurred a desire for bufeo "love charms." Like tigers and rhinos, bufeo pay for these magical potions and talismans with their lives.

The baiji was the first cetacean driven to extinction by humans, but we need to change our ways if we want it to be the last. ⤸

AFRICA

ASIA

RHINOCEROSES: TANK OF THE VELDT

EXTINCTION: the western black rhino and the Vietnam Javan rhino were both declared extinct in 2011

The rhinoceros is one of the toughest vegetarians nature ever built.

Its massive, several-ton physique, encased in thick folds of gun-metal-gray hide, is topped by a deadly, 3-foot-long spike at the end of its nose. Rhinos radiate danger standing still, and yet they are surprisingly agile athletes—set off their hair-trigger alarm, and rhinos can turn on a dime, barreling toward enemies in a rampaging fury. Nature's version of a living tank or a mounted, medieval knight, rhinos can sprint up to 30 miles per hour, toss a lion, and gore an elephant.

Rhinos are so strong and formidable they seem almost overdesigned. How tough do you need to be to feed on grass, leaves, and shrubbery? In the Pleistocene, apparently, pretty darn tough. Armed, armored, and dangerous, rhinos have almost no natural predators. Even sabertooth cats probably gave them a wide birth. For 50 million years, rhinos have been one of Earth's most successful herbivores, and over the last 4 million years, modern rhinos have changed hardly at all.

Why should they? Rhinos are perfectly adapted to take care of themselves. Until now.

Today, the opposite is true. For all their daunting attributes, rhinos find themselves in the same precarious position as so many other giant species whose fate is in our hands. Because of us, rhinos have become one of Earth's most endangered species; yet without us, they would be long gone already.

The reasons are familiar. The plights of tigers and lions are very similar. However, the rhino's story also embodies the sometimes violent, modern-day extremes of both wildlife poaching and wildlife preservation. Protecting rhinos might be one of the most dangerous jobs in conservation, since it amounts to volunteering to work in a war zone.

Horn of Gold

That horn is the problem. In a way, a rhino's horn is unlike any other animal's. It doesn't have a core of bone like an aurochs's horn or a moose's antler. It's not an errant tooth like a narwhal's spike. Rhino horn is made almost entirely of compressed keratin fibers, a similar protein to what's in hair, fingernails, and animal hooves. The keratin horn builds up over time, it can be polished and sharpened by rubbing it against wood or rock, and it will regrow if it breaks.

Rhino horns vary in size. Javan rhino horns are stubby, less than a foot long. Most other rhino species grow horns from 1 to 3 feet long. And Africa's white rhinos have the longest horns of all; theirs occasionally reach up to 5 feet, and the longest ever recorded was over 6 feet.

Earth's first rhinos didn't have horns. Most early species had tusks, which are overgrown canine teeth. We don't know why modern rhinos eventually developed horns instead, but it's an effective weapon for a creature who fights with its face.

In itself, keratin isn't valuable. We don't exactly treasure our fingernail clippings. But for different people in modern times, rhino horn has been literally worth its weight in gold.

For instance, in the 1960s and 1970s, it became extremely popular in Yemen and the Middle East to own ceremonial daggers with elaborately carved rhino horn handles. Called *jambiyas*, these daggers are bestowed upon young Muslim men as a male rite of passage, and how they're made signifies social status.

Like the ivory from an elephant's tusk, rhino horn has been used for centuries in art and ornamentation, such as for decorative cups. But the cultural frenzy for gilded, rhino horn daggers drove prices through the roof. At the time, one such *jambiya* might sell for $10,000, and poachers killed thousands of rhinos annually so they could sell their horns to feed this market. North Yemen once accounted for perhaps 40 percent of all illegal rhino horn imports.

Today, that particular rhino horn fashion has faded, though it has never disappeared entirely. In the mid-1980s, due to worldwide concern, North Yemen started enforcing bans on this illegal trade, and its rhino horn imports dropped significantly.

Now, rhino horn is desired almost solely for its alleged curative properties. Some of this demand relates to traditional Chinese medicine (TCM). In this, the tiger and the rhino face an identical threat. Like the tiger, all parts of the rhino have traditionally been used in TCM to treat a wide range of ailments, but rhino horn is considered the animal's most potent ingredient. Accounts and TCM practitioners vary, but historically rhino horn has been used to cure fevers, diphtheria, liver problems, flu, laryngitis, bad eyesight, nosebleeds, and food poisoning.

As with the tiger, China officially banned the use of rhino horn in TCM in 1993, but despite this, use of illegal rhino horn remedies continues among some practitioners of TCM and of other traditional medicines in Asia.

However, completely separate from TCM, recent myths about rhino horn have emerged. In the 2000s, some in Asia peddled the belief that rhino horn cures hangovers (while also being an intoxicant), and in Vietnam, a story spread that rhino horn could cure cancer. Though widely denounced as pure quackery, these claims have nevertheless led in the last five years to a spike in rhino horn poaching and in black market prices.

Estimating the true price of rhino horn on the black market is tricky guesswork. In the 1980s, one estimate was that a 2- to 5-pound horn was worth $50,000. In the 1990s, another source estimated that rhino horn was worth up to $8,000 a pound. Prices fell to about $2,300 a pound in

2009, and then they soared to over $30,000 a pound by 2013.

As famous conservationist Lawrence Anthony once wrote: "If you truly want to grasp the situation faced by conservationists, do what a poacher does and look at a rhino and see a three-foot-long horn made of pure gold…. What should be locked securely in a vault instead walks around on four legs in the bush."

The War Over Wildlife

Most wild rhinos are in fact confined and to varying degrees protected in wildlife preserves in Africa, India, and Southeast Asia. To poachers, these parks are not unlike banks, with the poachers being the bank robbers. To get rich, all a local poacher needs is a gun, some bullets, and a buyer willing to pay for the illicit goods.

Killing rhinos is relatively easy, especially compared to poaching tigers. Dehorning takes only a few minutes. As with the tiger, poverty drives some people to become poachers, while for others poaching is a profession: groups of well-armed, well-organized, international smugglers make it their business to keep demand and prices high.

To take a job guarding rhinos and tigers is deadly work. Both the animals and those who hunt the animals are willing to kill you. Rangers are trained and armed like soldiers. Some are outfitted with modern technology like GPS and the latest weaponry, and they wage what amounts to jungle warfare. But many more parks are underfunded, and park rangers are outnumbered and outgunned compared to poachers.

In India's Kaziranga National Park—one of the best protected parks in India, with one of the most aggressive stances against poachers—conservationist Steve Winter said rangers are still "a ragtag army, paid a pittance and lacking adequate gear, from threadbare uniforms and 70-year-old rifles that frequently misfire to flickering flashlights and poor footwear."

Given the dangers, why sign up for this job? In 2013, one Kaziranga ranger said, "These animals are like our family. We protect them from hunters like we would protect our own children."

Conservationist Ian Player found the same thing fifty years earlier during his time protecting white rhinos in South Africa. Player wrote, "I had seen rangers work day and night, prepared to give their lives to the cause of the Umfolozi Game Reserve and the white rhino, prepared to die for a piece of land they could never own, prepared to be maimed or blinded, not for a pittance of a salary but for love."

Yet as in any war, casualties pile up on all sides. Rhinos, rangers, and poachers are all shot, injured, and killed. Since 1985 in Kaziranga alone, over 100 poachers have been killed and over 600 people arrested, while poachers have killed over 500 rhinos. Meanwhile, across India from 2012 to 2014, seventy-two rangers lost their lives, either to wildlife or to poachers.

In any circumstance, this level of deadly conflict isn't sustainable. Force and violence are never long-term solutions, but particularly as an approach to wildlife conservation, even if military-style protections are currently necessary to keep rhino poachers at bay. Ultimately, the only thing that will secure the rhino's future is to change the economics that drive the war over wildlife. That means changing human attitudes, for it's always human desire that sets the price, both in lives lost and in money.

If people decided the rhino could keep its horn, then the problems of coexistence would revert to the usual ones: giving this ancestral giant the space it needs to attend to the business of living without hurting anyone.

Africa's White Rhino: The Extinction That Wasn't

Five species of modern rhino exist today, and Africa, the birthplace of the rhino, contains two: the white rhino (*Ceratotherium simum*) and the black rhino (*Diceros bicornis*). These names are famously inappropriate. All rhinos are shades of gray—gray like mossy granite, thunderclouds, and duct tape. Rhino species aren't distinguished by color, but by shape, behavior, and habitat.

The name "white" is possibly a corruption of the Afrikaans word *weit*, meaning "wide," to describe the square mouth of this grazing species, which

"RHINOS RADIATE DANGER STANDING STILL, AND YET THEY ARE SURPRISINGLY AGILE ATHLETES—SET OFF THEIR HAIR-TRIGGER ALARM, AND RHINOS CAN TURN ON A DIME, BARRELING TOWARD ENEMIES IN A RAMPAGING FURY."

lives to vacuum up grass in the savannah. Black rhinos, on the other hand, are browsers; they have an extended, prehensile upper lip ideal for grasping and tugging leaves and branches in Africa's bushy forests. Both have two horns but occupy different parts of the landscape.

In prehistoric times, these two rhino species essentially blanketed the continent south of the Sahara, and ancient rock art confirms that humans have always lived with and hunted rhinos, which are the world's second-largest land mammal after elephants. Among rhinos, whites are the biggest, standing 6 feet tall and ranging from 5,000 to well over 7,000 pounds, or 2.5 to almost 4 tons. Black rhinos are rarely larger than 3,000 pounds.

Early human hunting affected Africa's rhinos to some degree. People killed them with spears and drove them into stake-lined pits, and by about 4,000 years ago, early agriculturalists probably pushed white rhinos out of the best grasslands in east-central Africa. While the northern and southern white rhino subspecies diverged about 2 million years ago, people forced them to live at the extremes of their range.

In the early 1800s, the southern white rhino was the first to be discovered by Europeans, who, as they explored sub-Saharan Africa, found rhinos to be "excessively common," as one commentator said. If the species had suffered in its long acquaintance with humankind, you couldn't tell. This was great news to European big-game hunters, who turned killing rhinos into one of the nineteenth century's most popular sports.

One thing European hunters noticed right away: personality-wise, white rhinos and black rhinos differ like night and day. White rhinos can actually be very docile, while black rhinos are ticking time bombs. Startle a white rhino, and the animal's first instinct is to run away, unless it's protecting offspring. Startle a black rhino, and it will attack, "rushing and charging with inconceivable fierceness animals, stones, bushes—in short, any object that comes their way," as one nineteenth-century hunter wrote.

As a rule, it's hard to sneak up on a rhino. Despite being extremely near-sighted, rhinos compensate with excellent hearing and a phenomenal sense of smell. Their nasal passages are actually bigger than their brain, and one whiff of a sweaty hunter can set them off.

So naturally, deferring to prudence, big-game hunters targeted southern white rhinos almost exclusively, since they were bigger, had longer horns, and were easiest to kill. This hunting was so relentless and thorough that it's been compared to the slaughter of bison in America. By the 1890s, no southern white rhinos could be found, and most people considered the species extinct, joining Africa's extinct bluebuck, quagga, and Cape lion as one more nineteenth-century casualty.

Then, lo and behold, a dozen or so southern white rhinos were discovered near the Black and White Umfolozi Rivers in South Africa. As a result, in 1897, South Africa created several game preserves, with Umfolozi dedicated almost solely to protecting this species. Over the next six decades, now safe from hunters, the southern white rhino steadily recovered.

Yet this success occurred against a disturbing backdrop. At the same time that the southern white rhino was being protected, many large animals across southern Africa were, for a variety of reasons, being ruthlessly slaughtered. Vast stretches of land were cleared of wild megafauna to make way for livestock and agriculture, such as sugarcane. Native Zulu, themselves marginalized, squatted in reserve lands and killed game animals for food. And the rise of a domestic cattle disease spread by the tsetse fly led to an official wildlife extermination campaign (in order to get rid of the fly) that culminated in the widespread use of DDT, which decimated landscapes.

Today, it's hard to reconcile these events: why provide sanctuary for southern white rhinos while, often in the same parks, eliminating most other large charismatic species—like elephants and hippos, both of which were driven from Umfolozi?

To a degree, this reflected our lingering, contradictory, Victorian-era attitudes toward nature. People were fascinated by nature and wild animals when they were caged, contained, and no longer a threat, but they got rid of wildlife or eliminated wilderness if either impeded human progress or human society. Anything could be justified, since most felt nature only existed to serve humankind.

Attitudes toward nature have changed tremendously since then, but we still wrestle with this same conflict. Inevitably, all wildlife conservation must answer the same questions: When, or to what degree, does human self-interest trump the welfare of animals, and if we choose to preserve wildlife and wilderness, what cost are we willing to pay? What are we willing to give up, and how hard are we willing to work?

As for the southern white rhino, by 1953, the species had recovered beyond anyone's expectations, so much so that it was starting to overrun its environment. Over 400 rhinos crowded Umfolozi, and as the population kept growing, some would have to be killed if more space wasn't found. So more space was found. Starting in 1961, led by Umfolozi ranger and later parks chief Ian Player, Operation Rhino singlehandedly repopulated dozens of southern African parks by relocating white rhinos from Umfolozi (now called Hluhluwe-iMfolozi Park), and the program also sent southern white rhinos to zoos around the world.

This historic effort was a first in that it restored a species to some of its original range directly, without captive breeding, and it required pioneering new methods for darting, capturing, and transporting rhinos. Today, the southern white rhino population exceeds 20,000, which accounts for over 90 percent of all rhinos that exist.

Every other rhino species is considered threatened or critically endangered. For instance, the southern white's sibling, the northern white rhino, is one of the world's rarest animals. Its population count is down to three individuals. All live in a guarded preserve in Kenya, and all suffer from old age and illness. Captive-breeding efforts in recent years—attempts to breed northern white rhinos both with one another and with other rhino species—have been unsuccessful, and most consider those who remain "the walking dead." Extinction is only a matter of time.

The northern white rhino became extinct in the wild in 2006, when the last wild individuals were killed by poachers in Garamba National Park in the Democratic Republic of the Congo. That country was then in the midst of a civil war—leaving its parks essentially unguarded—and that year a last-ditch effort to find and rescue these rhinos failed. For an account of that attempt, and for a taste of what the war over wildlife is all about, read Lawrence Anthony's *The Last Rhinos*.

As Anthony wrote, "In African conservation you seldom win any war. Instead you win breathing space to hope that sanity will prevail."

Africa's Black Rhino: Dehorning Nature's Tank

Or, you could try thwarting poachers by beating them at their own game.

What if, instead of fighting to keep poachers out, you simply took away what they were after? What if you removed the rhino's horn first—but without killing the animal—thus eliminating the poacher's financial incentive?

If rhinos had no horns, would poachers leave them alone?

In the 1980s, African conservationists were desperate to stem the tide of rhino poaching, which was decimating the black rhino (as well as all but the southern white rhino). The accepted estimate is that Africa had a million black rhinos at the turn of the twentieth century, but by 1960 there were only 60,000, and by 1988, only about 3,500.

Dehorning was a crazy, controversial idea—the exact opposite of sanity—but if people didn't do something, the black rhino would soon be gone. So in 1989, Namibia embraced the strategy's cruel logic and became the first country to dehorn its black rhinos. Two years later, in 1991, Zimbabwe and Swaziland also dehorned their black rhinos.

All of which begged the question: without its horn, what is a rhino? And more importantly, could the rhino survive without it?

Rhinos occasionally use their horns to help them eat, by digging up roots and by pulling down branches. Mostly, though, the horn is used for fighting.

Rhinos are legendary combatants. Rhinos can kill lions, and they will even battle elephants for access to waterholes. An elephant has the size advantage, and its trunk is a deadly weapon, but rhinos are faster and more nimble, and if the elephant misses or miscalculates, the rhino will plunge in and gore the elephant in the belly.

Among rhinos, males and females sometimes fight, especially when they disagree over whether it's time to mate. Most often, though, males fight over territory. White rhinos are more territorial than black rhinos, but in both cases, territorial disputes are usually settled through ritualized confrontations that avoid direct violence. These can amount to nose-to-nose "staring contests" that end when one rhino defers, and then both back away while wiping their horns on the ground. At other times, rhinos will engage in "horn wrestling," or they charge with their shoulders, thus minimizing the risk of injury.

Sometimes, though, male rhinos fight in earnest, and when this happens, as Ian Player writes, "no quarter is given." Severe injury is common, and if neither submits, fights can last for hours, with each rhino charging and upthrusting its horn at the other's neck and belly or behind the foreleg. If one rhino falls, the other will descend instantly, goring it to death. During these epic battles, the forest shakes with the roars and screams of the bulls.

Without a horn, what exactly would rhinos do? In the early 1990s, conservationists tried to study and assess the impact of the dehorning programs. They found rhino behavior didn't change very much, nor did the animals' health seem to suffer. But the programs still turned out to be failures because, even when rhinos had no horns, poachers killed them anyway.

It didn't make sense. Some speculated that perhaps poachers killed rhinos before they realized the animals were hornless, or perhaps they killed rhinos out of spite, to show authorities that they could. Whatever the reason, rhinos still disappeared. In 1993, Zimbabwe suddenly revised the estimate of its black rhino population from about 2,000 animals to fewer than 500. Had 1,500 hornless rhinos been poached in two years, or had previous estimates been spectacularly wrong? Zimbabwe didn't explain, but within a few years, all the dehorning programs were canceled.

African parks returned to protecting black rhinos with their horns on, and by 2001, the black rhino population in Africa had dropped to about 2,300.

The Biggest Living Species

Here they are—the biggest animals alive. These sizes are the recorded extremes, but not always the biggest ever claimed. Many individuals are smaller.

On Land:

- Largest land mammal: African elephant; 11–13 feet tall, 6–7 tons
- Largest odd-toed ungulate: white rhinoceros; 13–15 feet long, 2.5–4 tons
- Largest even-toed ungulate: hippopotamus; 15–17 feet long, 2–3.5 tons
- Tallest land animal: giraffe; 18–20 feet tall, 1.5–2.5 tons
- Largest land carnivore: polar bear and Kodiak bear, tied; 9–10 feet tall (standing), 1,500–2,000 pounds,
- Largest snake: green anaconda; 20–30 feet long, 450–550 pounds
- Largest primate: Eastern lowland gorilla; 5.5 feet tall, 400–450 pounds

In the Water:

- Largest animal ever (and largest marine mammal): blue whale; 80–100 feet long, 160–200 tons
- Largest marine predator (and largest brain ever): sperm whale; 50–65 feet long, 40–50 tons; brain, 17–18 pounds
- Largest fish (and largest shark): whale shark; 32–42 feet long, 10–23 tons
- Largest carnivore: South Atlantic elephant seal; 19–23 feet long, 3.5-5.5 tons
- Largest ray: oceanic manta ray; 18–23 feet wide, 1.5–2.25 tons
- Largest freshwater fish: beluga sturgeon; 15–24 feet long, 2,500–3,450 pounds
- Largest reptile: saltwater crocodile; 17–20 feet long, 2,000–3,000 pounds
- Largest invertebrate (and largest cephalopod): colossal squid, 39–46 feet long, 1,100–1,650 pounds
- Largest amphibian: Chinese giant salamander; 4–6 feet long, 60–100 pounds

In the Air:

- Largest nonflying bird: ostrich; 7–9 feet tall, 300–350 pounds
- Heaviest flying bird: great bustard and kori bustard, tied; 4–5 feet long, 7.5–9 foot wingspan, 25–45 pounds
- Largest wingspan: wandering albatross, 3.5–4.5 feet long, 10–12 foot wingspan, 20–28 pounds
- Largest bird of prey: cinereous vulture; 3.5–4 feet long, 8–10 foot wingspan, 25–31 pounds

Fewer than ten of those were western black rhinos, one of four black rhino subspecies. These last western black rhinos lived in the forests of northern Cameroon, which was then engulfed in civil unrest and overrun with corruption. As with the northern white rhino, efforts to locate and protect the last of this subspecies were undermined by war itself. Governments rarely prioritize wildlife conservation when they are struggling to remain in power, and sometimes the authorities themselves become the poachers—using black market profits in the illegal wildlife trade to fund their militaries. This has been another aspect of the "war over wildlife."

In 2011, after it hadn't been seen in a decade, the western black rhino was declared extinct.

Still, since that low point in 2001, the black rhino has experienced a modest but notable recovery. Overall among its three remaining subspecies, the black rhino population has more than doubled, so that today they total about 5,000.

Southeast Asia: Rhinos in Love

There are three species of Asian rhino: the one-horned, classically wrinkled, and seemingly "armor-plated" Indian rhino (*Rhinoceros unicornis*); the woolly, two-horned Sumatran rhino (*Dicerorhinus sumatrensis*); and the one-horned Javan rhino (*Rhinoceros sondaicus*). Today, about 3,000 Indian rhinos live in India, and the vast majority, over 2,000, are protected within Kaziranga National Park.

Like Africa's northern white rhino, two of the Asian rhino species are among the rarest animals on Earth.

Fewer than fifty Javan rhinos remain in the wild, and they exist in only one place, Ujung Kulon National Park on Java. In the past, three subspecies of Javan rhino were once widespread across all of mainland Southeast Asia, from northeastern India to Vietnam. However, the Indian Javan rhino was hunted to extinction in the nineteenth century, and the Vietnam Javan rhino succumbed to poaching and was declared extinct in 2011, the same year as the western black rhino.

Sumatran rhinos number fewer than a hundred today, though they once extended from the Himalayan foothills south to Indonesia's islands. Like Africa's rhinos, they were once exterminated as agricultural pests, but the main threat today is poaching for rhino horn. They are the smallest rhino species, on average not weighing more than 2,000 pounds.

As Sumatran rhino numbers dwindled in the 1980s, some conservation organizations launched a controversial effort to restore the species through captive breeding. As with the red wolf, this was a last-ditch effort to stave off extinction. Rhinos are notoriously slow breeders, which is one reason why they decline so quickly under the pressure of hunting. In the wild, if rhinos don't kill one another, then almost nothing kills them except disease and old age. Occasionally, lions and hyenas will ambush a juvenile rhino, but most rhinos live about forty or fifty years.

Rhinos don't need to have kids very often, so they don't. A mother gives birth to a single calf (occasionally twins) every three to four years. Potentially, captive breeding is a way to speed up that process in a protected environment, but it was and remains a genuine challenge: it's expensive and labor-intensive; it further endangers wild populations by deliberately removing animals from the wild; and there's no guarantee of success.

At first, the Sumatran rhino program was an utter failure. Forty rhinos were taken from forests in 1984, and within a decade, half the rhinos had died and no births were recorded. Of the seven rhinos sent to the United States, four eventually died.

The worst fears of critics proved true: no one seemed to know how to care for this rare species. In America, keepers initially fed the Sumatran rhinos the same grasses that African rhinos eat, but Sumatran rhinos live in a rain forest. They couldn't survive on savannah grass. In 1994, keepers changed their meal plan to match the tropics, and finally the rhinos' health improved.

By then in the US, only three captive Sumatran rhinos remained: two females and one male at the Cincinnati Zoo. Yet getting them to breed was frustratingly impossible. Every time keepers put a male and a female together, the pair would fight as only rhinos can: slamming, screaming, and chasing each other until both were bloody. Water hoses were needed to separate them.

What on earth made rhinos fall in love?

Timing, apparently. Zoologists eventually realized that the female's receptive period lasts, at best, thirty-six hours. Once rhinos were paired within the narrow window of the female's estrus cycle, well… let's just say the fighting stopped.

Even then, babies were slow to follow. For years, the females miscarried until zoologists started giving them particular hormones to help the mother successfully carry a baby to term. Finally, in 2001, Andalas became the first captive-born Sumatran rhino, and in the years since, three more rhinos have been born in captivity.

Given the challenges, this qualifies as a tremendous victory. It's hard-won progress. Yet the lessons of the Sumatran rhino and the southern white rhino are complementary. They show how resilient species can be when they are left alone to take care of themselves, as well as how difficult it is for us to intervene and restore species once they are removed from the wild.

As conservationist Thane Maynard wrote about the Sumatran rhino program: "Does breeding a few rhinos save a species? Not by itself. Demonstrating the value of wild animals to the people in an area where they live is the number one way to help protect those species and their habitat." ↘

WRITTEN IN THE EARTH: THE SIXTH EXTINCTION & THE ANTHROPOCENE

My hope is that this book never needs a sequel. My hope is that so few species go extinct from this moment on that the only thing left to write about is how we kept today's giants in the world.

I hope we never have to explain where critically endangered species like the California condor, North Atlantic right whale, Asian elephant, Sumatran rhino, Amur tiger, and eastern gorilla went because they are still right here.

Inevitably, tales of extinct and endangered animals are sad, but this sadness shouldn't lead us to give up or give in to indifference. Numerous species, especially giants, live on the edge, with numbers so low it's hard to imagine how they will recover.

But with our help, they can. The red wolf, the Aldabra giant tortoise, and the southern white rhino are proof.

This epilogue is dedicated, then, to stepping back and taking the long view.

The Sixth Extinction: Defining a Crisis

The giants in this book are only a few of the species that have gone extinct over the last 500 years. In fact, more small species than large species are disappearing today, though that's partly because there are fewer giant species to begin with. In addition, the extinction rate has been increasing. Both of these things, the total number of extinctions and their pace, are what have led scientists to call what is happening the sixth extinction.

How many species and how fast? This is what everyone wants to know. The numbers scientists come up with vary widely, which is frustrating. There are no universally accepted, authoritative numbers. Here is a range of current estimates.

Among researchers who count only recorded extinctions, they calculate that some 77 to 111 mammal species have gone extinct since 1500. Of these extinctions, from 35 to 69 occurred since 1900, and one estimate is that 28 mammals have gone extinct in the last fifteen years. These are the lowest estimates, and they only count mammals.

Among all types of species, one source calculates that 1,200 have gone extinct since 1700, but at the higher end, another estimates that over *17,000 species* go extinct every year. While one source says 116 bird species have gone extinct since 1600, a different scientist calculates that, since 1200, over 2,000 bird species have gone extinct.

These estimates are extremely different, and seemingly in conflict, but partly they reflect different ways of counting. Scientists calculate using different assumptions. Each approach has flaws, but all may still reflect aspects of the truth. If we only count known, recorded extinctions, we're definitely underestimating the actual number—since some species are certainly going extinct without our knowing. But if we estimate a percentage of species that *might be* going extinct (based on estimates of how many species *may* exist), we can easily overestimate.

Further, scientists disagree over what counts as a full species, when to declare extinctions, and whether to include near extinctions or regional population losses. A species with two or three living members isn't dead yet, but it's "functionally extinct." If a species exists only in captivity, it's "extinct in the wild." If only a subspecies or regional population disappears, it's often said to be "extirpated." Three subspecies of tiger have gone extinct, but the tiger still lives, so is that three extinctions or none?

Some say we must count all these regional populations and partial extinctions to capture the true extent of the crisis, and some say this inaccurately overstates the problem.

The other important number to know is the extinction rate. To quantify our extinction crisis, we also need to compare the current extinction rate with the *average* extinction rate we'd expect under "normal" circumstances. As a rule of thumb, scientists estimate that the average extinction rate—called the "background extinction rate"—is 1 extinct species for every 10,000 species every 100 years. Expressed differently, that equals about one species in a million that goes extinct annually. This is just a guess, but it's the best tool we have. Scientists once tested a small sample size (like in a political poll), and they used it to calculate an overall percentage for all species.

One recent study tried to be deliberately conservative in order to confirm the *minimum* extinction rate that might be occurring. It found that, since 1500, that rate has been at least 8 to 15 times higher than normal among known vertebrate extinctions. Since 1900, it's been 22 to 53 times higher; for amphibians, the extinction rate may now be 100 times higher. Because this study counted only known extinctions, it risked underestimating to prove a point: that even the minimum extinction rate today qualifies as a serious problem. Many others calculate today's extinction rate as much higher.

In a nutshell, this means that, even using conservative estimates, more species are going extinct at a faster pace today than 500 years ago, 10,000 years ago, and maybe since the last mass extinction 65 million years ago.

By the time you read this, all these numbers will be higher. This can be said with confidence because extinction counts don't include endangered species. Today, over 190 species are listed as "critically endangered"; this status refers to species we think will probably go extinct in the near future no matter what happens. Plus, over 440 species are listed as "endangered"; this status refers to species we think will probably go extinct without serious conservation efforts. From 1996 to 2008, 156 species moved to a more endangered status.

Yet here's the underlying problem with all these numbers: we actually have no idea how many species exist, so we have no way of knowing how many species are going extinct. It may come as a surprise, but the level of our ignorance about species is astonishing. Scientists often argue heatedly over extinction rates, but it's a battle no one can win because *everyone* is guessing. We struggle to count species even as they are vanishing.

So far science has catalogued about 1.8 million species, and new species are named every year. Yet the total number of species on earth is usually estimated to be around 14 million. Some speculate that it's actually more like 100 million, but if we stick with 14 million species, that means humans have met, and named, at best 13 percent of all life on our planet, and maybe much less.

Bacteria, algae, fungi, insects—living beings all—we barely know. Most species fall into these four groups. We've named not even a million insects, and tens of millions may exist, and insects are some of the most successful and long-lasting species on Earth.

On the other hand, we know animal species the best, and large animals the best of all. We've catalogued 5,513 mammal species and 10,425 bird species, and that's believed to be most of them. We know possibly 88 percent of amphibians, and nearly 60 percent of all vertebrates. That's not *too* shabby.

So we can say at least this much: mammals, birds, amphibians, and vertebrates are leaving this world at an increasingly alarming rate. Estimating the entirety of the extinction crisis is like trying to measure the water in a waterfall. We grab a few cupfuls and guess at the rest.

The thirteen giants in this book are a cupful of species that we know have gone, or are going, over that waterfall. But their loss, and the reasons for it, illustrate what is happening everywhere.

The Anthropocene: Us, in the Picture

The sixth extinction is being driven mainly by the enormous impacts of human society on the globe. Stories about giants highlight this vividly. We are so influential that some scientists have proposed that we go ahead and rename the Holocene, which is our current geological era, the "Anthropocene."

Anthropo is Greek for "human."

If we're going to name an epoch after ourselves, does it have to be for such a lousy reason? But geologists aren't finger wagging. They are saying we should name the central force currently shaping Earth's environment. Human impacts on nature, the climate, and animals are so extensive that you can already read them in the geological record. With the violence of a meteor strike, our signature will be preserved forever in this particular sheaf of sediments.

Just as we once dug through layers of earth and discovered a long-lost world of enormous, vanished creatures—like glyptodonts and sabertooth cats—geologists in 10,000 years will dig through layers, reach today, and find that a great many strange and wonderful animals disappeared almost at once.

As we still do today, those geologists in the future, should they exist, will also ask why. What happened to all those animals? Written in the earth, the answer will be obvious.

Seven billion people leave a mark. Particularly over the last 500 years, our society has left no habitat untouched. Cleared forests, agriculture, industry, pollution, hunting, and even the spread of nonnative, invasive species will be read easily in the composition of the soil, the fossilization of animals, and the evidence of human life.

Despite all this, the story of the Anthropocene remains unfinished, and one critical difference separates this geological age and this extinction crisis from every other: us. We know what's happening as it's happening, and with this awareness, we can act in effective ways to repair damage, restore ecosystems, increase wilderness, and recover species. If we can accomplish those things, it will be written in the earth also.

Future geologists would read *that* story with awe, for it would look like nothing else in Earth's long history.

When Cro-Magnons painted their wondrous visions of prehistoric wildlife, they mostly left themselves out of the picture, but we can no longer do that. We are everywhere today, and we aren't going anywhere. Our presence, our attitudes, and our actions are now inseparable from the fates of Earth's species. Putting ourselves in the picture means seeing that we live in the landscape we're observing, and that our presence always has an impact. It also means accepting responsibility for that impact and acting in ways that take into account the welfare of everyone, including nature.

As this book's stories show, when we act in selfish ways at the expense of species, nature, and wilderness, we often harm and even destroy those things, and this hurts ourselves. The impacts may be felt directly, such as when wild species we love or depend on go extinct. Or they may be felt indirectly as harm to the overall environment. But ultimately, every ecosystem and species matters because we need a sustainable, healthy biosphere for our own survival, and the planet needs all its pieces in working order.

And yet, as this book's stories also show, we can't "save" species and preserve ecosystems at the expense of human welfare. The dynamics of poaching make that crystal clear: wildlife laws and park boundaries are meaningless if people don't respect them, and poverty makes people desperate, so that they will do, or take, whatever they need to survive.

This applies to nations. Impoverished countries are equally desperate to use their natural resources, and if conserving wildlife hurts more than it helps, then conservation will fail or never even be attempted.

Putting ourselves in the picture is recognizing that, at this point and perhaps forever, conservation, social justice, and economic well-being are all related.

Gardeners of Wilderness

What can any of us do? We can become gardeners of wilderness.

This sounds like an oxymoron. Gardens have borders; they are orderly, managed creations. Wilderness is creativity itself, unmanaged and free. The two are opposites, but merging them is the task we face. We must crossbreed these types of landscapes to make more robust, sustainable hybrids.

This book's stories describe many of things that are being done and that can be done to conserve wildlife (and Call to Action will lead you to more). All have their place; none are perfect in every situation. We will always need to be flexible and figure out the best approach each time, and as situations change, conservation will need to change, too.

However, how we conceptualize problems guides the solutions we come up with. That's why I suggest that this book's stories represent a "crisis of coexistence." We often present extinction as the problem, and conservation usually focuses on "saving species." But if keeping species alive were the only goal, then we could preserve many animals in zoos.

Animals in zoos don't help nature. Nature needs wild animals interacting in landscapes the way they evolved to do. Healthy, self-sustaining ecosystems depend on this biodiverse web of relationships to be whole. By definition, captive animals don't coexist with anyone; they are isolated from us, other animals, and the world.

At the other extreme, we often think that in order to preserve wilderness we have to keep people out, in essence defining wilderness as "nature without humans." This doesn't really exist anymore. No landscape remains unvisited by us or untouched by human impacts, even the wildest, most remote places—which is why scientists have proposed naming our age the Anthropocene. While we can certainly minimize human impacts, all ecosystems must now cope with and adapt to our presence.

So if wild animals belong in nature, and nature can't keep us out or escape our impacts, then our only choice is to figure out how to live together. Our problem is not how to keep species from going extinct. Our problem is learning how to coexist with nature and wild animals in ways that benefit everyone.

In other words, solving the crisis of coexistence means creating healthy relationships with wild animals in which everyone's welfare matters, even the welfare of the landscape itself. It means protecting wild places for the benefit of animals, but in ways humans can live with. To a degree, this means treating wilderness like a kind of garden—as special landscapes influenced, managed, and shaped by us to be healthy, sustainable homes for wild animals.

It also means letting our actual gardens become more wild, punching holes in the fences, as it were. Coexistence means accepting wild animals as part of the world humans live in—so that wild animals in parks, suburbs, cities, and farms are not automatically treated as "pests," or as weeds to pull. They are instead species who belong and that we need to care for. Granted, this is hardest of all, but one reason it can feel hard is because we aren't used to adjusting our lifestyles to benefit wildlife.

There is plenty of paradox and irony in this. It means protecting and caring for wild animals who might not tolerate us, who might disrupt our lives, and who are capable of injuring us. It means accepting that wilderness may not always be completely wild, nor civilization entirely tame and safe. It means becoming self-conscious caretakers who actively manage nature in part by managing ourselves and adapting to nature's needs. It means cultivating more wilderness in the world and accepting more wildness in ourselves and our society.

One tremendous benefit of this mind-set is that it empowers all of us to become conservationists within the context of our lives. If coexistence is our goal, then anytime we foster and cultivate our relationships with wild animals and wilderness, even in the smallest, most personal ways, we improve the world.

This, above all, is what I think we all want—to feel an integral part of the web of nature, in which our lives and our actions contribute to our planet's well-being. Humans were born into a world brimming with wild creatures and charismatic giants, and our sense of connection to them runs deep. It's bred in our bones. Who would ever want to live in a world without giants, or in which wilderness was a place humans were not meant to go?

Risking ourselves in wilderness, becoming comfortable with wildlife, meeting giants face to face: these are the experiences that inspire our love of nature in the first place. ⌇

CALL TO ACTION

Experiencing a call to action is both very simple and very profound. Our feelings of concern or caring give rise to a desire to become more involved. Perhaps we want, in our own small way, to help change the world for the better, or perhaps we merely want to foster a deeper connection to something we feel is important.

This section is devoted to helping you further explore this book's giant animals and wildlife conservation.

Here is a short list of things anyone, but particularly students, can do.

- Learn more about wildlife and endangered species, either for a school paper or on your own.
- Visit wilderness and wildlife and foster your own love of and connection to nature, perhaps as part of a guided trip run by a park, museum, zoo, or wildlife group.
- Raise awareness about conservation or a specific endangered species, such as for a class project.
- Take personal actions that help a species or an issue you care about; pick one specific project and see how it goes.
- Join or volunteer regularly with a local conservation or wildlife organization.
- Organize your own conservation effort related to a specific issue, perhaps by coordinating your effort with an established, local group.
- Coordinate a fundraising effort related to conservation in your class or school.

For Students and Teachers

This list of resources is specifically designed for kids, students, and teachers. Some provide class project ideas and lesson plans. Others run their own educational programs for young adults.

American Museum of Natural History, Center for Biodiversity & Conservation, www.amnh.org/our-research/center-for-biodiversity-conservation: educator resources and easy, environmentally friendly actions.

Bagheera, www.bagheera.com: resources and activities aimed at high school students.

Defenders of Wildlife, Kids' Planet, www.kidsplanet.org: games and information for kids and teachers.

EcoLibrary, www.ecolibrary.org: free, downloadable images and educational materials for school projects.

Earthwatch Institute, www.earthwatch.org: scientist-led educational trips for student groups and teens around the world.

Jane Goodall's Roots & Shoots, www.rootsandshoots.org: Jane Goodall Institute's global, youth-led community action and educational programs; coordinates service projects worldwide.

International Fund for Animal Welfare, Animal Action Education, www.ifaw.org/united-states/our-work/education: educational resources for students and teachers.

National Audubon Society, www.audubon.org: local Audubon centers foster hands-on education, and *Audubon Adventures* (www.audubonadventures.org) is for grades three to eight.

National Wildlife Federation, www.nwf.org/kids.aspx: NWF's kid-focused website has games, activities, teacher resources, and *Ranger Rick* magazine.

North Carolina Zoological Society, Field Trip Earth, www.fieldtripearth.org: wildlife information for students and teachers.

Wildlife Conservation Society, www.wcs.org: teen-focused field trips and programs related to five New York City–area zoos and aquariums.

Wildscreen Arkive, www.arkive.org: free, downloadable photos and videos, educational materials, and teacher resources.

Information on Extinct and Endangered Species

These resources are devoted to providing reliable, acccurate information on endangered and extinct species. Most of the conservation organizations also provide excellent species profiles.

Earth's Endangered Creatures, www.earthsendangered.com

EDGE, Evolutionary Distinct & Globally Endangered, www.edgeofexistence.org

Encyclopedia of Life, www.eol.org

Focusing on Wildlife, www.focusingonwildlife.com

International Union for Conservation of Nature (IUCN) Red List of Threatened Species, www.iucnredlist.org

NatureServe, www.natureserve.org

The Sixth Extinction, www.petermaas.nl/extinct

US Fish & Wildlife Service (USFWS), Endangered Species, www.fws.gov/endangered

Worldwide Conservation Organizations

These conservation organizations focus on saving endangered species, protecting the environment, and preserving nature across the globe. They share news and run projects for many species, including those in this book.

American Bird Conservancy, www.abcbirds.org

Born Free, www.bornfree.org.uk

Conservation International, www.conservation.org

Environmental Defense Fund, www.edf.org

Natural Resources Defense Council, www.nrdc.org

Nature Conservancy, www.nature.org

WildAid, www.wildaid.org

The WILD Foundation, www.wild.org

World Land Trust, www.worldlandtrust.org

World Wildlife Fund, www.worldwildlife.org

Species- and Place-specific Resources

Here are further resources and organizations related to specific species and places described in this book.

Moa

New Zealand Conservation Trust, www.nzconservationtrust.org.nz

New Zealand Department of Conservation, www.doc.govt.nz

Aurochs

Large Herbivore Network, www.lhnet.org

Rewilding Europe, www.rewildingeurope.com

Tauros Programme, www.taurosproject.com

Wild Wonders of Europe, www.wild-wonders.com

Elephant Bird

Lemur Conservation Foundation, www.lemurreserve.org

Lemur Conservation Network, www.lemurconservationnetwork.org

Wild Madagascar, www.wildmadagascar.org

Steller's Sea Cow

Save the Manatee, www.savethemanatee.org

Sirenian International, www.sirenian.org

Indian Ocean Giant Tortoises

Charles Darwin Foundation, www.darwinfoundation.org

Darwin Online, www.darwin-online.org.uk

The Galapagos Conservancy, www.galapagos.org

Galapagos National Park, www.galapagospark.org

La Vanille Réserve des Mascareignes, www.lavanille-reserve.com

Mauritian Wildlife Foundation, www.mauritian-wildlife.org

Passenger Pigeon

Long Now Foundation, Revive and Restore project, www.longnow.org/revive

The Messenger, www.songbirdsos.com

National Audubon Society, www.audubon.org

Passenger Pigeon Project, www.passengerpigeon.org

California Grizzly

Polar Bears International, www.polarbearsinternational.org

Yellowstone to Yukon Conservation Initiative, http://y2y.net

Thylacine

Tasmania Parks & Wildlife Service, www.parks.tas.gov.au

The Thylacine Museum, www.naturalworlds.org/thylacine

Thylacine Research Unit, www.thylacineresearchunit.org

Lion

African Conservation Experience, www.conservationafrica.net

African Conservation Foundation, www.africanconservation.org

African Wildlife Foundation, www.awf.org

Lion Conservation Fund, www.lionconservationfund.org

Living With Lions, www.livingwithlions.org

Red Wolf

International Wolf Center, www.wolf.org

Point Defiance Zoo and Aquarium, www.pdza.org/save-red-wolves

Red Wolf Coalition, www.redwolves.com

Red Wolf Recovery Project, www.fws.gov/redwolf

Tiger

Panthera, www.panthera.org

Tigers Forever, www.tigersforever.org

Tigers in Crisis, www.tigersincrisis.com

Wildlife Protection Society of India, www.wpsi-india.org

Baiji

Dolphins World, www.dolphins-world.com

Whale and Dolphin Conservation, http://us.whales.org

WDCS KidZone, www.wdcs.org/wdcskids/en/index.php

Rhino

International Rhino Foundation, www.rhinos.org

Save the Rhino, www.savetherhino.org

Save the Rhino Trust, www.savetherhinotrust.org

SavingRhinos.org, www.savingrhinos.org

World Rhino Day, www.worldrhinoday.org

SOURCES

General works and particularly important authors for the ideas in this book are listed under the Introduction, for easy reference. These resources contributed to all the stories in this book, in one way or another, and I highly recommend seeking them out.

Specific sources for each species story, the sidebars, and the boxed texts are provided in the order they appear in the book. Within each entry, sources are arranged alphabetically, and page numbers correspond to quoted material or specific topics. When a book is listed more than once, entries use short-title format. For more information on each species, see Call to Action.

Introduction: Meet the Giants

Ackerman, Diane, *The Human Age: The World Shaped by Us* (New York: W. W. Norton, 2014).

Bekoff, Marc, *Rewilding Our Hearts* (Novato, CA: New World Library, 2014).

Diamond, Jared, *Guns, Germs, and Steel: The Fates of Human Societies* (New York: W.W. Norton, 1997).

Flannery, Tim, *The Future Eaters* (New York: Grove Press, 1994/2002).

Goodall, Jane, *Hope for Animals and Their World: How Endangered Species Are Being Rescued from the Brink* (New York: Grand Central Publishing, 2009).

Grzimek, Bernhard, *Grzimek's Animal Life Encyclopedia: Extinction,* Vols. 1 and 2, editor in chief, Norman MacLeod (Farmington Hills, MI: Gale, Cengage Learning, 2013).

Kolbert, Elizabeth, *The Sixth Extinction* (New York: Henry Holt, 2014).

Leopold, Aldo, *A Sand County Almanac* (New York: Oxford University Press, 1949/1968), 199.

———, *Round River* (New York: Oxford University Press, 1953/1993).

MacPhee, Ross D. E., ed., *Extinctions in Near Time: Causes, Contexts, and Consequences* (New York: Kluwer Academic/Plenum, 1999).

Quammen, David, *Monster of God: The Man-Eating Predator in the Jungles of History and the Mind* (New York: W. W. Norton, 2003).

Shipman, Pat, *The Animal Connection: A New Perspective on What Makes Us Human* (New York: W. W. Norton, 2011).

Wilcove, David S., *No Way Home: The Decline of the World's Great Animal Migrations* (Washington, DC: Island Press, 2008).

Wilson, Edward O., *The Diversity of Life* (New York: Harvard University Press, 1992/2010).

Wuerthner, George, Eileen Crist, and Tom Butler, eds., *Protecting the Wild: Parks and Wilderness, the Foundation of Conservation* (Washington, DC: Island Press/Foundation for Deep Ecology, 2015).

Moa: The World's Largest "Chicken"

Adams, Douglas, and Mark Carwardine, *Last Chance to See* (New York: Harmony Books, 1991).

Anderson, Atholl, *Prodigious Birds: Moas and Moa-hunting in Prehistoric New Zealand* (Cambridge, England: Cambridge U Press, 1989/2003), 87, 89, 90.

Darwin, Charles, *The Voyage of the Beagle* (Washington, DC: National Geographic Adventure Classics, 2004), 373.

Day, David, *The Doomsday Book of Animals: A Natural History of Vanished Species* (New York: Viking, 1981).

Flannery, *Future Eaters*, 55, 65, 244, 249, 250.

Flannery, Tim, and Peter Schouten, *A Gap in Nature: Discovering the World's Extinct Animals* (New York: Atlantic Monthly Press, 2001).

Fromme, Alison, "Why Fly? Flightless Bird Mystery Solved, Say Evolutionary Scientists," *National Geographic*, May 13, 2014. http://news.nationalgeographic.com/news/2014/05/140513-flightless-birds-ostriches-moas-evolution-science.

Fuller, Errol, *Extinct Birds*, rev. ed. (Ithaca, NY: Cornell University Press, 2001/1987), 37–38, 51.

Grzimek, *Animal Life Encyclopedia*, vol. 2, 595–98.

Kolbert, *Sixth Extinction*, 232.

Nicholls, Henry, *Lonesome George: The Life and Loves of a Conservation Icon* (New York: Macmillan, 2006).

Yong, Ed, "The Surprising Closest Relative of the Huge Elephant Birds," *National Geographic*, May 22, 2014. http://phenomena.nationalgeographic.com/2014/05/22/the-surprising-closest-relative-of-the-huge-elephant-birds.

For "Island Dwarfism: The Incredible Shrinking Giants"

Balouet, Jean-Christophe, *Extinct Species of the World: Lessons for Our Future* (London, England: Charles Letts & Co., 1990), 102–7.

Tyson, Peter, *The Eighth Continent: Life, Death, and Discovery in the Lost World of Madagascar* (New York: William Morrow, 2000).

Aurochs: The Original Wild Bull

Balouet, *Extinct Species*, 39, 112-15.

Day, *Doomsday Book*, 188-89.

Diamond, *Guns, Germs & Steel*.

Goderie, Ronald, Wouter Helmer, Henri Kerkdijk-Otten, and Staffan Widstrand, *The Aurochs: Born to Be Wild: The Comeback of a European Icon* (The Netherlands: Roodbont Publishers, 2013), 118. http://issuu.com/kristjanjung/docs/the_aurochs_-_born_to_be_wild.

IUCN Red List of Threatened Species, "Bos primigenius," 2008, www.iucnredlist.org/details/136721/0.

Rewilding Europe, www.rewildingeurope.com.

Shipman, *Animal Connection*, 202–13.

Vuure, Cis van, *Retracing the Aurochs: History, Morphology, and Ecology of an Extinct Wild Ox*, trans. by KHM van den Berg (Sofia, Bulgaria: Pensoft Publishers, 2005), 68–71, 89–90, 91, 93, 106.

For "Chauvet Cave: 'They Have Been Here!'"

Clottes, Jean, "Chauvet Cave," Metropolitan Museum of Art website, www.metmuseum.org/toah/hd/chav/hd_chav.htm, accessed September 22, 2015.

Hammer, Joshua, "Finally, the Beauty of France's Chauvet Cave Makes its Grand Public Debut," *Smithsonian*, April 2015. www.smithsonianmag.com/history/france-chauvet-cave-makes-grand-debut-180954582/?no-ist.

Herzog, Werner, *Cave of Forgotten Dreams* (Creative Differences and Werner Herzog Filmproduktion, 2010), DVD.

Quammen, *Monster of God*, 404–10.

Thurman, Judith, "First Impressions: What Does the World's Oldest Art Say About Us?" *The New Yorker*, June 23, 2008, www.newyorker.com/magazine/2008/06/23/first-impressions.

Vuure, *Retracing the Aurochs*, 130.

The Pleistocene Extinctions: Rise of the Mammoth Hunters

Diamond, *Guns, Germs, and Steel.*

Diamond, Jared, *The Third Chimpanzee: The Evolution and Future of the Human Animal* (New York: HarperCollins, 1992), 40–41, 47.

Flannery, *Future Eaters.*

Grzimek, *Animal Life Encyclopedia*, vols. 1 and 2, 366, 595–98.

Kolbert, *Sixth Extinction*, 226, 237–47, 253.

Mann, Charles C., *1491: New Revelations of the Americas Before Columbus* (New York: Knopf, 2005).

Martin, Paul S., and David W. Steadman, "Prehistoric Extinctions on Islands and Continents," in *Extinctions in Near Time: Causes, Contexts, and Consequences*, ed. Ross D. E. MacPhee (New York: Kluwer Academic/Plenum, 1999), 17–56.

Owen-Smith, Norman. "The Interaction of Humans, Megaherbivores, and Habitats in the Late Pleistocene Extinction Event" n *Extinctions in Near Time,* ed. MacPhee (New York: Kluwer Academic/Plenum, 1999), 57–70.

Peacock, Doug, *In the Shadow of the Sabertooth: A Renege Naturalist Considers Global Warming, the First Americans and the Terrible Beasts of the Pleistocene* (Oakland, CA: AK Press, 2013).

Quammen, *Monster of God.*

Stone, Richard, *Mammoth: The Resurrection of an Ice Age Giant* (Cambridge, MA: Perseus Publishing, 2001), 20–23.

Elephant Bird: A Legend Come to Life

Balouet, *Extinct Species*, 51–53

Brown, Mervyn, *A History of Madagascar* (Princeton, NJ: Markus Wiener Publishers, 1995/2000), 12–14.

Burney, David, and Ramilisonia, "The Kilopilopitsofy, Kidoky, and Bokyboky: Accounts of Strange Animals from Belo-sur-Mer, Madagascar, and the Mega-faunal 'Extinction Window,'" *American Anthropologist*, vol. 100, no 4 (1998).

Day, *Doomsday Book*, 20–21.

Fuller, *Extinct Birds*, 12, 34–35.

Goodall, *Hope for Animals*, 317–21.

Grzimek, *Animal Life Encyclopedia*, vol. 2, 587, 590.

IUCN News, "Lemurs of Madagascar Three-Year Conservation Plan Launched," August 1, 2013, www.iucn.org/news_homepage/news_by_date/?13487/ Lemurs-of-Madagascar-three-year-conservation-plan-launched.

Kay, James, "Etienne de Flacourt, *L'Histoire de le Grand Ile de Madagascar* (1658)" in *Curtis's Botanical Magazine,* vol. 21 (Oxford, England: Blackwell Publishing for the Royal Botanic Gardens Kew, November 2004).

MacPhee, Ross D. E., "Remember the Islands" in Rosamond Wolff Purcell, *Swift as a Shadow: Extinct and Endangered Animals* (New York & Boston: Mariner Books/Houghton Mifflin, 1999), 142–49.

MacPhee, Ross D. E., and P. A. Marx, "The 40,000-year plague: humans, hyperdisease, and first-contact extinctions," in Steven M. Goodman and B. D. Patterson, eds., *Natural Change and Human Impact in Madagascar* (Washington, DC: Smithsonian Institution Press, 1997), 169–217.

Tyson, Peter, *The Eighth Continent: Life, Death, and Discovery in the Lost World of Madagascar* (New York: William Morrow, 2000), 1, 136, 138.

Yong, Ed, "The Surprising Closest Relative of the Huge Elephant Birds," *National Geographic*, May 22, 2014, http://phenomena.nationalgeographic. com/2014/05/22/the-surprising-closest-relative-of-the-huge-elephant-birds.

For "Cryptozoology: Hunting the Snark"

Balouet, *Extinct Species*, 102–8.

Grzimek, *Animal Life Encyclopedia*, vol. 2, 543.

Wikipedia, "Cryptozoology," https://en.wikipedia.org/wiki/Cryptozoology, accessed September 22, 2015.

Steller's Sea Cow: Elephant of the Ocean

Balouet, *Extinct Species*, 56.

Day, *Doomsday*, 216–18.

Domning, D. P., "Sea cow family reunion," *Natural History* 96, no. 4 (April 1987): 64–71.

Flannery, *Gap in Nature*, 6–7.

Haley, D., "Saga of Steller's Sea Cow." *Natural History* 87, no. 9 (November 1978): 9–17.

IUCN Red List of Threatened Species, "Hydrodamalis Gigas," 2008, www.iucnredlist.org/details/10303/0.

Self-Sullivan, Caryn, Daryl P. Domning, and Jorge Velez-Juarbe, "Evolution of the Sirenia: An Oultine," Sirenian International (2007, updated 2014), www.sirenian.org/sirenianevolution.pdf, accessed April 28, 2015.

Stejneger, Leonhard, "How the Great Northern Sea-Cow (Rytina) Became Exterminated," *The American Naturalist* 21, no. 12 (1887): 1047-54, www.jstor.org/stable/2451162?seq=1#page_scan_tab_contents.

Steller, Georg Wilhelm, *De Bestiis Marinis, or, The Beasts of the Sea (1751),* trans. Walter Miller, Jennie Emerson Miller, and Paul Royster, *Faculty Publications, UNL Libraries,* Paper 17 (Lincoln, NE: University of Nebraska-Lincoln), 13–16, 19, 21, 25, 43, 44–45, http://digitalcommons.unl.edu/libraryscience/17.

————, *Journal of a Voyage with Bering, 1741-1742,* ed. O. W. Frost (Stanford, CA: Stanford University Press, 1988), 134, 136, 159–60, 161, 162, 163–64.

Turvey, S. T. and C. L. Risley, "Modelling the Extinction of Steller's Sea Cow, Bilogical Letters 2, no. 1 (March 22, 2006): 94–97, www.ncbi.nlm.nih.gov/pmc/articles/PMC1617197.

For "Hardtack & Scurvy: A Sailor's Diet in the Age of Exploration"

Balouet, *Extinct Species,* 48.

MacDonald, Janet, *Feeding Nelson's Navy* (London: Frontline Books, 2004/2014).

Steller, *Journal of a Voyage,* 134.

Wikipedia, "Scurvy," https://en.wikipedia.org/wiki/Scurvy, accessed September 15, 2015.

The Pros & Cons of Being Giant

Flannery, *Future Eaters.*

Grzimek, *Animal Life Encyclopedia,* vols. 1 and 2, 369, 533.

Kolbert, *Sixth Extinction,* 224.

Owen-Smith, "Interaction of Humans, Megaherbivores," 57–70.

Quammen, *Monster of God*, 70–72.

Wilson, *Diversity of Life*, 36, 210.

Ray, Justina C., et al., eds., *Large Carnivores and the Conservation of Biodiversity*, (Washington DC: Island Press, 2005), 87–95, 212–28.

Indian Ocean Giant Tortoises: Antediluvian Old Souls

Balouet, *Extinct Species*, 46, 48, 49, 247.

Chambers, Paul, *A Sheltered Life: The Unexpected History of the Giant Tortoise* (Oxford, UK: Oxford University Press, 2006), 17, 18, 125, 214–15.

Darwin, Charles, *The Voyage of the Beagle* (Washington, DC: National Geographic Adventure Classics, 2004), 333–34, 335, 342–43, 350–51.

Day, *Doomsday Book*, 249.

Flannery, *Future Eaters*, 188–89.

IUCN Red List of Threatened Species, "Geochelone gigantea," 1996, www.iucnredlist.org/details/summary/9010/0.

Nicholls, Henry, *The Galápagos: A Natural History* (New York: Basic Books, 2014), 85, 86, 99–100, 109.

———, *Lonesome George: The Life and Loves of a Conservation Icon* (New York: Macmillan, 2006).

Stanford, Craig B., *The Last Tortoise: A Tale of Extinction in Our Lifetime* (Cambridge, MA: Belknap Press/Harvard University Press, 2010), 4, 20, 34, 43, 143.

For "The Dodo: Not Such a Stupid Bird"

Day, *Doomsday Book*, 28–32.

Flannery and Schouten, *Gap in Nature*, 4

Fuller, Errol, *Dodo: A Brief History* (New York: Universe Publishing, 2003).

Quammen, David, *The Song of the Dodo* (New York: Touchstone, 1997).

Passenger Pigeons: Meteors from Heaven

Balouet, *Extinct Species.*

Flannery and Schouten, *Gap in Nature*, 124.

Fuller, *Extinct Birds*, 189–190.

Fuller, Errol, *Lost Animals: Extinction and the Photographic Record* (Princeton, NJ: Princeton University Press, 2013).

———, *The Passenger Pigeon* (Princeton, NJ: Princeton University Press, 2015), 52–55, 66–67, 73, 79–80.

Greenberg, Joel, *A Feathered River Across the Sky: The Passenger Pigeon's Flight to Extinction* (New York: Bloomsbury, 2014), 3, 11, 15, 31, 33–34, 40, 52, 94, 131–32, 135, 155.

IUCN Red List of Threatened Species, "Ectopistes migratorius," 2012, www.iucnredlist.org/details/22690733/0.

Leopold, *Sand County Almanac*, 111.

Mann, *1491: New Revelations.*

Master, Larry. Email with author, September 15, 2015.

Rich, Nathaniel, "The New Origin of Species," *New York Times Magazine*, March 2, 2014.

For "The Pyrenean Ibex & Frozen Arks: Extinction Insurance"

Ackerman, *Human Age*, 151, 160, 163.

Ambrose Monell Cryo Collection, American Museum of Natural History, www.amnh.org/our-research/sackler-institute-for-comparative-genomics/facilities/amcc.

CryoBioBank, Cincinnati Zoo, http://cincinnatizoo.org/conservation/crew/crew-animal-research/cryobiobank.

Frozen Ark, University of Nottingham, www.frozenark.org.

Frozen Zoo, San Diego Zoo, www.sandiegozooglobal.org/what_we_do_banking_genetic_resources/frozen_zoo.

Kolbert, *Sixth Extinction*, 260–61.

Rich, "The New Origin of Species."

Rincon, Paul, "Fresh Effort to Clone Extinct Animal," *BBC News*, November 22, 2013, www.bbc.com/news/science-environment-25052233.

Zimmer, Carl, "Bringing Them Back to Life," *National Geographic*, April 2013, http://ngm.nationalgeographic.com/2013/04/125-species-revival/zimmer-text.

California Grizzly: Elder Brother, Cousin, Great-Grandfather

Brunner, Bernd, *Bears: A Brief History*, trans. by Lori Lantz (New Haven and London: Yale University Press, 2007), 1–3, 17, 80.

Busch, Robert H., *The Grizzly Almanac* (New York: Lyons Press, 2000), 4–10, 98–104, 106, 109, 115, 161–96.

Cunningham, Laura, *A State of Change: Forgotten Landscapes of California* (Berkeley, CA: Heyday, 2010), 19–33.

IUCN Red List of Threatened Species, "Ursus arctos," 2008, www.iucnredlist.org/details/41688/0.

Master, Larry, communication with author, September 20, 2015.

Peacock, *Shadow of the Sabertooth*, 43, 51.

Quammen, *Monster of God*, 289–90.

Snyder, Susan, ed., *Bear In Mind: The California Grizzly* (Berkeley, CA: Heyday Books, 2003), x, 4, 5–6, 13, 16, 32–33, 48–52, 116–17.

Storer, Tracy I., and Lloyd P. Tevis, Jr., *California Grizzly* (Berkeley and Los Angeles: University of California Press, 1955), 44–47, 90, 94, 120–23, 140–49, 194–95, 221–23.

US Fish and Wildlife Service, Marine Mammals Management, "Polar Bear," www.fws.gov/alaska/fisheries/mmm/polarbear/pbmain.htm, accessed September 16, 2015.

Yellowstone National Park. "Grizzly Bears," National Park Service, www.nps.gov/yell/learn/nature/grizzlybear.htm, accessed September 16, 2015.

Yellowstone to Yukon Conservation Initiative, http://y2y.net, accessed September 16, 2015.

For "How to Hunt a Grizzly"

Snyder, *Bear In Mind*, 16–17, 20.

Australia: A Lost Continent

Alroy, John, "A Multispecies Overkill Simulation of the End-Pleistocene Megafaunal Mass Extinction," *Science* 292 (2001): 1893–96.

Diamond, *Guns, Germs, and Steel*, 41–42.

Flannery, Tim, *Chasing Kangaroos*, (New York: Grove Press, 2004), 124, 155–64, 175–76, 205, 207.

———, *Future Eaters*, 69–87, 108–28, 153, 199–207, 242.

Flannery, Tim, and Peter Schouten, *A Gap in Nature: Discovering the World's Extinct Animals* (New York: Atlantic Monthly Press, 2001), xv–xvii.

Grzimek, *Animal Life Encyclopedia*. vols. 1 and 2, 366, 533, 541–43.

Kolbert, *Sixth Extinction*, 225, 231–32.

MacPhee, "Remember the Islands," 142–49.

Martin, "Prehistoric Extinctions on Islands," 17–56.

Owen-Smith, "Interaction of Humans, Megaherbivores," 57–70.

Thylacine: The Great Ghost Tiger

Day, *Doomsday Book,* 223–25.

Flannery, *Chasing Kangaroos.*

———, *Future Eaters*, 315–18, 383.

Flannery and Schouten, *A Gap in Nature*, 146.

Fuller, *Lost Animals,* 173, 177–78.

Grzimek, *Animal Life Encyclopedia*, vol. 2, 581.

IUCN Red List of Threatened Species, "Thylacinus cynocephalus," 2008, www.iucnredlist.org/details/21866/0.

Owen, David, *Tasmanian Tiger* (Baltimore, MD: Johns Hopkins Press, 2004), 25–26, 48, 58–61, 82, 86–87, 92–93, 109–11, 115, 118–19.

Paddle, Robert, *The Last Tasmanian Tiger* (Cambridge, England: Cambridge University Press, 2000), 20–22, 29–31, 55, 57, 68, 70–71, 72, 118–19, 237–39.

Australian Screen, "Tasmanian Tiger Footage (1932)," Beaumaris Zoo, http://aso.gov.au/titles/historical/tasmanian-tiger-footage/clip1, accessed August 2, 2015.

YouTube, "Last Tasmanian Tiger, Thylacine, 1933," www.youtube.com/
watch?v=6vqCCI1ZF7o, accessed August 2, 2015.

YouTube, "Tasmanian Tiger Filmed in Central Tasmania 2012," a video hoax,
www.youtube.com/watch?v=9DLL0ELg-y8, accessed August 2, 2015.

For "It's Happened Before: The Five Other Mass Extinctions"

Ackerman, *Human Age*, 154.

Grzimek, *Animal Life Encyclopedia*, vol. 1, 26.

Jablonski, David, from Rick Gore, "Extinctions," *National Geographic,* June
1989, 673, as cited in David Rains Wallace, *Beasts of Eden: Walking Whales,
Dawn Horses, and Other Enigmas of Mammal Evolution* (Berkeley and Los
Angeles: University of California Press, 2004), xxvii, 194.

Kolbert, *Sixth Extinction*, 90.

Quammen, *Song of the Dodo*, 606.

Wilson, *Diversity of Life*, 29–31.

Lion: Long Live the King

Clutton-Brock, Juliet, "Competitors, Companions, Status Symbols, or Pests:
A Review of Human Associations with Other Carnivores," in *Carnivore
Behavior, Ecology, and Environment*, vols. 1 and 2, John Gittleman, ed. (Ithaca:
Comstock Pub. Associates, Cornell University Press, 1989/1996), 375–92.

Day, *Doomsday Book*, 175–78.

Eveleth, Rose, "Lions and Tigers Bear Vocal Cords for Roars," *Scientific American*,
podcast, November 2, 2011, www.scientificamerican.com/podcast/episode/
lions-and-tigers-bear-vocal-cords-f-11-11-02.

Grzimek, *Animal Life Encyclopedia,* vol. 2, 376, 536.

Hancock, Colin, and Daisy Carrington, "Maasai Warriors: How Do They Choose
a Chief? They Dance," *CNN*, March 25, 2105, www.cnn.com/2015/03/25/
africa/maasai-warriors-they-used-to-hunt-lions-now-they-dance.

IUCN Red List of Threatened Species, "Panthera leo," 2015, www.iucnredlist.
org/details/15951/0.

Maasai Association,. www.maasai-association.org, accessed September 21, 2015.

Martin and Steadman, "Prehistoric Extinctions on Islands," 17–56.

Morris, Desmond, *The Animal Contract* (London: Virgin Books,1990), 22–25, 98–100.

Quammen, David, "Can Good Come from Maasai Lion Killings in the Serengeti?" *National Geographic*, April 29, 2014, http://news. nationalgeographic.com/news/2014/04/140428-serengeti-ngorongoro- conservation-area-tanzania-lions-maasai-craig-packer-lion-guardians-world.

Quammen, *Monster of God*, 6–8, 21–23, 25–26, 28–29, 260–74, 401–10.

Platt, John R., "African Lion Populations Drop 42 Percent in Past 21 Years," *Scientific American*, June 24, 2015, http://blogs.scientificamerican.com/ extinction-countdown/african-lion-populations-drop-42-percent-in-past- 21-years.

———, "When Did the Barbary Lion Really Go Extinct?" *Scientific American*, April 22, 2103, http://blogs.scientificamerican.com/extinction- countdown/2013/04/22/when-did-the-barbary-lion-really-go-extinct.

Ray, *Large Carnivores*, 5.

Schaller, George B., *Serengeti: A Kingdom of Predators* (New York: Alfred A Knopf, 1972), 2.

———, *The Serengeti Lion: A Study of Predator-Prey Relations* (Chicago: University of Chicago Press, 1972).

Sinha, Sanskrity, "Extinct Barbary Lions of Africa Could Be Back to Life Soon," *International Business Times*, April 3, 2014, www.ibtimes.co.uk/extinct- barbary-lions-africa-could-be-back-life-soon-1443182.

Turner, Alan, and Mauricio Anton, *The Big Cats and Their Fossil Relatives* (New York: Columbia University Press, 1997), 60–72, 96, 130, 151.

Wilcove, *No Way Home*, 82–96.

For "Sabertooth Cats: Long in the Tooth"

Peacock, *Shadow of the Sabertooth*, 30–32.

Quamman, *Monster of God*, 319–25.

Turner, *Big Cats*, 30, 57, 116–18, 197, 207–15.

Red Wolf: Dog of the Woods

Beeland, T. Delene, *The Secret World of Red Wolves: The Fight to Save North America's Other Wolf* (Chapel Hill: University of North Carolina Press, 2013), 4, 7–9, 13–14, 105–24, 127, 129–31, 137–38, 167, 171, 177–85, 206–8, 226.

Boitani, Luigi, "Wolf Conservation and Recovery," in *Wolves: Behavior, Ecology, and Conservation*, eds. Mech and Boitani, 317–40.

Busch, Robert H., *The Wolf Almanac: A Celebration of Wolves and Their World* (Guilford, CT: Lyons Press, 1995/2007), 6–8, 25–33, 47–63, 114–16, 123–25, 137, 188–92.

Day, *Doomsday Book*, 154

Fritts, Steven H., "Wolves and Humans,." in *Wolves: Behavior, Ecology, and Conservation*, eds. Mech and Boitani, 289–316.

Goodall, *Hope for Animals*, 47–59, 145–47.

IUCN Red List of Threatened Species, "Canis rufus," 2008, www.iucnredlist.org/details/3747/0.

Mech, David, and Luigi Boitani, eds., *Wolves: Behavior, Ecology, and Conservation* (Chicago and London: University of Chicago Press, 2003); see also individual chapter citations.

Nicholls, *The Galápagos,* 82.

Phillips, Michael K., V. Gary Henry, and Brian T. Kelly, "Restoration of the Red Wolf," in *Wolves: Behavior, Ecology, and Conservation*, eds. Mech and Boitani, 272–88.

Red Wolf Coalition, www.redwolves.com, accessed September 28, 2015.

Red Wolf Recovery Project, www.fws.gov/redwolf, accessed September 28, 2015.

Ronald M. Nowak, "Wolf Evolution and Taxonomy," in *Wolves: Behavior, Ecology, and Conservation*, eds. Mech and Boitani, 239–58.

Velasquez-Manoff, Moises, "Lions and Tigers and Bears, Oh My!" *New York Times Magazine*, August 17, 2014, 32–37.

Wilson, *Diversity of Life*, xii, 38–42.

For "Trophic Cascades: Gray Wolves in Yellowstone"

Berger, Joel, and Douglas W. Smith, "Restoring Functionality in Yellowstone with Recovering Carnivores: Gains and Uncertainties," in *Large Carnivores*, Ray, 100–109.

Busch, *Wolf Almanac*, 194–200.

Eisenberg, Cristina, *The Wolf's Tooth: Keystone Predators, Trophic Cascades, and Biodiversity* (Washington, DC: Island Press, 2010).

Goodall, *Hope for Animals*, 145–47.

Grzimek, *Animal Life Encyclopedia*, vol. 1, 26–27.

"Wolves in Yellowstone," Yellowstone National Park, www.nps.gov/yell/learn/nature/wolves.htm, accessed September 23, 2015.

"Wolf Restoration," Yellowstone National Park, www.nps.gov/yell/learn/nature/wolf-restoration.htm, accessed September 23, 2015.

Discovering the New World: The Americas

Alroy, John, "A Multispecies Overkill Simulation of the End-Pleistocene Megafaunal Mass Extinction," *Science* 292 (2001): 1893–96.

———, "Putting North America's End-Pleistocene Megafaunal Extinction in Context," in *Extinctions in Near Time*, ed. MacPhee, 105–44

Balouet, *Extinct Species,* 102-7.

Ceballos, Gerardo, et al., "Accelerated Modern Human-induced Species Losses: Entering the Sixth Mass Extinction," *Science Advances* 1 (June 2015),. doi:e1400253.

Diamond, *Guns, Germs, and Steel*, 46.

Fariña, Richard A., Sergio F. Vizcaíno, and Gerry de Iuliis, *Megafauna: Giant Beasts of Pleistocene South America* (Bloomington, IN: Indiana University Press, 2013).

Grzimek, *Animal Life Encyclopedia*, vols. 1 and 2, 366–68, 536, 538–41.

Haynes, Gary, and B. Sunday Eiselt, "The Power of Pleistocene Hunter-Gatherers: Forward and Backward Searching for Evidence about Mammoth Extinction," in *Extinctions in Near Time*, ed. MacPhee, 71–94.

Kolbert, *Sixth Extinction*, 225, 233–35.

MacPhee, "Remember the Islands," 142–49.

MacPhee, Ross D. E., and Clare Flemming, "*Requiem Aeternam*: The Last Five Hundred Years of Mammalian Species Extinctions," in *Extinctions in Near Time*, ed. MacPhee, 333–66.

Mann, *1491: New Revelations*, 16–17, 166–69.

Martin, "Prehistoric Extinctions on Islands," 17–56.

Owen-Smith, "Interaction of Humans, Megaherbivores," 57–70.

Peacock, *Shadow of the Sabertooth*, 17, 24, 28–33, 40–43, 56–57, 64–71, 84, 148–51, 168, 185–87, 199.

Quammen, *Monster of God*, 321.

Tigers: The Perfect Predator

Coggins, Chris, "King of the Hundred Beasts: A Long View of Tigers in Southern China," in *Tigers of the World*, eds. Tilson and Nyhus, 431–34.

Day, *Doomsday Book*, 178–79.

Dell'Amore, Christine, "Hybrid Panthers Helping Rare Car Rebound in Florida," National Geographic, September 24, 2010, http://news.nationalgeographic. com/news/2010/09/100924-science-florida-panthers-texas-hybrids- endangered-animals.

Ghose, Tia, "House Cats and Tigers Share 95.6 Percent of DNA, Study Reveals," *Christian Science Monitor*, September 18, 2013, www.csmonitor.com/Science/ 2013/0918/House-cats-and-tigers-share-95.6-percent-of-DNA-study-reveals.

Grzimek, *Animal Life Encyclopedia*, vol. 1, 377–78.

IUCN Red List of Threatened Species, "Panthera tigris," 2015, www.iucnredlist. org/details/15955/0.

Jackson, Peter, "Fifty Years in the Tiger World: An Introduction," in *Tigers of the World*, eds. Tilson and Nyhus, 3–14.

Luo, Shu-Jin, et al. "What Is a Tiger? Genetics and Phylogeography" in *Tigers of the World*, eds. Tilson and Nyhus, 36–47.

Mills, Judy A., *Blood of the Tiger* (Boston: Beacon Press, 2015), 51–55, 116, 125, 129–32.

Nowell, Kristin, "Tiger Farms and Pharmacies: The Central Importance of China's Trade Policy for Tiger Conservation," in *Tigers of the World*, eds. Tilson and Nyhus, 464-469.

Quammen, *Monster of God*, 365, 385–86.

Sunquist, Mel, "What Is a Tiger? Ecology and Behavior," in *Tigers of the World*, eds. Tilson and Nyhus, 20–23.

Tilson, Ronald, and Philip Nyhus, eds., *Tigers of the World: The Science, Politics, and Conservation of* Panthera Tigris, 2nd ed., Foreword by George Schaller (London: Academic Press, 2010), vii-xiv, 128–37, 377–88; see also individual chapter citations.

Tilson, Ronald, Philip Nyhus, and Jeff R. Muntifering, "Yin and Yang of Tiger Conservation in China," in *Tigers of the World*, eds. Tilson and Nyhus, 439–48.

Turner and Anton, *Big Cats,* 60–68, 73–74, 80.

Winter, Steve, and Sharon Guynup, *Tigers Forever: Saving the World's Most Endangered Big Cat* (Washington DC: National Geographic Society, 2013), 7–10, 42, 47–50, 60, 105, 154, 163.

Wright, Belinda, "Will the Tiger Survive in India?" in *Tigers of the World*, eds. Tilson and Nyhus, 88–98.

For "Pleistocene Park: Restoring Mammoths & the Mammoth Steppe"

Grzimek, *Animal Life Encyclopedia*, vol. 1, 30.

Long Now Foundation, "Woolly Mammoth Revival," http://longnow.org/revive/projects/woolly-mammoth, accessed October 16, 2015.

Pleistocene Park, www.pleistocenepark.ru/en, accessed September 27, 2015.

Rich, Nathaniel, "The New Origin of Species," *New York Times Magazine*, March 2, 2014.

Wikipedia, "Pleistocene Park," https://en.wikipedia.org/wiki/Pleistocene_Park, accessed September 27, 2015.

Zimmer, Carl, "Bringing Them Back to Life," *National Geographic*, April 2013, http://ngm.nationalgeographic.com/2013/04/125-species-revival/zimmer-text.

Zimov, Sergey A, "Pleistocene Park: Return of the Mammoth's Ecosystem," *Science* 308, no. 5723 (May 2005): 796–98,. doi:10.1126/science.1113442.

Baiji: Goddess of the Yangtze

Adams, Douglas, and Mark Carwardine, *Last Chance to See* (New York: Harmony Books, 1991), 153, 164, 170, 172, 175.

Fuller, *Lost Animals*, 189, 193

Goodall, *Hope for Animals*.

Grzimek, *Animal Life Encyclopedia*, 403.

IUCN Red List of Threatened Species, "Lipotes vexillifer," 2008, www.iucnredlist.org/details/12119/0.

Miller, Gerrit S., Jr., "A New River-Dolphin from China," Smithsonian Miscellaneous Collections, vol. 68, no. 9 (Washington, DC: Smithsonian Institution, March 30, 1918), www.biodiversitylibrary.org/page/29836424#page/298/mode/1up.

Ruiz-Garcia, Manuel, and Joseph Shostell, "An Introduction to River Dolphin Species," in *Biology, Evolution, and Conservation of River Dolphins*, eds. Manuel Ruiz-Garcia and Joseph Shostell (New York: Nova Science Publishers, 2010), 1–3, 11–18, 20–25.

Turvey, Samuel, *Witness to Extinction: How We Failed to Save the Yangtze River Dolphin* (Oxford, England: Oxford University Press, 2008), 3–5, 11–14, 15–24, 25, 33–39, 46–53, 74–78, 202–5.

Turvey, Samuel, et al., "First Human-Caused Extinction of a Cetacean Species?" *Biology Letters* 3, no. 5 (October 2007), doi: 10.1098/rsbl.2007.0292, http://rsbl.royalsocietypublishing.org/content/3/5/537.short.

Wilkinson, Philip, *Yangtze* (London: BBC Books, 2005), 12–14, 45, 101–2, 122, 133–34.

Winchester, Simon, *The River at the Center of the World: A Journey Up the Yangtze, and Back in Chinese Time* (New York: Henry Holt, 1996), 10–13, 97, 98, 99.

For "Room to Live: Biodiversity & SAR"

Kolbert, *Sixth Extinction*, 165–67.

MacPhee, "Remember the Islands," 148–49.

Ray, Justina C., et al., "Conclusion: Is Large Carnivore Conservation Equivalent to Biodiversity Conservation and How Can We Achieve Both?" in *Large Carnivores and the Conservation*, Ray, 401–2.

Wilson, *Diversity of Life*, 205, 221, 227–28, 275–80.

Rhinoceroses: Tank of the Veldt

Adams and Carwardine, *Last Chance to See*, 88–93.

Anthony, Lawrence, with Graham Spence, *The Last Rhinos: My Battle to Save One of the World's Greatest Creatures* (New York: Thomas Dunne Books/St. Martin's Press, 2012), 2, 4, 14, 310.

Bass, Rick, *The Black Rhinos of Namibia: Searching for Survivors in the African Desert* (New York: Houghton Mifflin Harcourt, 2012), 41–44, 47.

Cunningham, Carol, and Joel Berger, *Horn of Darkness: Rhinos on the Edge* (New York: Oxford University Press, 1997), vix, 3, 8–9, 17, 32–33, 50, 64–68, 96, 186–87, 212.

Erlich, Paul, and Anne Ehrlich, *Extinction: The Causes and Consequences of the Disappearance of Species* (New York: Random House, 1981), 30–32

Goodall, *Hope for Animals*, 140–44.

Gray, Denis D., "Kazaringa Park Rhino Poaching Persists Despite India's Efforts," Huffington Post, March 12, 2013, www.huffingtonpost.com/2013/01/10/kaziranga-park-rhino-poaching-india_n_2445023.html.

Grzimek, *Animal Life Encyclopedia*, 394.

Heath, Kevin, "The Killing Fields of India—Rangers Under Attack," *Wildlife News*, September 8, 2014, http://wildlifenews.co.uk/2014/09/the-killing-fields-of-india-rangers-under-attack.

Hluhluwe-iMfolozi Park, www.kznwildlife.com/imfolozi-mpila.html, accessed September 18, 2015.

IUCN Red List of Threatened Species, "Diceros bicornis," 2012, www.iucnredlist.org/details/6557/0.

Jacobsen, Rowen, "Number One with a Bullet," *Outside*, August 30, 2011, www.outsideonline.com/1819076/number-one-bullet.

Kolbert, *Sixth Extinction*, 219–23.

Kumar, Hari, "Kazaringa Remains a Success Story, Despite Rising Poaching," *New York Times,* India Ink blog, April 11, 2013, http://india.blogs.nytimes.com/2013/04/11/kaziranga-remains-a-success-story-despite-rising-poaching.

Owen-Smith, "Interaction of Humans, Megaherbivores," 57–70.

Penny, Malcolm, *Rhinos: Endangered Species* (New York: Facts on File Publications, 1988), 5–19, 36–43, 79–81, 83.

Platt, John, "Great News for Lions, Terrible News for Rhinos," *Scientific American*, May 12, 2015, http://blogs.scientificamerican.com/extinction-countdown/great-news-for-lions-terrible-news-for-rhinos.

———, "How the Western Black Rhino Went Extinct," *Scientific American*, November 13, 2013, http://blogs.scientificamerican.com/extinction-countdown/2013/11/13/western-black-rhino-extinct.

———, "Only 4 Northern White Rhinos Remain in Africa: Inside the Last Attempts to Breed and Save Them," *Scientific American*, January 29, 2014, http://blogs.scientificamerican.com/extinction-countdown/only-4-northern-white-rhinos-remain-in-africa-inside-the-last-attempts-to-breed-and-save-them.

———, "Poachers Drive Javan Rhino to Extinction in Vietnam," *Scientific American*, October 25, 2011, http://blogs.scientificamerican.com/extinction-countdown/poachers-drive-javan-rhino-to-extinction-in-vietnam/.

———, "Rhino Poaching: An Extinction Crisis," *Scientific American*, October 18, 2012, http://blogs.scientificamerican.com/extinction-countdown/rhino-poaching-extinction-crisis.

Player, Ian, *The White Rhino Saga* (New York: Stein and Day, 1973), 17–20, 23, 30–38, 138–40, 170, 214–39.

———, *Zulu Wilderness: Shadow and Soul* (Golden, CO: Fulcrum Publishing, 1998), xi–xiii, 118.

Wei-Haas, Maya, "Rare White Rhino Dies, Leaving Only Four Left on the Planet," *National Geographic*, July 29, 2015, http://news.nationalgeographic.com/2015/07/150729-rhinos-death-animals-science-endangered-species.

Winter and Guynup, *Tigers Forever*, 58, 66, 68, 73.

Written in the Earth: The Sixth Extinction & the Anthropocene

Ackerman, *The Human Age*, 116, 154, 308.

Bekoff, *Rewilding Our Hearts*.

Ceballos, Gerardo, et al., "Accelerated Modern Human-induced Species Losses: Entering the Sixth Mass Extinction," *Science Advances* 1 (June 2015), doi: e1400253.

Cunningham, *State of Change*, 297–99.

Cunningham and Berger, *Horn of Darkness*, 229–30.

Diamond, *Guns, Germs, and Steel*.

Grzimek, *Animal Life Encyclopedia*, vols. 1 & 2, 25, 357, 369, 372.

Kolbert, *Sixth Extinction*.

MacPhee, "Remember the Islands," 143.

MacPhee, Ross, and Clare Flemming, "*Requiem Aeternam*: The Last Five Hundred Years of Mammalian Species Extinctions," in *Extinctions in Near Time*, ed. MacPhee, 333–66.

Mann, *1491: New Revelations*, 326.

Nyhus, Philip J., and Ronald Tilson, "The Next 20 Years of Tiger Science, Politics, and Conservation" in *Tigers of the World*, eds. Tilson and Nyhus, 510.

Ray, *Large Carnivores*.

Wilcove, David, *The Condor's Shadow: The Loss and Recovery of Wildlife in America* (New York: W. H. Freeman, 1994).

Wilson, *Diversity of Life*, xvii, 311–51.

ACKNOWLEDGMENTS

All books are collective endeavors, and I have a core group of people to thank for their help with this one. That said, any and all errors, mistakes, or mistatements are mine alone.

First of all, I am indebted to my wonderful editor, Dan Harmon. Dan's enthusiasm and sharp mind helped shape this project through many long conversations, and I feel lucky for his encouragement and support.

I am also grateful to the entire team at Zest, especially designer and illustrator Adam Grano, whose incredible artwork brought these giants to life, and copyeditors, Judith Dunham and Olivia Ngai, who helped me dot the i's and more.

I owe a huge, unpayable debt to conservationist Larry Master, who graciously agreed to review the manuscript and helped correct and improve my science. He was generous and kind to a fault, for no other reason than his love of animals. I also must thank Eric Quiñones and Princeton professor David Wilcove for helping connect us.

Carolyn Keating was another early reader, as well as a dear friend and editorial colleague, whose eagle eye helped me craft the book. As always, animal advocate Marc Bekoff has been a guiding inspiration; his work has deeply influenced my own.

I owe a huge shout-out to the dedicated librarians in Morristown, Morris County, and at the New York Public Library, who patiently fielded my requests and helped me find many obscure volumes.

Finally, I thank my family for their endless, steadfast support. This book would not exist without the love, care, and editorial savvy of my wife, Deanna, whose companionship and inspiration along every step of our shared journey have helped me realize my dreams.